Language Planning and Educatic..

Edinburgh Textbooks in Applied Linguistics

Titles in the series include:

Edinburgh Textbooks in Applied Linguistics
Series Editors: Alan Davies and Keith Mitchell

Language Planning and Education

Gibson Ferguson

Edinburgh University Press

© Gibson Ferguson, 2006

Transferred to Digital Print 2010

Edinburgh University Press Ltd
22 George Square, Edinburgh

Typeset in Garamond
by Norman Tilley Graphics, Northampton,
and printed and bound in Great Britain
by CPI Antony Rowe, Chippenham and Eastbourne

A CIP record for this book is available from
the British Library

ISBN-10 0 7486 1261 0 (hardback)
ISBN-13 978 0 7486 1261 1
ISBN-10 0 7486 1262 9 (paperback)
ISBN-13 978 0 7486 1262 8

Published with the support of the Edinburgh
University Scholarly Publishing Initiatives Fund.

Contents

Series Editors' Preface

This series of single-author volumes published by Edinburgh University Press takes a contemporary view of applied linguistics. The intention is to make provision for the wide range of interests in contemporary applied linguistics which are provided for at Master's level.

The expansion of Master's postgraduate courses in recent years has had two effects:

1. What began almost half a century ago as a wholly cross-disciplinary subject has found a measure of coherence so that now most training courses in Applied Linguistics have similar core content.
2. At the same time the range of specialisms has grown, as in any developing discipline. Training courses (and professional needs) vary in the extent to which these specialisms are included and taught.

Some volumes in the series will address the first development noted above, while the others will explore the second. It is hoped that the series as a whole will provide students beginning postgraduate courses in Applied Linguistics, as well as language teachers and other professionals wishing to become acquainted with the subject, with a sufficient introduction for them to develop their own thinking in applied linguistics and to build further into specialist areas of their own choosing.

The view taken of applied linguistics in the Edinburgh Textbooks in Applied Linguistics Series is that of a theorising approach to practical experience in the language professions, notably, but not exclusively, those concerned with language learning and teaching. It is concerned with the problems, the processes, the mechanisms and the purposes of language in use.

Like any other applied discipline, applied linguistics draws on theories from related disciplines with which it explores the professional experience of its practitioners and which in turn are themselves illuminated by that experience. This two-way relationship between theory and practice is what we mean by a theorising discipline.

The volumes in the series are all premised on this view of Applied Linguistics as a theorising discipline which is developing its own coherence. At the same time, in order to present as complete a contemporary view of applied linguistics as possible, other approaches will occasionally be expressed.

Each volume presents its author's own view of the state of the art in his or her topic. Volumes will be similar in length and in format, and, as is usual in a textbook series, each will contain exercise material for use in class or in private study.

Alan Davies
W. Keith Mitchell

Author's Preface

This book is one volume in a series on applied linguistics and it is natural, therefore, that the subject matter – language planning and language policy – is approached from an applied linguistics perspective, meaning that educational concerns and the relationships of language planning to education feature prominently.

The book has been written at the level of an advanced introduction and thus assumes some prior acquaintance with basic sociolinguistic concepts. In other respects, however, it is intended to be widely accessible, and a potential basis, therefore, for MA-level courses in language planning (LP) or for research work by those pursuing particular interests. The contents will also be of interest more generally to applied linguists, language teachers and educational policy-makers.

As others have remarked before, language planning/language policy is an interdisciplinary field with a very wide scope, geographically as well as conceptually. It is difficult, therefore, for any one volume to encompass more than a small proportion of the issues and sites that could potentially be considered, and this work is no exception. Thus, while we have included examples of LP activity from a variety of geographical locations – in Europe, North America, Africa, and Asia – there are inevitably omissions: little will be found here on Latin America or the Arab world, for example.

Similarly, there are omissions regarding the range of issues addressed, an example being the absence of any detailed discussion of normative theories of language rights. That said, the book does engage, as outlined below, with a number of themes many would see as central to contemporary LP and education.

THE SCOPE AND ORGANISATION OF THE BOOK

The first two chapters provide overviews respectively of the development of LP over the past fifty years or so, and of key concepts in the practice of LP. This sets the scene for the following two chapters (Chapters 3 and 4) which discuss LP/policy with respect to immigrant and autochthonous minorities.

In Chapter 3, the focus is on the educational and political dimensions of bilingual education for linguistic minorities in the United States. One reason for focusing so specifically on the USA is that there are few other settings, with the possible exception of Canada, where the educational effects of various forms of bilingual education have been more thoroughly researched, and where, in consequence, a substantial body of high quality literature on the subject has accumulated. Another is that recent developments (for example, Proposition 227) have laid bare with particular clarity the politics of bilingual education, a central issue being the re-imagining of national identities in an era of mass migration.

With Chapter 4 there is shift of scene and topic – to Europe and to regional autochthonous minorities, now reasserting their distinctive cultures and languages. The first part of the chapter provides an overview of the topic of language decline and revitalisation; the second moves to a case study of two Celtic language minorities, Welsh and Breton, and examines in detail how and why they appear to be set on different trajectories of revival.

Chapter 5 focuses on the contested causes and effects of the global spread of English, considering in particular the impacts on other languages and cultures, and on inequalities of various kinds. An emergent theme is that language policy alone cannot contain the spread of English, and therefore democratisation of access may be one of the more realistic ways of managing, or mitigating, some of the more negative impacts.

Maintaining the focus on English but this time giving greater attention to policy as it directly relates to pedagogy, Chapter 6 discusses that other concomitant of spread – the linguistic diversification of English, focusing in particular on the debate over New Englishes, English as a Lingua Franca (ELF) and the choice of appropriate models for teaching English around the world.

The reason, incidentally, for giving the English language more attention than it might command in some other books on language policy is straightforward: many readers are likely to be, or to have been, teachers of the dominant global language, interested in reflecting on their how their work relates to broader policy issues. And it is true, of course, that responses to the global spread of English are, in themselves, a major theme in policy debates the world over.

In the final chapter (Chapter 7), we explore one of the major topics of language planning in education: the choice of media of instruction in developing post-colonial societies. The chapter considers the socio-political and economic factors that help sustain the retention of English as a medium – despite very evident educational disadvantages – arguing that these so strongly constrain the likelihood of radical policy reform that applied linguists may need to complement advocacy of reform with the investigation of practical measures; measures that might, in the interim, mitigate some of the adverse effects attaching to the use of foreign language media of instruction.

A recurring motif throughout these chapters (3–7) is the tension between the local and the national or global, between identity and access, between belonging and opportunity, which – in the sphere of language – so often appears to place languages in opposition to each other. No wonder, then, that the most commonly urged solution is bilingualism: personal plurilingualism and institutional bilingualism at state level. The idea behind this is that while one language conserves identity, the other, often a language of wider communication, offers access to opportunities in a wider world.

This solution is not unproblematic, however: personal plurilingualism is not always easy to maintain, and societal bilingualism/multilingualism not always congenial to traditional conceptions of the nation and national identity. Bilingualism can, moreover, be unstable, and the precursor, as we see in Chapter 4, of a shift to a dominant language. Stability, where it does occur, is usually the result of functional differentiation between languages, but this can leave the language of affect subordinate to that of public, formal domains. Nor, finally, is it always easy to demarcate so precisely the functions of identity and utility, and pin them neatly on different, complementary languages.

All that said, the alternatives – usually monolingual ones – are no better, leading, as Wright (2004: 250) observes, in one direction toward confinement and parochialism and in the other toward the loss of diversity and possible anomie. Persistence with policies supportive of bilingualism may, then, be the least disadvantageous path to follow, which implies, as we argue in forthcoming chapters, that bilingual education be more actively considered and investigated as an educational option than has sometimes been the case in the past.

Acknowledgements

Identifying and thanking all those who have helped me write this book, whether by commenting on drafts or by shaping my understanding of language planning over many years of discussion, is no easy task; impossible in fact, for there are so many of them. I would, however, like to record my particular thanks to Alan Davies and Keith Mitchell, the series editors, for their patient support throughout the writing of this book and for the careful, constructive feedback they provided on draft chapters.

I must also record my gratitude to colleagues at Edinburgh and to students on the language planning courses I have taught both there and at Sheffield, whose comments and reactions have so enriched my understanding of language planning issues. Finally, I would like to thank my wife, Karen, for her encouragement and support, without which the writing of this book and much else besides would scarcely have been possible.

Chapter 1

The discipline of language planning: a historical overview

'Language planning' denotes both language planning practices, that is, organised interventions by politicians, linguists and others in language use and form (Christian 1989: 193), and the academic discipline whose subject matter is the study of these practices. In the first chapter of this introductory overview, therefore, we focus on the latter, charting the changes that have taken place in the academic discipline over the past half century, while in the second we review the concepts and terminology the discipline has furnished for describing and theorising language planning activities. We turn first, however, to the emergence of the discipline.

1.1 THE EARLY YEARS OF THE DISCIPLINE OF LANGUAGE PLANNING

The academic discipline has a comparatively recent provenance, with the first use of the term 'language planning' attributed to Haugen's (1959, 1966a) description of the development of a new standard national language in Norway following independence from Denmark in 1814 (Karam 1974: 105; Fettes 1997: 13).

Its early years are most strongly associated, however, with decolonisation and the language problems of newly emergent states, as is reflected in the title of the now classic language planning publications of this period – *Language Problems of Developing Nations* (Fishman, Ferguson and Das Gupta 1968), *Can Language Be Planned? Sociolinguistic Theory and Practice for Developing Nations* (Rubin and Jernudd 1971), *Advances in Language Planning* (Fishman 1974a), and in Fishman's (1974b: 79) definition of language planning as 'the organised pursuit of solutions to language problems, typically at the national level'. The reference here to the 'national level' is indicative of the historic importance in language planning of nation-building and associated processes of national identity formation, including language standardisation.

The decolonised states of Africa and Asia were regarded as a particularly apt arena for language planning and policy partly because their patterns of language allocation were felt to be more flexible and less settled than those of the older states of Europe, offering opportunities thereby for the application of theory to practice, and partly because the challenges facing the new states were all too evident. These comprised modernisation and development, the evolution of more democratic forms of governance, and traditional nation-building; that is, the construction of a cohesive state to which citizens could give their allegiance in place of more local ethnic attachments. This latter enterprise was viewed as particularly problematic, for the new states inherited the artificial, arbitrary borders imposed in the colonial era, and consequently encompassed a diversity of ethnic and linguistic groups. There was, therefore, no pre-existing ethnic or linguistic cohesion on which the new ruling elites could draw to fashion a new national identity.

Analysing this problem from a language policy perspective, Fishman (1968: 7) described a tension between **nationalism**, the cultivation of a national identity (or authenticity) to supersede 'ethnic–cultural particularisms', which pointed to the espousal of some indigenous language as the national language, the emblem of national identity, and **nationism,** meaning operational efficiency in administration and economic management for the maintenance of political stability, which pointed in an opposite direction – to the official use of a non-indigenous, and therefore non-authentic, former colonial language.

In an ideal world, 'ideal' for being modelled on European nationalist solutions, the official language of state administration and the national language, with its identity functions, would be one and the same, but such a solution was difficult to achieve – particularly in Africa. The hope nonetheless was that in the fullness of time, with nationist requirements satisfied, it might be possible with careful language planning to displace the former colonial language from its roles as official language and language of wider communication (Fishman 1968: 7).

In fact, however, such hopes have not been realised, and in most post-colonial states English or other metropolitan languages (such as French or Portuguese) have been retained as languages of the state and of education. Post-independence, the immediate justification was practical: the new states were mostly poor and fragile; there was little indigenous experience in implementing radical policy change; and changing the language medium of education, even, would have entailed considerable preparation, not least retraining teachers and the expensive redesign of teaching materials. A second justification was political: allocation of any one, or any one set of, indigenous languages to official functions was seen as having the potential to excite accusations of ethnic favouritism, threatening the national unity the new political leaders were keen to foster.

Behind these rationales there also lurked less openly declared considerations. While the retention of former colonial languages may have reduced the risk of ethnic division, it did very little for greater socio-economic equality, serving in particular to bolster the power of ruling elites who owed their privileged position to their proficiency in English or French, a language few others could readily acquire as long as access to formal education remained limited.

To this pattern there were exceptions, however, as in a number of states it was possible to identify an indigenous language that could both signify a distinct, authentic national identity and serve official state functions, the most cited examples being Tanzania, Indonesia and, eventually, Malaysia (see Wright 2004, Foley 1997,

Omar 1992). As a long-standing regional lingua franca with a Bantu grammatical base and relatively few resident native speakers, Swahili – in a highly heterogeneous Tanzania – was well suited to serve as a national official language, a role for which it was soon selected.[1] A similar situation obtained in Indonesia, which, like Tanzania, but to an even greater degree, encompassed a great diversity of ethnic and linguistic groups scattered through an archipelago extending over 5,000 kilometres. Here, the early nationalist leaders preferred a variety of Malay (subsequently known as *Bahasa Indonesia*) over dominant ethnic languages such as Javanese for the role of national language.[2] The advantage of Malay was that it was an established and prestigious regional lingua franca not associated with any dominant ethnic group yet historically linked to Islam, and therefore relatively acceptable, and accessible, to a wide range of the Indonesian population. In post-independence Malaysia, meanwhile, a ten-year transition period, during which English was retained as an official language, came to an end in 1967 with the passage of a language bill installing *Bahasa Malaysia* as the sole official language (Omar 1992: 113). Not long after it also became the medium of instruction throughout the education system, though significantly in 2003 the government took the decision to reinstate English as the medium for mathematics and science at secondary school.

If these three cases, all of which involved intense language planning input, can be portrayed as language planning successes, the larger picture was distinctly gloomier. In the decades after independence the economies of many post-colonial African states first faltered, and then in the 1980s went into frank decline. A number of states also entered a period of internal ethnically-based conflicts, and in some extreme cases there followed in the late 1980s and early 1990s a total collapse of state authority (for instance in Somalia, Sierra Leone, Liberia and Zaire/Congo).

Against this background of failure, confidence in the efficacy of all kinds of planning – language included – that characterised the early efforts to address the language problems of developing nations dissipated, and interest waned. Hardly encouraging either was the changing intellectual climate, which by the 1980s had turned away from the grand projects for development with which language planning had become associated.

1.2 CRITICISMS OF LANGUAGE PLANNING

By the 1980s and early 1990s language planning (henceforth LP), as a discipline and an activity, had also become the object of a battery of criticisms deriving from Marxist, post-structural and critical sociolinguistic perspectives. It was accused, for example, of serving the interests and agendas of dominant elites while passing itself off as an ideologically neutral, objective enterprise; of embracing a discourse of 'technist rationality' that transformed into 'simple matters of technical efficiency' problems that were actually value-laden and ideologically encumbered; of neglecting the inevitable implications LP enterprises held for power relations and socio-economic equality (Luke, McHoul, Mey 1990: 25; Williams 1992).

In its approach to the language problems of the new African states, LP was also criticised for being wedded to, and for projecting, traditional European notions of the nation state, in which citizens are unified around a common standard language. Such conceptions, with their emphasis on the ideal of a coincidence of nation, state and language, inevitably helped propagate the view that multilingualism was problematic, a potential source of inefficiency and disunity, thereby lending justification to LP interventions that sought to discipline or tame it. Bamgbose (1994: 36), in a much cited passage, makes this point forcefully, remarking additionally that a common language cannot in and of itself unify:

> In Africa, it seems that we are obsessed with the number 'one'. Not only must we have one national language, we must also have a one-party system. The mistaken belief is that in such oneness of language and party we would achieve socio-cultural cohesion and political unity in our multi-ethnic, multilingual and multi-cultural societies.

Another strand of criticism focuses on the tendency of LP to objectify language(s); that is, to treat languages as natural, 'out-there', discrete entities (Blommaert 1996, Ricento 2000b), a view contrasting sharply, of course, with more recent conceptions of languages as political constructions (see Joseph 2004: 125), and of language names (for example, Malay, Swahili, English) as labels sheltering 'a disparate set of language practices' (Wright 2004: 98). Applied to Africa, such objectification lent support to the practice of enumerating a diverse set of distinct languages for each country – 41 in Zambia, 125 in Tanzania, 54 in Ghana, and so on. The impression thus created of an unruly multilingualism, of a veritable Tower of Babel, provided arguments for language planners to discipline multilingualism, and to 'reduce sociolinguistic complexity' (Blommaert 1996: 212). In fact, however, as Makoni and Meinhof (2003: 7) suggest, these diverse, distinct languages are inventions in the specific sense that they are the product of decisions to divide a linguistic continuum into discrete named entities, decisions determined in the African case 'by outsiders without any reference to the socio-linguistic identities of the local communities' (Makoni and Meinhof 2003: 7).[3]

Though not all the criticisms outlined above might stand up to close examination, they did collectively have a cumulative effect. By the end of the 1980s LP as a discipline had diminished in prominence and prestige, appearing, almost, to be set on a downward trajectory. The term itself, even, had a somewhat dated resonance, eliciting unfavoured images of manipulation, positivist social engineering, and technical rationality.

1.3 THE RESURGENCE OF LANGUAGE PLANNING AND LANGUAGE POLICY

All the more striking, therefore, has been the recent resurgence of interest in language policy and planning, signalled most obviously by the appearance in 2000 and 2001 of two new journals dedicated to the subject – *Current Issues in Language Planning* and *Language Policy*, and by the publication in 2004 of two major book-length treatments (Wright 2004 and Spolsky 2004).

For an explanation of this renaissance one needs to look to the major geopolitical developments that have marked the closing years of the twentieth century and set new challenges for LP, a problem-oriented and profoundly political discipline, to address. Particularly significant among these developments for the changes they have wrought in the context of LP work are the following:

1. The collapse of communism in the former Soviet Union and Eastern Europe (1989–91), and the ending of the Cold War, two principal effects of which have been the resurgence of ethno-nationalisms suppressed under communism and the formation of new states in Central Asia (e.g. Kazakhstan, Uzbekistan, Azerbaijan, Georgia) and in the former Yugoslavia (e.g. Slovenia, Croatia, Bosnia), not forgetting the resurrection of states in the Baltic (Estonia, Latvia, Lithuania). The resultant processes of nation-building, and of identity construction, have led to LP interventions not very dissimilar to those associated with decolonisation and earlier phases of European nation-state formation – for example, the selection of official languages, standardisation and purification.

   One might add here that the ending of the Cold War also indirectly hastened the final, formal decolonisation of Africa, specifically in Namibia and South Africa,[4] both of which have been sites of intense and ongoing language planning/policy work. In South Africa, for example, the 1996 post-apartheid constitution bestowed official status on eleven languages,[5] and charged the newly established LP agency (the Pan South African Language Board) with the task of elevating the status of the indigenous languages among them.

2. Not unrelated to the above developments has been the re-emergence of small nations and regional languages within the old established European nation states. In the UK, for example, devolution has given new levels of political autonomy to Wales and Scotland, paralleling the autonomy previously granted to Catalonia and the Basque country in Spain. Concomitantly, the languages of these groups (Welsh, Catalan, Basque, and so on) have been revalorised, achieving – in some cases – co-equal status in their region with the dominant majority language.

   The reasons for the resurgent assertiveness of minority nationalisms are complex and not altogether clear. Wright (2004: 201) argues persuasively, however, that the weakening of the nation state due to globalisation and the consolidation of supranational economic, political and military institutions (such as the European Union and NATO) have in combination opened up space for regional and national minorities to assert their distinctive identities and press for a commensurate degree of political autonomy. That this has, by and large, been conceded also reflects, one might argue, the emergent view that intolerance of separate regional identities is not easily reconciled with the democratic principles on which the European Union is founded. More than democratic idealism is involved here, however: many European governments have come round to believing that devolution – the granting of a degree of political and cultural autonomy to regions – is one of the more effective ways of defusing minority nationalisms and of preserving the overarching unity of the state in the long run.[6]

However one analyses the causes, one consequence has been a noticeable intensification of language planning/policy work on behalf of autochthonous regional languages in Europe, some of which has been of the traditional nation-building kind, albeit on a smaller, sub-national scale – defending the purity of the language, or promoting the standard variety throughout the speech community, for example.[7] The main focus, however, it would be fair to say, has been on revitalisation, on reintroducing the minority language to the public domains from which it had previously been excluded (a process known in Spain as 'normalisation') and on spreading knowledge of the language through school and adult education (see Chapter 4).

All this has been accompanied, and supported, by legislation on minority languages at regional, national and supranational levels (for example, The European Charter for Regional or Minority Languages 1992), and by a burgeoning of interest in normative theories of language rights on the part of political theorists (such as Kymlicka and Patten 2003), to whose work language planners, reflecting the interdisciplinary character of their subject, are increasingly turning for guidance.

3. A third set of global developments reshaping the context of LP may be brought together under the label 'globalisation' – a fashionable term for a fashionable concept that has spawned a voluminous literature. The initial debate over the very existence of the phenomenon – a myth, a fundamental dynamic of our age, or neither – has been broadly settled, Giddens (2004) affirms, in favour of the globalists: globalisation is real rather than mythical, and is a genuinely new rather than old phenomenon. That said, and reflecting no doubt its multiple material, cultural and cognitive dimensions, there appears to be no settled, definitive characterisation. It tends instead to be defined in terms of a cluster of related features – 'action at a distance', deterritorialisation, time-space compression, the increasing mobility of people and capital, interdependence and integration, and the weakening of the nation state (Held and McGrew 2003: 3).

Fortunately, a language planning/policy perspective licenses a selective focus on language-related aspects, three of which seem of particular relevance and are summarised briefly below:

Migration: As is well known, North America, Europe and Australasia have been receiving increasing numbers of migrants, becoming as a result ever more obviously multilingual and multicultural, especially in urban centres. The historic policy response of most Western countries has been assimilative in education and in the civic realm more generally: that is, they have encouraged, sometimes obliged, migrants to learn the dominant majority language while tolerating the use of the minority language in private but not public domains.

Historically, these assimilationist policies have been underpinned by socio-linguistic patterns of language shift leading typically to the loss of the ethnic minority language by the third generation, but recent developments give reason to question whether this pattern will continue. One factor here is the increased scale of recent migration, which – in amplifying the size of minority residential communities – raises the possibility that many of their members will be able to live out their lives using only, or predominantly, the minority language. Another is the rise of a more assertive multicultural ideology, making claims for the greater representation of minority languages and identities in the public realm. A third factor is the emergent phenomenon of transnationalism, referring – among other things – to the tendency of migrants to maintain closer and more regular connections with their countries of origin.

For some,[8] these developments are experienced as a vexatious challenge to national identities as traditionally conceived; for others they represent a welcome break with the monoculturalism traditionally associated with nation-state politics. Whichever analysis one prefers, there can be little doubt that language policy, specifically language education policies (see Chapter 3), have been close to the centre of debates over how best to manage contemporary migration flows to Western countries, and that, again, LP discussion in this area has intensified as a result.

Loss of indigenous languages: Of concern to many for its adverse impact on global linguistic diversity is the predicted loss of up to 90 per cent of the world's 'small' indigenous languages, most of which are unwritten and spoken by poor marginalised communities (Nettle and Romaine 2000, Crystal 2000). Their demise can be linked to globalisation in so far as they have been hitherto sustained by geographical isolation, socio-economic marginalisation and the perceived absence of opportunities for joining the mainstream, all of which traits tend to be undone by the increased interconnectedness, urbanisation and time-space compression associated with globalisation.

Our purpose here, however, is not to discuss causation (see Chapter 4 for a fuller discussion) but simply to highlight the fact that this issue has acted as a further stimulant to increased intellectual engagement with matters of language policy and planning. So much so, in fact, that for those who adopt an ecology of language perspective (see Mühlhäusler 1996, 2000; Phillipson and Skuttnab-Kangas 1996) the preservation of linguistic diversity is a central, even overriding, goal for language policy. At the same time, indigenous language loss coupled with the migration mentioned above has added a language dimension to political theorists' preoccupation with issues of pluralism, diversity and minority rights.

The global spread of English: Most obviously associated with globalisation is the global spread of English, a phenomenon whose causes and effects continue to be widely debated (see Chapter 4), and which needs, Spolsky (2004: 91) reckons, to be taken into account by policy-makers the world over. Just how this is done varies considerably, depending on the political and sociolinguistic situation of individual countries and on how English is perceived – as a threat to linguistic diversity and to the vitality of national languages, as a means of accessing technological knowledge, as a useful lingua franca or as all of these simultaneously. In the majority of instances, however, national governments, even those historically most anxious about the spread of English such as the French, have felt obliged to accommodate their language education policies to the massive popular demand for English language skills, illustrating in the process the limited control language policy-makers can exert over the dynamics of language spread.

4. A final development of considerable significance for language policy/planning, and the focus also for a growing literature (see, for example, Coulmas 1991, Phillipson 2003), has been the construction of supranational political communities, most notably the European Union (EU), which in May 2004 admitted ten new members bringing the total membership to 25 states and the number of languages officially recognised for communication between EU institutions and citizens from 11 to 20.

Inevitably, this degree of linguistic diversity, valued and acknowledged as part of the European cultural heritage, poses considerable practical challenges, as is indicated by the large cadre of interpreters and translators employed to service the communication needs of the European Commission, the European Parliament, and the European Court of Justice – the largest, some say, of any organisation worldwide.

The expense and inconvenience involved[9] have led some commentators to wonder just how long present arrangements can be sustained and how long the EU's politically expedient reticence on language policy matters can be continued: 'It is difficult to see how serious contemplation of both present arrangements and the need for reform can, in real terms, be postponed for much longer' (Shuibhne 2001: 69).

One could equally well argue, however, that it is exceedingly difficult, nor necessarily desirable, for the EU to retreat from the principle of equality for all its official languages, especially in the formal, public deliberations of the Council of Ministers or European Parliament, given that the equality of treatment of member states is a central, founding principle of the Union.

Behind the scenes, however, in the internal workings of the EU administration, it has been possible for officials to evolve pragmatic, de facto arrangements for working in a restricted number of languages – typically French, English or some communicatively effective 'franglais' mix. Given the understandable reluctance of the member states to address language issues explicitly, not to mention the difficulty of reaching agreement, it seems quite likely that such pragmatic accommodations may well entrench themselves, though, as

Phillipson (2003) suggests in critical vein, this 'laissez-faireism' is only likely in the longer run to further consolidate English as a European lingua franca within as well as outside the institutions of the EU (see also de Swaan 2001: 174).

Our purpose here, however, is not to examine language policy issues in the EU in any detail but to suggest simply that the emergence of supranational political communities is another development shaping the contemporary context of language planning/policy. What the European Union case does in particular illuminate, however, with rather special clarity, is the relative ease – in the absence of explicit policy formulation – with which language practices can harden into a kind of undeclared, implicit policy, and how non-decisions can in practice influence language practice and use as surely as explicit policy declarations (see de Swaan 2001: 144).

1.4 CHANGES IN THE DISCIPLINE OF LANGUAGE PLANNING

As Blommaert (1996: 205) points out, LP is one of those disciplines that is strongly rooted in 'contingent historical and socio-political realties'. Such theoretical frameworks as it possesses owe much to the perspicacious analyses by single authors of the sociolinguistic and political histories of particular countries (e.g. Haugen 1966a on Norway), to the accretion of knowledge through case studies and to the observation of correlations between types of polities – sociolinguistically considered – and language policies (see Lambert 1999, Spolsky 2004). It is unsurprising, then, that the major geopolitical developments outlined above have coincided with significant changes in the discipline of language planning, which we now discuss briefly.

1.4.1 The widening scope of language planning

One of the more obvious changes, perhaps, has been an enlargement of the range of topics addressed within language planning/policy and an extension of the discipline's geographical purview relative to the early days of the 1960s and 1970s. Thus, the processes of language standardisation, codification and dissemination of the standard so strongly associated with the nation-building projects attending decolonisation, while still important, are no longer quite so central and have been joined by other issues – language revitalisation, minority language rights, globalisation and the spread of English, the preservation of linguistic diversity and bilingual education, for example – all of which are among the staples of the journal literature as well as recent textbooks (e.g. Kaplan and Baldauf 1997, Wright 2004, Spolsky 2004), including this one.

The discipline's attention is also no longer so geographically biased toward the post-colonial states of Africa and Asia. With migration and the rise of regional nationalism, the language policies and patterns of language distribution of the old established nation states of the West now appear less settled than was once assumed, and they too are therefore viewed as experiencing 'language problems', meriting the attention of language policy/planning specialists as much as those of economically less developed societies. Similarly, the emergence, or re-emergence, of successor states to the Soviet Union in Central Asia, the Caucasus and the Baltic, and the distinct language policies they have embarked on, have attracted the attention of language policy/planning specialists, providing ample scope for analysis and publication.

The overall trend, then, has been toward a geographical diversification in the coverage of the literature, such that it is now difficult to find any region or country omitted from consideration. The advantage of this trend is, as Spolsky (2003: xi) observes,[10] that there is now a more extensive body of data on language policies at the national level, creating the possibility thereby for better-founded generalisations.

1.4.2 Changing postures toward linguistic diversity

A more fundamental change, however, has been in the posture of language planning towards linguistic diversity and multilingualism. Omitting nuance for the sake of rough generalisation, one might argue that in the decolonisation era of the 1960s and 1970s those involved in LP – whether politicians or academics – tended, in the spirit of earlier European nationalists, to see language diversity as predominantly a problem, a centrifugal force, and thus an impediment to nation-building. The thrust of policy, therefore, was to identify a limited set of languages for official uses, so 'reducing sociolinguistic complexity' (Blommaert 1996: 212) to manageable proportions in what were felt to be the interests of efficiency and integration.

In the last decade or so, however, linguistic diversity has undergone revalorisation in academic LP circles and beyond, being seen now as something to be cherished, maintained and promoted – a public good even on a par with fresh, clean air. One illustrative manifestation of this heightened regard is the enthusiastic reception given to the 1996 post-apartheid South African constitution, which, in sharp contrast to the practice of most African states attaining independence in the early 1960s, extends official status to eleven languages and calls on the state to promote the status of previously marginalised languages. Another, in a different context, is the qualified welcome given to the 1992 European Charter for Regional or Minority Languages, which calls on signatory states to protect and promote these languages.

Explaining this change of orientation is not straightforward, for, as with many intellectual paradigm shifts, a variety of contributory causes appear to have coalesced. One factor may be the criticisms levelled at traditional LP by Marxists, post-structuralists and critical social theorists to which we referred earlier. The effect has been to alert language planners to the ineluctably ideological and political character of their endeavours, which therefore become ever more appropriate objects for sustained critical scrutiny. The accusation that LP serves the interests of dominant elites may also have prompted greater interest in, and concern for, the languages spoken by subordinate or marginalised speakers.

Another factor, one may venture to suggest, has been historical developments to which we have already alluded – the spread of English as a dominant global lingua, globalisation and the loss of indigenous languages (see Chapter 4), all of which have brought into clear focus the prospect, real or imagined, of diminished linguistic diversity, and the need, therefore, for interventions to reduce the likelihood of this actually occurring.

Influential also, perhaps, in converting opinion to the desirability, inevitability even, of diversity are late twentieth-century intellectual developments, which, in opposing grand narratives and universalised ideologies, can be seen as sympathetic toward heterogeneity and pluralism of perspective. The contemporary intellectual climate, then, is more favourable to diversity of various kinds, and LP, in common with other socially oriented disciplines, has not escaped its influence, turning a more critical eye as a result on traditional LP nation-building interventions that involve any suppression of diversity – for instance, the promotion of a single standardised national language over other language varieties. Also contributing to this greater academic scepticism towards nation-building activity in LP, is, Wright argues (2004: 98), an emergent post-nationalist ethos that globalisation has done much to foster as we move, she suggests (2004: 251), 'beyond the national model' into a post-national era.

Some aspects of this thesis may be overstated, however. To be sure, the powers of the nation state have been considerably attenuated economically and politically by globalising forces, but there is as yet no firm evidence that it has been superseded as the dominant form of political organisation or as an important locus for popular sentimental attachments. Indeed, as Giddens (2004) has suggested, far from witnessing the demise of the nation state we may be living through an era of its universalisation, marked by the emergence of new states from the debris of older empires (e.g. the Soviet Union) and by the claims for recognition as distinct nations which minority groups within old nation states have recently advanced.[11] That said, it does seem that global, supranational developments are impinging more and more on the nation-state unit, and that LP is attending more to the interface of the national and local with the global. One might agree, therefore, that – in academic circles at least – nationalism as a motivating force in LP is more critically regarded than previously, and that there is greater concern that nation-building projects, where they continue, should be more accommodating to minority cultures and aspirations than has historically been the case.

We can conclude, then, that, alongside a broadening in the range of topics studied within the discipline, the principal changes in LP since the early days of the 1960s have been ideological in character, with two tendencies particularly salient: first, linguistic diversity has been revalorised so that contemporary language planning interventions aim as much, or more, to maintain diversity as to restrain it; second, responding perhaps to the critiques of critical theorists, the discipline displays greater concern with issues of social disadvantage, equality and access to state institutions as they affect minority groups, this being signalled most clearly by the growth of literature on minority language rights.

1.4.3 The interdisciplinary character of language planning

In the area of minority language rights, as in others, LP has maintained its traditionally interdisciplinary character, the influence in this instance coming from political and legal theory, whose impact may be expected to increase as political theorists engage more with language diversity and language rights (see Kymlicka and Patten (2003), for example). Economics, too, is a discipline to which language planners have traditionally looked for guidance,[12] and its influence continues through the work of scholars such as Grin (2002, 2003a, 2003b), who has argued (2003a: 87) that its principal contribution lies in the provision of a framework for explicitly identifying alternative policy alternatives, and for assigning costs and benefits to them; in short, for facilitating policy analysis. He admits (2003b: 5), though, that because language policy-making is fundamentally a political process and because non-market values (e.g. matters of identity and culture) attach to languages individually and collectively, economics can never be central, only complementary, as an instrument assisting decision-making.

1.4.4 The limitations of language planning and language policy

The final point one may make regarding contemporary language planning/policy is that there now seems to be a greater readiness to acknowledge its often limited efficacy in a range of policy areas such as revitalising threatened languages and curbing the spread of English. Wright (2004: 169), for example, points out that top-down policy has a limited capacity to contain, let alone reverse, the spread of lingua francas like English, whose success owes much to 'factors largely outside the control of individual governments' (see Chapter 4 for a more detailed discussion). Romaine (2002: 3), too, is similarly sceptical about the efficacy of language policies – in this case those aimed at supporting endangered languages. She attributes their ineffectiveness mainly to 'weak linkages between policy and planning', meaning by this that policies are frequently announced but much more rarely implemented. For example, Quechua was declared a co-official language with Spanish in Peru in 1976, but resistance from the dominant Spanish-speaking majority has impeded meaningful implementation. Six African languages have been declared official in Senegal, but lack of resources and political will severely limit their use in education (Romaine 2002: 13).

Romaine's wider point, however, is that language policy is not autonomous from the economic, social, political and attitudinal forces that shape patterns of language use, and is rarely effective when it attempts to operate against rather than with sociological dynamics.

Spolsky (2004: 223), meanwhile, citing the inability of government action to revitalise the Irish language, draws attention to LP's unimpressive record: 'there are comparatively few cases where language management has produced its intended results'. The same theme of past failure and consequent loss of optimism also surfaces in Tollefson's (2002b) paper entitled 'Limitations of Language Policy and Planning'.

Discussion of the reasons for this greater pessimism, or realism, regarding the efficacy of language policy and planning lies beyond the scope of this chapter, so the best one can offer is a brief enumeration of some contributory factors. These would include the unimpressive record of planning success, to which we have already alluded, and an intellectual climate both distrustful of planning as potentially authoritarian and sceptical as to its ability to deliver.

Relevant here as an underlying influence is the collapse of communism in Eastern Europe at the end of the 1980s, a set of events interpreted, by neo-liberals mainly, as signalling the failure of central economic planning and as confirming, supposedly, market forces as more appropriate arbiters for the allocation of resources. Turning finally to intellectual developments within the field, there is, as we have previously noted, a growing recognition of the complexity of the social ecology of language status and use, and a correspondingly enhanced appreciation that LP targeting these areas can only be effective to the extent that it takes account of, and works with, the economic, political and social structures that more substantially influence language behaviour than language policy itself can.

1.5 CONCLUSION

As we have seen, language planning is a resurgent academic discipline revived by the policy challenges of late twentieth- and early twenty-first-century global developments: globalisation, migration, resurgent ethno-nationalisms, language endangerment, the global spread of English, new states and failing states.

It is, however, a different discipline in several respects from the early years of the immediate post-colonial era of the 1960s and 1970s. First of all, as we have observed above, there is now greater scepticism regarding the efficacy of LP. A second striking difference is the much more positive stance toward linguistic diversity, manifested in increased interventions on behalf of regional minority languages, the languages of migrants and the endangered languages of indigenous peoples. Evident also, and clearly linked to the above, is a greater interest in questions of power, access, inequality, discrimination and disparity, and how all these are impacted by language policies.

Behind this ideological reorientation is a combination of influences: the criticisms levelled at the technist positivism of traditional LP by critical linguists and others, for example; the effect of which has been to heighten awareness of the ideological bases and biases of LP. Then there are the socio-political developments that have so radically changed the context of language planning and policy. Large-scale migration, for example, has compelled greater recognition of multicultural realities, and provoked a re-examination of the traditional foundations on which national identities have been constructed. Receding into the past, also, is the era of most intense nation-building, when linguistic diversity was typically viewed as a potential threat to national unity, and when the dominant preoccupations of language planners were with standardising, codifying and disseminating official languages of state. This is not to say that nation-building has come to halt – nations are ongoing construction projects; only that it is a less central concern than previously, and that space has opened up, therefore, for the reappraisal of the value of linguistic diversity within these political units.

Alongside change, meanwhile, there are continuities. As ever, the language problems addressed by LP are not just, or only, problems of language and communication but typically arise from, and can only be fully understood against, a background of political, economic, social and cultural struggle. And, for this very reason, the study of LP cannot help but remain an interdisciplinary enterprise.

NOTES

1. Tanganyika gained independence in 1961, and was renamed Tanzania following union with Zanzibar in 1964. In 1967 Swahili was declared the national official language. In the same year it was made the medium of primary education.

2. The choice of a prestigious variety of written Malay as the national language of Indonesia following independence from the Dutch in 1949 was in fact neither surprising nor controversial. It had been the language of administration and education during the Japanese occupation (1942–5), and had been identified as a suitable national language by nationalists as early as 1928. At independence, Javanese speakers were easily the largest ethno-linguistic group, comprising around 48 per cent of the total Indonesian population.

3. Linguistic diversity in Africa is not typically experienced as a significant problem at the grassroots level. Most Africans are individually plurilingual, but this is somewhat less remarkable or exotic than Europeans sometimes perceive it to be. In Central, East and southern Africa, many 'languages' are closely related, sharing a high proportion of lexis and grammatical structures. Furthermore, Africans tend to be socialised into multilingual practices from an early age. As Fardon and Furniss (1994b: 4) point out:

> multilingualism is the African lingua franca. Any African national or ethnographer will testify to a transcontinental genius for facilitating communication by drawing on language competences, however partially these might be held in common. The African lingua franca might best be envisaged not as a single language but as a multilayered and partially connected language chain that offers a choice of varieties and registers in the speaker's immediate environment.

4. Under apartheid, South Africa had many of the features of old settlement colonies, and is therefore assimilated here to the colonial category.

5. These eleven languages are: isiZulu, isiNdebele, siSwati, isiXhosa, Xitsonga, Tshivenda, Sesotho, Setswana, Sepedi, Afrikaans and English.

6. This appears to be the case thus far in Scotland. Devolution (following a referendum in 1997) and the establishment of a Scottish parliament has not thus far led to an increase in votes for the Scottish National Party (SNP).

7. Language planners in Catalonia have been concerned, for example, to maintain the distinctiveness of Catalan from Castilian Spanish, to which it is closely related linguistically. In the Basque country, meanwhile, effort has been invested in diffusing, and gaining acceptance for, a common standard variety.

8. For example, supporters of 'Official English' in the United States (see Chapter 3).

9. De Swaan (2001: 172), drawing on figures from Truchot (2001), reports that in 1999 the translation and interpreting costs of the European Commission amounted to 325 million Euros, 30 per cent of its internal budget. There are other figures in circulation, however, and Grin, for example, has claimed that translation and interpreting costs account for a relatively small proportion of the EU's overall budget.

10. Spolsky's comments appear in the preface to a volume by Kaplan and Baldauf (2003) on language planning in the Pacific Basin (covering twelve states). Other volumes edited by these authors, drawing on papers from the journal Current Issues in Language Planning, deal with Nepal, Taiwan and Sweden (Baldauf, Kaplan and Baldauf 2000), Malawi, Mozambique and the Philippines (Baldauf and Kaplan 1999) and Botswana, Malawi, Mozambique and South Africa (Baldauf and Kaplan 2004).

11. For example, Basques, Catalans, Welsh, Corsicans.

12. See, for example, Thorburn's 1971 contributions on the application of cost-benefit analysis to language planning.

Chapter 2

The practice of language planning: an overview of key concepts

In this chapter we turn to a review of key concepts in the study of language planning practices, starting with some initial terminological clarification regarding the scope of the terms 'language policy' and 'language planning', which are sometimes used interchangeably and sometimes to mark distinct domains.

For commentators such as Baldauf (1994), Schiffman (1996) and Kaplan and Baldauf (2003) there is a clear difference in denotation, the former (language policy) referring to decision-making processes and the setting of goals, and the latter (language planning) to the implementation of plans for attaining these goals. The distinction seems justified when one considers the frequency with which policies are declared but not implemented (see Bamgbose (2000) for examples). But it also tends to encourage a view of language planning as primarily a set of technical activities, or managerial operations, undertaken after the really important decisions have been made by politicians or administrators; a characterisation resisted by some language planning scholars on the grounds that political and social considerations intrude as much into implementation as they do into initial decision-making.

Some, therefore, would subsume policy formation under language planning (LP), an example being Rubin (1971), whose influential framework of LP procedures provides for four separate phases: fact-finding, policy determination (formulation), implementation and evaluation.

Clearly, then, there is a certain indeterminacy about the range of reference of the two terms, a complicating factor being that it is sometimes difficult, as Schiffman (1996: 13) and others note, to ascertain just what policies are actually in force – there being some that are formalised and overt but many others also that are inchoate, de facto and highly informal. It may be preferable, therefore, not to overplay the discreteness of planning and policy as separate categories but instead regard them as so closely related that they can profitably be brought together for purposes of exposition and analysis, this being an increasingly common tendency, it would appear, if one considers the co-ordinate phrase 'language policy and language planning' in the title of Wright's (2004) recent volume.

A similar indeterminacy attaches to the vertical scope of language policy/planning; that is, to the question of whether families, individuals even, may be said to have language policies. Again, different commentators take differing views. Spolsky (2004: 43), for example, following the lead of Cooper (1989: 38), appears content to speak of 'family language policy'. Grin (2003: 29), on the other hand, argues that this is an overextension of the concept and proposes that it be restricted to the activities of larger-scale social actors that seek to influence the linguistic environment of whole communities. Questionable though such circumscription may be, it is at least practically useful in managing discussion of the field, and for this reason we will follow Grin (2003) and regard language planning policy as prototypically undertaken by agencies of the state at national or regional level, leaving open the question whether individual or family decisions on language constitute policy-making.

2.1 LANGUAGE, NATIONS AND NATIONALISM

LP's historical association with nation-building and state formation derives from, and reflects, the importance of language in European nationalism. It is appropriate, therefore, in this introduction to LP concepts to comment briefly on the relationship between language, nation, state and nationalism.

This, in fact, is not straightforward, for there is, and has been, considerable variability in the role of language in the construction of European national identities and in state formation – the Scots, for example, giving it less weight as an identity marker than the Welsh. Particularly helpful, therefore, is Wright's (2004) distinction between state nations and nation states, the two being distinguished by the different state formation processes they have undergone. Thus, in the state nations – prototypical examples of which are France, Britain and Spain – the boundaries of the state, or kingdom, were fixed and stabilised first. Thereafter, their rulers initiated a long-term process of cultural, religious and linguistic unification to construct a cohesive national community from previously rather disparate populations.

In the nation states, by contrast – Germany being a commonly cited exemplar – national consciousness, a group's sense of itself as ethnically and historically cohesive, is the antecedent of, and justification for, the group's attainment of self-government and a political state. Important here is a teleological conception of nationhood deriving from nationalism, an ideology that Kedourie (1960: 9), one of very many academic commentators on nationalism, famously describes as 'a doctrine invented in Europe at the beginning of the nineteenth century'. Its central tenets, he adds, are that humanity divides naturally into nations (which are thus seen as primordial), that nations have distinct characteristics and that self-government is the rightful, manifest destiny of nations.

For Kedourie, the intellectual roots of nationalist ideology lie in the work of German Romantics, specifically, Herder (1744–1803), Fichte (1762–1814) and von Humboldt, W. (1767–1835), who – writing at a time when Germany was no more than a geographical expression – saw in the German language the most plausible evidence for the existence of a German nation, which, because it was a nation, was entitled to its own state. This linkage of language and nation, with a distinct language taken to be an important defining characteristic of a nation, had a profound influence on succeeding generations of nationalist thinkers and can be seen as giving language a foundational role in European nationalism.

A common, though not universal, feature of European nationalist movements, then, has been the active consideration given to language matters, one of the more common objectives being the differentiation of the language of the group from related varieties on the same dialect continuum – the North Germanic or Romance continuum, for example – and the fusion of language varieties believed to be internal to the group into a single variety so as to forge a distinct language. This could then form part of the case for political independence where the group had yet to achieve a state of its own, nations being entitled to states. Or, where political autonomy had already been attained, it could reinforce the solidarity and cohesion of the national population.

Even where the language of the group was already sufficiently distinct linguistically not to require differentiation from related varieties, an *Abstand* as opposed to an *Ausbau* language, to use Kloss's (1967) terms, nationalist-inspired intervention was not absent. A case in point is Greece, which achieved independence from Ottoman rule in 1832 following an extended nationalist struggle, and whose national self-definition could draw on the resources of a distinctive Orthodox Christianity, a unique alphabet, a glorious past and a language readily identifiable as separate on linguistic grounds. For the new state, however, the issue of what form the written, standard language should take remained open.

The solution eventually adopted by the Greek government, albeit in a more extreme form than originally envisaged (Trudgill 2000: 247), was that advocated by a group of purists under the leadership of Adamantios Korais (1743–1833), who had argued for a vernacular form of Greek, but one purified of Turkish and regional dialect influences and closer to classical Greek, this being known as *Katharevousa*. Progressively institutionalised as the language of government and education during the nineteenth century, this was a variety quite distinct from the everyday spoken vernacular, *Dhimotiki*, this difference becoming in the twentieth century a major focus of contestation in Greek politics (see Trudgill 2000).

Illustrated here is a thesis increasingly upheld by contemporary commentators on language and national identity (e.g. Joseph 2004), which is that – far from being primordial as Fichte proclaimed – national standard languages are cultural and political constructs. The German language itself, specifically standard German, is an example: as Joseph (2004: 98) points out, it emerges from a patchwork of dialects in the sixteenth century, a product both of individuals' contributions (e.g. Luther's translation of the Bible) and of wider socio-cultural developments – the introduction of printing, for instance.

If the German case can be interpreted as an instance of speakers accepting that their related but sometimes barely mutually intelligible varieties are dialects of a single standard language (Barbour 2000b), there are converse cases where speakers of related and mutually intelligible varieties come to view themselves, because they have distinct ethnic sensibilities and affiliations, as speaking separate languages. Not uncommonly, such perceptions are encouraged by interventions consciously designed to emphasise, and deepen, any relatively small differences between varieties as may already exist, as the cases of Norwegian (see below) in the nineteenth century and Serbian and Croatian in the twentieth century illustrate. The general point here, now a sociolinguistics commonplace, is not just that national standard languages are constructs but that they are often delimited as much, or more, on political as on linguistic grounds. Indeed, as Barbour (2000a: 13) suggests, the emergence of nation states and national standard languages are profoundly implicated in each other: standard languages, he remarks, can be seen 'as products of modern nations, and nations partly as products of modern communications that allow the effective functioning of states'.

This is not to say that political borders necessarily demarcate separate languages. For instance, despite repeated efforts to evolve a distinct standard, speakers of *Vlaams* (Flemish) in Belgium acknowledge the same official standard, *Algemeen Nederlands* (Standard Dutch), as Dutch speakers across the border in the Netherlands (see Howell 2000), this example illustrating the complex, variable and contingent nature of the relationship between language and nation.

If national standard languages are constructions, the same – in the view of many contemporary scholars – may be said of nations. One part of the construction process of nations is often the forgetting, or psychological denial of just this, and the assertion of exactly the opposite: namely, that the nation's roots lie in antiquity and that it is an entity 'so "natural" as to require no definition other than self-assertion' (Hobsbawm 1983, in Hutchinson and Smith 1994: 76).

Among the exponents of these constructivist analyses of nations and national identity are Hobsbawm (1983), cited above, who stresses the role of 'invented traditions', national rituals and symbols (e.g. the mass production of statuary) in the production of feelings of solidarity and belonging, and Anderson (1991: 6), whose notion of the nation as an imagined community is much cited:

> It is imagined because the members of even the smallest nation will never know most of their fellow-members, meet them, or even hear of them, yet in the minds of each lives the image of their communion.

For Anderson, print language and the products it gives rise to – newspapers and novels – are especially instrumental in the forging of national consciousness. Billig (1995), meanwhile, in an extension of Anderson's ideas, draws attention to a phenomenon he calls 'banal nationalism', meaning the daily deployment of national symbols – flags, coins, anthems, airline livery, sporting uniforms, botanic emblems (e.g. the thistle) and the like – all of which function to continually reproduce and reinforce national sentiments in the populace.

It would be wrong, however, to suppose that there is any unanimity of interpretation. Gellner (1983), for instance, another influential commentator, conceives nationalism somewhat differently. He does not deny that nationalism, with its selective exploitation of rural folk elements, constructs nations (rather than the reverse), but does insist that it should not on that account be taken to be solely an ideological invention of particular intellectuals. It emerges, rather, out of specific social conditions, and has, moreover, a camouflaged sociological content he characterises as follows:

> The basic deception and self-deception practised by nationalism is this: nationalism is, essentially, the general imposition of high culture on society. It means that generalised diffusion of a school-based, academy-supervised idiom, codified for the requirements of a reasonably precise bureaucratic and techno-logical communication. It is the establishment of an anonymous, impersonal society, with mutually substitutable atomized individuals, held together above all by a shared culture of this kind in place of a previously complex structures of local groups, sustained by folk cultures reproduced locally and idiosyncratically by the micro-groups themselves. (Gellner 1983: 57)

Different again is Carmichael (2000: 282), who criticises Hobsbawm and Anderson's emphasis on the constructedness of national cultures for failing 'to take nationalism seriously as a phenomenon', for failing to empathise with the 'real emotional need' that the invention of traditions can fulfil. In an echo of Edwards (1994: 133), she makes the further point that even if national identities are constructed, they are not constructed out of nothing, but derive from some 'actual', non-fictive past solidarity.

Illustrated here, one might conclude, is the continuing elusiveness of agreed definitions of nations and nationalism, including the balance of subjective and objective elements in the former's constitution (see Hutchinson and Smith 1994: 4). To pursue this issue further, however, would take us too far beyond our central focus, which is the role of LP in the processes of construction outlined above – a topic to which we now turn.

2.2 THE ROLE OF LANGUAGE PLANNING IN THE CONSTRUCTION OF NATIONAL LANGUAGES AND NATIONS

In this section we review – with suitable exemplification – the processes of standard-isation, differentiation, codification, elaboration and purification that are central to the language planning tradition, especially as it relates to nation-building. First, however, we locate these processes with respect to the influential distinction between corpus and status language planning

2.2.1 Corpus and status language planning

The conscious, organised interventions that make up LP are customarily divided, following Kloss (1969), into two categories: status and corpus planning. Status planning addresses the functions of language(s) in society, and typically involves the allocation of languages to official roles in different domains – government and education, for instance. Inevitably, these allocative decisions enhance, or detract from, the status of these languages – hence status planning. Corpus planning, by contrast, addresses language form, the code itself, and seeks to engineer changes in that code, central among which, as summarised by Ferguson (1968), are graphisation (the development of writing systems), standardisation and modernisation. The involvement of persons with linguistic expertise is, therefore, typically greater than in status planning, which remains the province mainly of politicians and administrators.

It would be unhelpful, however, to overplay the distinction, useful though it is, for not only are corpus and status planning intertwined – changes in the form of a language being a usual prerequisite of its allocation to new functions – but both are typically driven by political considerations extending well beyond language per se. Moreover, the once commonly accepted notion that corpus planning follows, and is dependent on, status planning has recently been questioned (see Fishman 2000: 44): corpus planning, the evidence suggests, can in fact prepare the ground for status changes as well as consolidate them after they have taken place, or both can, indeed, proceed simultaneously. Nowhere, perhaps, is such interdependence better observed than in one of the main activities of LP – standardisation, which we now discuss along with codification and differentiation, its close associates.

2.2.2 Differentiation, standardisation and codification

In both state nations and nation states linguistic unification, or convergence (see Wright 2004: 42), was an important instrument for fashioning a cohesive national culture with which the population could identify. One aspect of this (see above) was conscious differentiation of the national language variety from other related varieties through a process known, following Kloss (1967), as *Ausbau* (German for 'building away'), involving the selection and promotion of those variants in the national variety dissimilar to equivalents in the other varieties on the same dialect continuum (Wright 2004). A classic example is the nineteenth-century differentiation of Norwegian from Danish, but similar interventions can also be observed in the cases of Macedonian/Bulgarian, Serbian/Croatian and Urdu/Hindi – in all of which linguistic distancing served to underscore political and national difference (see Fishman 2000: 45).[1]

A second aspect of unification, equally important, is standardisation, the construction – and subsequent dissemination – of a uniform supradialectal normative variety. This, it is widely agreed (Milroy and Milroy 1998, Joseph 2004), has both a linguistic and an ideological dimension. Linguistically, a key feature is the creation of a uniform written variety, achieved by replacing optional variants with invariable forms (Milroy, J. 1999), the ultimate aim being, in Haugen's (1966b) celebrated phrase, minimal variation in form and maximal variation in function. Complementary here, and necessary – since without it there could be no enduring standard – is codification, the process of giving explicit definition to the norm, principally through the production of authoritative grammars, dictionaries, spellers and the like. These contribute to the dissemination of the standard by making clear its rules and boundaries. This standard is, however, an abstract idealisation rather than an empirically verifiable reality in that while some speakers may approximate to the standard they never 'exactly conform to the idealisation' (Milroy, J. 1999: 18), an observation that has led several scholars (e.g. Milroy and Milroy 1998, Joseph 2004) to refer to the standard language as an 'idea in the mind', a sort of platonic form.

Standardisation is also an ideological process in a number of respects. First of all, the standard is commonly based on the variety (or variants) spoken by the most powerful sector of society, whose norms are subsequently held up for less privileged social groups to emulate. This, it is sometimes argued, consolidates and helps legitimate the economic and social dominance of elites. Acceptance and acquisition of the standard becomes necessary for socio-economic mobility. Second, standard-isation gives rise to what Milroy and Milroy (1998) refer to as a 'standard language ideology', a constellation of beliefs propagated by the media, government agencies or influential opinion formers, and widely accepted by the public, whose principal constituents may be summarised as follows:

1. Identification of the standard language (e.g. standard English) with the whole language (see Milroy, J. 1999: 18)
2. Belief in the superiority of the standard language over other varieties or dialects
3. Development of the notions of correct and incorrect language, and the idea that there is only 'one correct form of the spoken language' (Milroy, L. 1999: 174), part of the population coming to stigmatise their own speech as 'incorrect' or 'ungrammatical'. Language change also comes to be associated with decay or corruption
4. Identification of the standard language with the national language, a symbol of national identity and source, potentially, of national pride.

Turning now to the role of LP in standardisation, we immediately encounter a complicating factor, inimical to generalisation, which is the considerable variation in the routes taken toward the building of a standard language. In some cases, for example, standardisation is a protracted process, in others relatively swift; in some a standard is imposed from above, in others it emerges gradually from below in a more organic process; in some standardisation commences before the era of high nationalism, in others it coincides with or post-dates that era; in some standard-isation produces a single accepted standard, in others the outcome is two or more competing standards; and so on. It may be more appropriate, therefore, to proceed with some illustrative and contrasting examples.

A convenient example of standardisation as a long-term process, and one, more-over, where formal, state-directed LP is not especially evident, would be English. In this case, the standardising process is generally thought to have commenced in the Renaissance period with Caxton's introduction of printing to England in 1476 and his adoption of the prestitious south-east Midlands variety, centred on London, as the basis of the print language. The position and prestige of this variety was steadily entrenched by its use in administration and literary production (e.g. in the works of Spenser, Marlowe and Shakespeare). In due course it received the attention of the eighteenth-century prescriptivists, all of whom were desirous of linguistic order and keen to secure the language from decay, and whose works – the proposals of Swift (1712), the grammars of Duncan (1731) and Bishop Lowth (1762) and, most notably, the dictionary of Dr Johnson (1755) – advanced the construction of modern standard English.[2]

Alongside the efforts of these individuals, and not forgetting the nineteenth-century creation of the Oxford English Dictionary (OED), one also needs to set wider social forces conducive to linguistic convergence and the dissemination of a uniform standard: the rise of print capitalism (Anderson 1991), industrialisation and increased urbanisation in the eighteenth and nineteenth centuries, military conscription, the introduction of mass education after 1870 and, finally, the twentieth-century development of a mass media. The general picture, then, is of a steady, gradual evolution of a standard language from the speech of an elite sector of society, a process sometimes quickened by the interventions of individuals (e.g. Johnson), or by non-governmental institutions, but facilitated fundamentally by the social forces cited above, all of this occurring with little direct intervention by the state.

Contrasting with English, and now – thanks to the seminal writings of Haugen (1966a) – a regular textbook example of LP, is the case of the development of standard Norwegian. This differs from English both in its chronology – the standardisation of a distinct Norwegian only commencing in the nineteenth century following independence from Denmark in 1814 – and in its very clear exemplification of the influence of nationalism and romanticism in the standardisation process.

At independence there was no standard Norwegian, Danish having long been entrenched as the written language of Norway.[3] Such a situation, however, was profoundly uncongenial to contemporary nationalist and Romantic notions of the nation, which emphasised, as we have seen, the importance of a distinctive language as a significant, even defining, element of a unique national identity. It is no surprise, therefore, to find that as the century progressed and especially from the 1830s on (see Vikør 2000: 112), questions of language and national identity loomed large in the preoccupations of the Norwegian intellectual class.

There were, however, opposing views as to how a distinct Norwegian identity could be defined. One influential strand of opinion sought – in true Romantic fashion – to retrieve a Norwegian identity not from the sullied present but from a more pristine and distant past, from a medieval Norse culture, traces of which lived on, it was believed, in the popular culture of remote rural Norway. The implication, in linguistic terms, was that if there was to be a true Norwegian, it would need to be based on the popular rural dialects of the time.

Inspired by this Romantic vision, and instrumental to its practical realisation, was Ivar Aasen (1813–96), a self-taught linguist and himself a native speaker of a rural dialect, who set out to codify a common written standard out of, and for, the diversity of rural dialects. His grammar of 1864 and dictionary of 1873, the fruit of long travels around the Norwegian countryside collecting and comparing dialect forms (see Linn 1997), laid the foundations for what – with some refinements and modifications – became known as *Landsmål* (the language of the country), a variety recognised by parliament in 1885 to have equal validity with Dano-Norwegian and renamed *Nynorsk* (New Norwegian) in 1929. Today, despite the unfavourable prognostications of some of Aasen's contemporaries (see Linn 2004: 228), who believed it to be too much of an artificial contrivance,[4] *Nynorsk* persists as one of Norway's standard languages – albeit a lesser used one than its competitor.

This competing standard, the product of a second line of nineteenth-century language reform, emerged from an alternative conception of Norwegian nationhood, one that looked to the urban, middle-class culture of the time rather than the distant past as a more relevant resource for the construction of a modern Norwegian identity (see Vikør 2000: 113). In linguistic terms, the implication was that the Norwegian-ised Danish spoken in the towns rather than Aasen's rural dialects was an appropriate foundation for a modern written Norwegian standard. What was needed, therefore, were adjustments to the existing Danish standard to mark it as more distinctively Norwegian: the replacement, specifically, of foreign lexicon with 'native' Norwegian vocabulary, and orthographic changes that would more authentically reflect the everyday pronunciation of educated, middle-class Norwegians. Leading this reform programme, or more precisely one faction within it, was the teacher Knud Knudsen (1812–95), whose work is generally acknowledged as laying the basis of a Dano-Norwegian that received recognition in the official revision of the standard of 1907 and that was subsequently renamed *Bokmål* (book language) in 1929.

By the early twentieth century, then, there were two standard languages in Norway, a situation sufficiently uncomfortable as to encourage attempts at a rapprochement between *Bokmål* and *Nynorsk*, from which, it was hoped, a single fused standard would emerge. The story of these ultimately unsuccessful endeavours, fascinating though they are, lies, however, beyond the scope of this chapter, since the main aim of this thumbnail sketch has been to bring out the contrast with English, this lying primarily in the more obvious nationalist motivation driving Norwegian standardisation, the more direct and self-conscious LP involved, and in the more overtly political character of the process.

There is, however, a further reason for citing the Norwegian case here, which is that it was one of the sources for Haugen's (1966c) elaboration of a model of language planning, since refined (Haugen 1983), which continues to be influential. The model, in its original form (Haugen 1966c/1972: 110), identifies four processes involved in developing a standard language: (a) selection of norm, (b) codification of form, (c) elaboration of function and (d) acceptance by the community.

Selection here refers to the choice of one or more dialects to serve as the basis of the standard, and is exemplified in the Norwegian case by Knudsen's preference for the speech of the urban middle class over rural dialects as the basis of a new Norwegian standard. Codification, of which we have already spoken, involves stabilising, or fixing, the form of the language through the production of normative grammars and dictionaries: Aasen's 1864 grammar and 1873 dictionary would be examples here. Elaboration, sometimes referred to as 'cultivation', aims at an expansion of the language's functional range, allowing it to serve, for example, as a medium of scientific and technical discourse. Typically, this requires the development of new registers and the creation of new lexical items – especially in the fields of science, technology and economy, an activity that has led some writers (e.g. Ferguson 1968) to prefer the term 'modernisation' and others to equate elaboration with language modernisation.

If codification lies firmly in the domain of corpus planning, and elaboration is a combination of corpus and status planning, the final element in Haugen's (1966c) model – acceptance – can reasonably be placed in the category of status planning in that it involves conscious dissemination of the standard and orchestrated efforts to persuade the community to accept the norm. That this is necessary, and often difficult, is amply illustrated in the numerous instances where the standard, as developed by committees, academies or individuals, is rejected, or resisted, by the community.

One example of this, discussed in more detail in Chapter 4, is the ambivalent and sometimes hostile attitude of many native Breton speakers toward the standardised, literary variety of Breton developed in the twentieth century, a form they feel is somewhat artificial and strained. Not altogether dissimilar is the situation in the *Biskaia* province of the Basque country, where the new unified written Basque, *Euskara batua*, has yet to gain full acceptance, principally because it tends to reflect more closely the *Gipuzkoa* variety (Fishman 1991; Gardner, Serralvo, Williams 2000: 330). Illustrated here, and a quite general phenomenon,[5] is the reluctance speakers may experience in accepting a standard based on a dialect quite different from their own, and one that they feel does not, therefore, adequately acknowledge their particular identity.

Estrangement from the standard may also occur, however, for other reasons. If, for example, the path to standardisation is an archaising one in which the written standard is constructed from some older, more classical and therefore putatively more authentic variety, then a diglossic situation may develop in which the standard is used in high (H) functions (e.g. education and administration) and a more demotic, everyday variety in low (L) functions (e.g. home, informal interaction). Over time, however, resistance to the written standard, the high form, may set in, simply because it comes to be perceived as remote from everyday life, as an unwelcome artifice and as an impediment to education

Such, one might argue, has been the situation in Greece, where, as we remarked earlier, the contrast between *Katharevousa*, a purified, artificial variety harking back to a classical Greek past, and *Dhimotiki*, a popular, vernacular variety, was a focus of political contestation for much of the twentieth century up to 1974, when – with the overthrow of the ruling military junta – the former lost all official and popular support (see Trudgill 2000: 248).

Gaining acceptance of the standard is, then, a potentially fraught business, but – recalling Romaine's (2002: 19) point that LP interventions tend to be more effective to the extent that they work with rather than against prevailing social currents – it is possible to identify, at a very general level, circumstances that are conducive to success. Thus, where a standard emerges gradually out of the speech of the elite and steadily accrues prestige, where there are material and social incentives for acquisition and access is relatively easy, or where there are clear and widely understood ideological reasons for adoption – nationalist reasons for example – acceptance of a dominant standard language is more likely; this, almost paradoxically, rendering conscious LP intervention less necessary. Conversely, where standardisation proceeds relatively swiftly and is more obviously orchestrated, and the standard consequently has less time to accrue prestige to itself, where it is seen as an artificial construction imposed from above, where regional identities remain strong, or where material incentives and ideological motives are relatively weaker, acceptance will be correspondingly more difficult, rendering conscious promotion simultaneously more necessary and less likely to succeed.

One might add here that the prestige of the standard, a factor crucial to its successful dissemination, is widely acknowledged to be significantly enhanced by the literary output of creative writers, translators, and other literary figures. An example would be William Morgan's 1588 translation of the Bible into Welsh, which is recognised (see Chapter 4) as laying the foundation for a prestigious and eventually widely accepted standard written Welsh. Similarly, Yannis Psicharis's (1854–1929) celebrated novel *To Taxidhi Mou* ('My Journey'), the first literary work published in *Dhimotiki* (Trudgill 2000: 247), is recognised as immeasurably enhancing the credibility of *Dhimotiki* as a potential alternative standard to *Katharevousa*.

With this mention of individuals who have had a significant impact on language standardisation, we arrive at a juncture where it is convenient to introduce other agencies active in LP. In the next section, accordingly, we turn attention to language academies and their role, specifically, in elaboration and language purification.

2.2.3 Elaboration, purism and the role of language academies

Individual writers, philologists and linguists – such as Johnson, Webster, Aasen and Psicharis – have, as we have seen, been significant players in LP, but ranking alongside them in historical importance are formal institutions, the academies, to whose activities we now turn.

2.2.3.1 Language academies

The earliest of these were the *Accademia della Crusca* of Florence founded in 1572 and, more eminent still, the *Académie Française*, which started out as a literary grouping led by Valentine Conrart before it was converted into an official state organisation by Cardinal Richelieu in 1634. Operating at a time when France was beginning to emerge from a period of civil disorder and religious wars, and when the French vernacular was beginning to displace Latin in literary and administrative functions, Richelieu's aim was to pull the literary elite into the orbit of his influence and harness it to his objective of consolidating civil order and the power of the monarchy. The particular function of the new Academy, however, as set out in the statutes of foundation, was to purify the vernacular, expand its functions and regulate the language so as to 'render it pure, eloquent and capable of treating the arts and sciences' (cited in Cooper 1989: 10). From the outset, therefore, the Academy, like its Florentine counterpart, was a prescriptive, purifying institution dedicated to the codification of a literary standard that could not, and did not, admit words felt to have no place in polite society.

The members of the Academy, the forty 'immortals' as they became known, were in fact largely untutored in linguistic matters, which may partly explain the slightness of their corpus planning efforts, a rather poorly regarded dictionary only appearing in 1694. Nonetheless, the Academy's very existence, and the prestige it commanded, set an example for others beyond France to follow, most notably the Bourbon monarch Philip V, who established the *Real Academia Española* in Madrid in 1713. Its motto, *'Limpia, fija y da esplendor'* (purify, stabilise and glorify), is an apt summary of its aim and of its work, which in due course led to the production of a dictionary in 1730 and a grammar in 1771, the latter building on Nebrija's *Gramática castellana* of 1492 (see Joseph 2004: 103; Edwards 1994: 157).

The Spanish Academy, in turn, served as a model for the establishment in the nineteenth century of a string of independent Latin American academies – Colombia (1871), Mexico (1875), Ecuador (1875), El Salvador (1880), Venezuela (1881), Chile (1886), Peru (1887) and Guatemala (1888) (Guitarte and Quintero 1974: 324), which in the twentieth century came together with the *Real Academia Española* to found an overarching *Asociación de Academias de la Lengua española*, dedicated, among other things, to combating centrifugal tendencies among national varieties of Spanish. The *Académie Française*, meanwhile, which today acts as a bulwark against the contaminating influence of the English language, was more directly the inspiration for the foundation of academies in other European countries – the Swedish Academy (1786), the Russian Academy (1783) and the Hungarian Academy (1830), for example. Notably absent here is any English language academy. Proposals for such an institution, along French lines, were in fact advanced by Defoe (1702) and Swift (1712) in England and by John Adams (1780) in the United States, but they foundered on the objections of influential individuals (e.g. Johnson) and on the Anglo-Saxon aversion to formal institutional regulation of language. The work of codification and elaboration thus fell to individuals and private institutions (e.g. the OED).

In the twentieth century many more academies and LP agencies were founded, most conspicuously this time in colonial and post-colonial Africa and Asia. Well-known examples include *Dewan Bahasa dan Pustaka* (the Institute of Language and Literature), established in Malaysia in 1956,[6] the Indonesian National Language Council, set up in 1947 and later retitled the Centre for the Development and Preservation of the National Language in 1975, and the International Language Committee (for East Africa) established in 1930 to promote the standardisation of Swahili. With Tanzanian independence in 1961 this body was renamed the Institute of Swahili Research and transferred to the University of Dar-es-Salaam, where – alongside the National Swahili Council (*Baraza la Kiswahili*) – it is today responsible for Swahili research, vocabulary elaboration and language promotion.

Like the older European academies on which they were modelled, the central focus of these newer agencies has been the development of the national language, principally through codification, publication and elaboration of vocabulary. The latter, always a more iterative undertaking than either graphisation or codification (see Fishman 1974: 23), has been a particularly energetic area of activity: by the 1980s, for example, up to 500,000 new terms had been created for *Bahasa Indonesia* (Alisjahbana 1984), and a significant, though lesser, number for Kiswahili (Ohly and Gibbe 1982), the majority in the fields of science, technology and education. That these were the domains predominantly targeted for lexical elaboration indicates that the dominant motive was not the reinforcement of good taste or refinement – as with some of the older academies – but modernisation; that is, the expansion of the lexicon to facilitate scientific/technical discourse and to provide for 'intertranslatability with other languages in a range of topics and forms of discourse' (Ferguson 1968: 28).

Recent decades have seen the establishment of a further wave of LP agencies, but these operate in a quite different socio-political and intellectual context, one that is more suspicious of 'linguistic streamlining'. Compared to their predecessors, they also tend to have a wider remit, reflected in a greater degree of engagement in status planning. One of the main tasks of the recently established Welsh Language Board (*Bwrdd yr Iaith Gymraeg*),[7] for example, is the supervision of measures intended to bring Welsh to a position of equality with English in Wales (see Chapter 3). Similarly, the (Catalan) General Directorate for Language Policy (DGPL), established in 1980 following the enactment of the 1979 Catalan Statute of Autonomy, is involved in implementing and overseeing legislation aimed at 'normalising' Catalan; that is, elevating it to functional equality with Spanish (*castellano*). In South Africa, meanwhile, the Pan South African Language Board (PANSALB), formally inaugurated in 1996 as an independent statutory body and a key South African language planning agency, is charged – among other things – with working to promote the use of previously marginalised languages now awarded official status – languages such as Tshivenda, Xitsonga, isiNdebele and siSwati – and with investigating alleged violations of language rights provisions (see Marivate 2000).

We can conclude, then, that formal institutions backed by the state continue to play an important role in LP. With the passage of time, though, their functions have diversified into status planning, and their ideological biases have altered – at least in some cases. This is perhaps most clearly exemplified by PANSALB, which, far from standardising and promoting a single hegemonic national language within the borders of the state, as might once have been the case, today promotes an officially sanctioned multilingualism.

2.2.3.2 Lexical elaboration

Turning now to examine in a little more detail the operations involved in lexical elaboration, we find that they too have an ideological as well as a technical dimension in that developers of new terminology confront a set of choices, each of which carries a political or ideological charge. One choice, for example, and sometimes the soundest for being least prescriptive and most realistic in a world of easy electronic communication, is to give official recognition to borrowed terms already widespread in popular usage. This, of course, circumvents the problem of acceptance but may encounter puristic and nationalistic objections: academies in some countries, for instance, are resistant to borrowings from English. Where, however, there is no term currently available for a particular concept, or where spontaneous, popular borrowings are considered unacceptable, then intervention to coin a new lexical item ('lexication') may be thought necessary, in which case further options present themselves.

An initial binary choice is between creating a new term from indigenous linguistic resources or systematic borrowing from another language. If systematic borrowing is preferred, yet further decisions are needed: for example, on the source language, and on the degree to which the loan should be indigenised through phonological, graphological or morphological modification. If creating new terms from indigenous linguistic resources is favoured, then a variety of techniques can be exploited: for example, loan translation (translating a foreign word); semantic shift or meaning transfer (that is, giving new meanings to existing words); building new terms from the roots and affixes of indigenous words; and compounding.

These processes are commonly illustrated with examples from Indonesian (see Cooper 1989; Foley 1997; Kaplan and Baldauf 2003) – probably because terminology elaboration in this case has exploited not one but a variety of sources and techniques, and because the operations involved are well documented (Alisjahbana 1976). For convenience, then, we also use Indonesian as our source of examples, as in Table 2.1.

Whether one borrows a word from a foreign language or draws on indigenous resources to coin new lexical items, there are practical and ideological consequences. Borrowing, for example, can facilitate 'intertranslatability', but it may also make the word more difficult to understand – at least for some sectors of the population. It may also, more seriously, be seen as compromising the authenticity of the national language, though such sentiments usually vary in strength depending on the source language.

The use of indigenous language sources is not problem-free either, however. For modernisers, for example, it may be seen as an atavistic parochialism. Uncomfortable questions may also arise regarding which indigenous languages and varieties are to be the providers of roots and affixes. And finally, looming over all, is the issue of the acceptability of new coinings. Here, there appears to be agreement that it is easier to gain acceptance for a coining where there is no alternative term already in use, or no usage at all (Cooper 1989: 151). Far more difficult is gaining acceptance for coinings intended to replace spontaneous borrowings already established in popular discourses on science, sport, economics and commerce, politics, popular entertainment, computing and so on. Indeed, all too often the neologisms devised by academies never catch on, becoming 'dead butterflies pinned into collections' (Lewis 1999: 75) – beautiful but lifeless because they remain unused in newspapers, books or conversation.[8]

Table 2.1   Vocabulary elaboration: examples from Indonesian
(see Foley 1997, Kaplan and Baldauf 2003, Alisjahbana 1976)

'Lexication' technique	Examples
1 Borrowing from European languages (e.g. English) with graphological/phonological adaptation	*taksi* [taxi] *universitas* [university] *demokrasi* [democracy]
2 Semantic shift/meaning extension	*urak* [root] ⇒ [tendon] *pembulah* (*pem* [to] + *bulah* [bamboo] ⇒ [vein]
3 Borrowing of Sanskrit roots and affixes	a. *wan* [person of] + *warta* [news] ⇒ *wartawan* [journalist] b. *wan* [person of] + *sastera* [literature] ⇒ *sasterwan* [man of letters]
4 Use of roots and affixes of indigenous Indonesian languages	affixes: *ke- -an.* root: *bangsa* [people] ⇒ *ke-bangsa-an* [nationality]
5 Compounding	*anak kalimat* [child of a sentence] ⇒ [phrase] *anak uang* [child of money] ⇒ [interest]

Comments: Cooper (1989: 152) observes that borrowings from English and other European languages tend to be more common in the domains of science, technology, economics and politics, and those from Sanskrit in literature and the arts. Foley (1997: 414) remarks, meanwhile, that in coining new words Indonesian language planners tend to look first to indigenous languages as a source, then to Sanskrit (the Indic language of past Indonesian empires) and finally to English; priorities which reflect, of course, a concern for national identity and authenticity.

This is not to say that there have not been successes in the dissemination of new terms, especially where nationalist sentiments have been mobilised behind the replacement of foreign borrowings – as, for example, in the Turkish language reform of the 1930s (see below). Generally, however, it is difficult to disagree with Wright's (2004: 60) view that today, in an age of globalisation, open borders and electronic communication, it is increasingly difficult, and less acceptable, to police the national language and shut out foreign borrowings, which these days often derive from English. There has, moreover, been a shift in attitudes towards borrowings, which are now just as likely to be regarded by linguists and academics as indicators of vitality as of corruption. An example might be the reflections of Kuneralp (1981), a Turkish diplomat and writer, on the Turkish language reform (cited in Lewis 1999: 152):

if we are fanatical partisans of pure Turkish, when we cannot find a pure Turkish word to express the meaning we want, we load that meaning on to some other word and, for the sake of our socio-political beliefs, cast aside the Arabic, Persian or Western word that perfectly meets our needs. In this way we impoverish our language, we obliterate its nuances, we deprive it of clarity and thrust it into a tasteless form. Whereas, the more numerous the sources a language can draw on for words, the more explicit, the more colourful, the more copious it becomes ... The world we live in is steadily diminishing in size, the nations are growing closer together, their languages are influencing one another and thereby becoming jointly enriched. (Translation from Lewis 1992: 2–3)

2.2.3.3 Linguistic purism

Implicitly and explicitly, we have made reference in the preceding discussion to linguistic purism, an ideology that has been influential in the work of language academies and individuals and that therefore merits brief attention. As Thomas (1991: 75) suggests, there are various types of purism: elitist purism, for example, which scorns non-standard and regional usages, or archaising purism, that locates the purest, truest expressions of the language in the remote past. Another type, perhaps more common, and one we concentrate on here, is 'xenophobic purism' (Thomas 1991), which seeks to purge the language of foreign elements.

As one might expect, xenophobic purism is closely connected to ideologies of nationalism, to the Herderian notion that the national language cannot be authentically national if it too obviously or abundantly contains borrowed elements. It tends, therefore, to be more evident in periods of intense nation-building. It also tends to give most attention to the lexicon, though, as Thomas (1991) points out, any area of language – phonology, morphology, orthography – can in principle be the focus of puristic agitation. Typically, then, puristic interventions target foreign borrowings in the lexicon, and endeavour to replace them with words constructed from indigenous national sources – dialects, archaic popular forms, ancient texts.

Examples of this kind of intervention abound – both today in, say, the continuing struggle of the *Académie Française* against incursions from English and, more prolifically, in the nineteenth and early twentieth centuries, eras of high nationalism. In nineteenth-century Finland, for instance, linguists strove hard to eject Swedish terms in favour of authentically Finnish neologisms (Wright 2004: 58), and the Italian fascist regime (1922–45) was keen to eliminate any words of obvious foreign origin from public display. One of the most remarkable cases of language intervention, however, and one where there is a clear fusion of purism and nationalism, was the Turkish language reform, initiated in the 1930s.

The political context of the reform – essential to understanding its motivation – was the emergence in 1923 of a new Turkish republic from the debris of the old Ottoman empire. Its first president and founding father, Kemal Atatürk (1881–1938), was determined to forge a new national identity that was distinctively Turkish, secular and modern, and to this end introduced a whole battery of social, legal and cultural reforms. These included a western calendar system (1925), a new secular legal code, western-style surnames (1934), an extension of the rights of women, the closure of madrasas (religious schools) and a ban on the wearing of the fez (1925).

Language did not long escape the attention of the reformers, and in 1928 the

Arabo-Persian alphabet was formally replaced by a Latin alphabet, the so-called 'Gazi alphabet' (Lewis 1999: 35). Radical though this was, it was soon eclipsed by a still more ambitious project: the wholesale purging of the large number of words of Arabic or Persian origin that had over centuries infiltrated into written Ottoman Turkish,[9] and their replacement with words of Turkish origin so as to forge a pure Turkish (*Öztürkçe*), free of the 'yoke of foreign languages'[10] and less distant from popular speech.

The project was unleashed in its fullest vigour at the close of the first Kurultay (Turkish Language Congress) in October 1932 with what can appropriately be described as a language mobilisation. All over Turkey, teachers, doctors, civil servants, tax collectors and administrators were sent out to collect words from Anatolian dialects to replace those of Arabic origin. Scholars, meanwhile, scoured old texts and dictionaries of Turkic languages in search of replacements for the offending Arabic-Persian words. The results of these endeavours were published in 1934 in a volume titled *Tarama Dergisi*. The following year – for the benefit of a wider public – lists of replacement words proposed by the press were published under the title *Cep Kılavuzu* (Pocket Guide from Ottoman to Turkish) (Lewis 1999: 55).

Inevitably, perhaps, in such a large undertaking, involving many persons with little or no linguistic expertise, there were excesses. Thus, while some neologisms were created on sound philological principles by, say, compounding existing Turkish roots and affixes, others were little more than concoctions arbitrarily plucked from the imagination (see Lewis 1999). And, in cases where no Turkish equivalent could be found for an essential word, ingenious efforts were often made to fabricate a Turkish etymology for them.

The details of this neologising, and of the purification work conducted by the *Türk Dil Kurumu* (TDK) (Turkish Society for the Study of Language) after Atatürk's death, lie beyond the scope of this chapter however. All we can include here is a brief mention of the overall outcome, which is that by the 1970s written Turkish had been so utterly transformed that young Turks could barely comprehend texts from the 1920s or 1930s. And it is this, combined with the impoverishment of the lexicon and of register variation resulting from the whittling away of Ottoman words, that leads Lewis (1999) to refer to the reform as a 'catastrophic success'. He admits (1999: 150), though, that not all is lost: old words are re-emerging, there is greater willingness to countenance useful borrowings and the object of puristic concerns is now not so much Ottoman vocabulary but incursions from English.

For language planners, then, the Turkish language reform is a remarkable, and somewhat unusual, example of successful corpus planning. But it also illustrates the unforeseen and adverse consequences that can flow from such large-scale intervention.

2.2.4 The role of status planning

Unlike corpus language planning, whose domain is language itself (see above), status planning – that is, intervention targeted at the societal functions of language – usually involves simultaneous activity across several social domains: the workplace, local government, the family/home, the law, the media, education and so on. An example would be Quebec in the 1970s, where the ruling nationalist party, the *Parti Québécois*, implemented a series of measures to enhance the status of French relative to English. The most far-reaching of these – enacted in 1977 – was Bill 101 (the 'Charter of the French Language'), which required, among other things, businesses with over fifty employees to obtain a 'francisation' certificate attesting that French was the normal language of internal communication (the workplace domain). Newly-arriving immigrants were required to send their children to French-medium public schools (the education domain), and, most controversially, languages other than French were banned from outdoor signs (e.g. shop signage, advertising hoardings, traffic signs).

Provisions of this restrictiveness amounted to a rejection of the federal government's bilingual/bicultural policy, the rationale being that in a country where the dominant language, English, was so strongly associated with opportunity and social mobility, liberal pluralist policies offering freedom of language of choice could only condemn French to long-term decline. The only effective remedy, it was believed, was an active counter-hegemonic policy aimed at turning Quebec into a unilingual French sphere (see Schmidt 1998).

Another example of status planning implemented across a range of domains is the 'Speak Mandarin' campaign in Singapore. Initiated in 1979 by the then prime minister Lee Kuan Yew for a mixture of educational, cultural and communicative reasons (see Bokhorst-Heng 1999 for more detail), the aim was to persuade Chinese Singaporeans to give up speaking 'dialects' (e.g. Hokkien, Teochew, Hakka, Cantonese) in favour of Mandarin. As with the promotion of French in Quebec, a variety of instruments were used: advertisements in the press and on television urged a shift to Mandarin, and a prohibition was placed on the use of 'dialects' on public service radio and television (the media domain); provision of adult education classes teaching Mandarin was expanded (the education domain); for some occupational groups (e.g. the army) promotion and salary enhancements were linked to passing Mandarin tests (the workplace domain); and shop owners and stallholders were asked to provide Hanyu Pinyin[11] signs or names for their premises.

Recent census statistics suggest that the campaign has enjoyed a fair degree of success, not just in the public domains overtly targeted but also in the family/home domain. By 2000, for instance, the reported use of 'dialects' in the home had fallen to 23.8 per cent of respondents from the higher figure of 59.5 per cent in 1980 while over the same period use of Mandarin in the home rose from 10.2 per cent to 35.0 per cent (census figures cited in Pakir 2004: 122).

2.3 LANGUAGE PLANNING IN EDUCATION

Of all the domains mentioned above, education is probably the most crucial, sometimes indeed bearing the entire burden of LP implementation. The reasons are straightforward: education in most countries is largely funded and thus controlled by the state; schools are one of the key agencies of socialisation; school pupils are a captive audience, and the curriculum affords the state unequalled opportunities to shape the attitudes and behaviours of the next generation. Unsurprisingly, then, it has often been a cornerstone in processes of national transformation.

To take one example, the national mass education systems introduced in England and Wales in 1870, and in France in the 1880s under the Jules Ferry laws have, like those in many other countries (e.g. Japan – see Coulmas 2002), been absolutely central to the dissemination of national standard languages, which are, of course, often quite different to the vernacular varieties spoken in the home. In such cases, inculcation of literacy in the standard calls for mastery not only of a different medium – writing – but also of a syntactically and lexically different variety.

Education has also more recently been a key instrument for language revitalisation in societies emerging from, or rejecting, the old linguistic/cultural hegemony of a dominant, centralised state – in Wales, Catalonia and the Basque country, for example – where teaching the regional language is seen as an essential complement to intergenerational transmission within the family and as generally uplifting to the prestige of the language.

Evidence for the efficacy of teaching in revitalising a language is mixed, however. The recent small rise in the number of Welsh speakers recorded in the 2001 national census can, for instance, very plausibly be attributed to greater school exposure to Welsh; but, as explained more fully in Chapter 4, it remains to be seen whether Welsh language skills acquired at school will be retained over a lifetime and handed down to the next generation.

In the very different circumstances of Ireland, however, teaching the minority language[12] has not proved to be an effective instrument for language revitalisation (see Ó'Riagáin 2001). The lesson many commentators draw, following Fishman (1991), is that while minority language schooling is helpful, even necessary, for language revitalisation, it is insufficient and likely in fact to be ineffective in the absence of actions in other domains that reinforce the effects of teaching (see Chapter 4).

If language education very often functions as an instrument for the attainment of wider status planning goals (e.g. the dissemination of a national standard language), it may also be a focus of language policy in its own right, one sufficiently distinct to merit a separate label. One possibility, proposed by Cooper (1989: 33), is 'acquisition planning', which refers to planning directed at increasing the numbers of users/speakers of particular languages. Another, perhaps preferable for being more encompassing, is 'language planning in education' within the scope of which would fall the following policy issues, many of which are discussed in later chapters:

1. The choice of medium of instruction for various levels of the education system – primary, secondary, tertiary (see Chapters 3 and 7)
2. The role of the home language (or 'mother tongue') in the educational process (see Chapter 3)
3. The choice of second/foreign languages as curricular subjects of instruction, along with associated decisions on:

when these languages will be introduced into the curriculum

whether foreign language study will be made compulsory, for whom and for how long

what proportions of the school population will be exposed to second/foreign language instruction

4. In the case of English and a few other pluricentric languages, what variety of the language will serve as a model (or norm) for teaching purposes (see Chapter 6).

Worth noting immediately is that few of the issues above can be considered exclusively educational; they clearly have much wider social and political ramifications. For example, use of an ethnic minority language for teaching certain school subjects certainly does have important educational consequences, but in such societies as the United States (see Chapter 3) it is also a key focus of identity politics in that while some Americans welcome bilingual education (involving minority languages) as the realistic embrace of multilingualism in a multicultural society, others oppose it, fearful that it corrodes national identities traditionally constructed on monocultural lines and that it is a harbinger of future social strife.

Similar points might be made about media of instruction in multilingual post-colonial societies (e.g. Malaysia, Hong Kong, India, Tanzania, South Africa, Kenya), where the choice of media is very evidently a political as well as an educational matter (see Chapter 7 for a fuller discussion). Indeed, the consequences for society, and not just the individual learner, of choosing one medium in preference to another are so far-reaching that political considerations usually trump educational ones, as many commentators repeatedly observe (including those in Tollefson and Tsui's 2004 volume.)

This same theme – the mixing of the political and the educational in language education policy debates – emerges strongly in the next chapter, where we turn to a discussion of migration and the education of linguistic minorities, this time in the United States.

NOTES

1. English, too, cannot be forgotten here, if we bear in mind Noah Webster's eighteenth-century spelling reforms (e.g. American 'color' in place of British 'colour'), designed in part to highlight the independence of American from British English.

2. These works are titled as follows: Swift, J. (1712) *Proposal for Correcting, Improving and Ascertaining the English language*; Duncan, D. (1731) *A New English Grammar*; Lowth, R. (1762) *A Short Introduction to English Grammar*; Johnson, S. (1755) *A Dictionary of the English Language*.

3. Norway had been under Danish rule since 1380, a four-hundred-year period during which Danish was established as the formal written language.

4. The reference here is to Johan Storm (1836–1920), who, as Linn (2004: 228) notes, was not optimistic regarding the future of Landsmål:

We do not wish for Landsmål's demise; let those, for whom it is natural to do so, write it [...] but if it is forced on those for whom it is alien, then it will not be possible to conceal the fact that it is an artifical and randomly put together dialect language, and it will suffer the fate of all artificial languages: it will pass quietly away. [Storm, J. 1896: 114–15. Cited in Linn, A. 2004: 228]

5. One might cite the case of Swahili here as a further example, in that the decision taken in the 1930s under British colonial rule to standardise the language on the basis of the Zanzibari dialect Ki-Unguja was badly received by speakers of the rival northern dialect, Ki-Mvita, centred on Mombasa. There is no evidence, however, that this has impeded the spread of Kiswahili as a lingua franca in Kenya.

6. By 1966 the Dewan Bahasa dan Pustaka (DBP) had published 475 titles, mainly educational books for schools and readers for the general public. A Dictionary of Malay followed in 1970. (Alishjahbana 1974: 407). The DBP is also involved in coining new terminology (70,000 items by 1967).

7. The Welsh Language Board was given statutory recognition in 1993 (see Chapter 3).

8. Lewis (1999: 75) attributes this metaphor to the Turkish language reformer Falih Atay (1894–1971). Speaking of coinings that do not catch on, one thinks of the Spanish term 'balompie' for football ('*futbol*'), which all too evidently has fallen out of popular use (except in the title '*Real Betis Balompié*').

9. One survey (see Lewis 1999: 158) estimated that by 1931, 51 per cent of the vocabulary of five well-known Turkish newspapers was of Arabic origin as against 35 per cent of Turkish origin.

10. These words are those of Atatürk himself (1930), as cited and translated by Lewis (1999: 42).

11. Hanyu Pinyin is a romanised writing system used for transcribing Chinese characters based on Mandarin pronunciation.

12. Irish is a compulsory school subject.

Chapter 3

Educational and political dimensions of bilingual education: the case of the United States

One of the more striking features of globalisation is the increased rate of migration over recent years into the industrial societies of Western Europe, Australasia and North America. For some the ever more obvious linguistic and cultural diversity of the recipient countries is experienced as a problem; for others it is an opportunity and a societal and personal resource (see Ruiz's 1984 'Three orientations in language planning'[1]). The orientation adopted ultimately reflects underlying language ideology, conceptions of nationhood and beliefs about the place of minority cultures in the nation state, all of which have a critical influence on policy towards the education of the children of linguistic minorities. For this reason we return to address these issues later.

Initially, however, we discuss the educational rather than the political dimension of bilingual education, focusing on the United States – partly because the vast literature requires a selective approach and partly because bilingual education in that country is a high profile, contested area of language policy. North America also happens to be the setting for a considerable body of theoretical and empirical work on educational programmes for linguistic minority pupils, which, though specific and non-generalisable in some respects, nonetheless has relevance and interest for the implementation of bilingual education in other regions of the world, as does the political debate.

Bilingual education is, of course, powerfully influenced by the social, political and educational context in which it takes place, and it is appropriate, therefore, that we start with a review of relevant contextual factors.

3.1 THE CONTEXT OF BILINGUAL EDUCATION IN THE UNITED STATES

For convenience of discussion, contextual factors are broken down into four categories: demographics, social context, the history of bilingual education and types of bilingual education. We turn first to a consideration of the changing ethnic demography of the United States.

3.1.1 The demographics of migration and minority groups in the United States

A new era of immigration into the United States was inaugurated by the Immigration and Nationality Act Amendments of 1965, abolishing the national origins quota system.[2] A major consequence has been that Asia and Latin America have displaced Europe as the major source of migrants. Macias (2000: 17), for example, drawing on the US decennial census, reports that whereas in the first decade of the twentieth century 92.5 per cent of all immigrants came from Europe, the corresponding figure for the 1981–90 decade was 9.6 per cent. The proportion of immigrants from Asia had risen to 38.4 per cent and that from Latin America, especially Mexico, to 32.1 per cent.

A second very significant change has been in the accelerated rate of immigration. Whilst the US population increased by 10 per cent between 1980 and 1990, the number of persons reporting the use of a language other than English in the home rose over the same period by 38.6 per cent to a total of 31.8 million (14 per cent of the national population) as against 23.1 million or 11 per cent of the national population in 1980 (Macias 2000). Of these 31 million, the largest proportion at 54.4 per cent (17 million) were Spanish speakers, with Mexican Americans constituting comfortably the largest subgroup.[3]

Also significant is the uneven distribution of minority language speakers across the United States: over 50 per cent live in three states – California, New York and Texas – with particular concentrations of Spanish speakers in Los Angeles, New York, Miami, Chicago and the San Francisco Bay area (Macias 2000; Schmid 2001).

As regards English language learners, the data is slightly less secure, mainly because there are different definitions across the states of what constitutes an English language learner or a Limited English Proficient (LEP) student.[4] Nonetheless, both August and Hakuta (1997) and Macias (2000) offer persuasive evidence of a rapid rise through the 1990s in the number and proportions of LEP students enrolled in US public and private schools. One estimate (Macias 2000: 43) claims around 3.4 million LEP enrolments from kindergarten through to twelfth grade (K–12) in 1997, of whom 73 per cent were Spanish speakers. A more recent estimate (Kindler 2002) talks of over 4 million LEP enrolments across the mainland United States, constituting 10 per cent of all public school enrolments K–12. Again, however, the distribution across the nation is uneven. Gandara (1999), for example, reports that 25 per cent of California's K–12 enrolment is Limited English Proficient with 88 per cent of these students coming from Spanish-speaking homes. Meanwhile, states with little previous experience in serving LEP students have also seen rapid rises in such students, admittedly from a low base – Kansas up 290 per cent, Georgia 392 per cent, Oregon 480 per cent (Crawford 2002). Demographic projections suggest that this population group could constitute as much as 40 per cent of the US school age population by the 2030s (Thomas and Collier 2002: 1).

3.1.2 Minorities: the social context

In the United States, as elsewhere, there is considerable diversity within the linguistic minority population. Asian Americans, for instance, are obviously different from Native Americans and Latinos, all three appellations referring to meta-ethnic groupings with very considerable internal variation.[5] One way of approaching this diversity is through Ogbu's distinction (1978) between autonomous, caste-like and immigrant minorities,[6] later resolved (Ogbu 1992) into a contrast between voluntary and involuntary minorities: coarse distinctions, certainly, but they do at least highlight power, status and degree of subordination as factors distinguishing minority groups. They also help draw attention to the fact that some minorities have suffered involuntary incorporation into US society through military conquest or violence. The cases of African Americans, Native Americans and Mexican Americans (following the 1846–48 war) spring immediately to mind.

Asian Americans, by contrast, are sometimes classed as a voluntary minority on the grounds that they have migrated voluntarily, though this is problematic for two main reasons. First, and less importantly, the socio-economic disruption suffered by such countries as Vietnam and Cambodia raise questions as to whether emigration from these countries can always be classed as voluntary; second, whether voluntary or not, once they arrive most immigrants are, irrespective of their wishes, incorporated into pre-existing and long-standing racialised ethnic identities.

> Countless daily interactions with those from other groups (e.g. Anglos, African Americans, Asian/Pacific Island Americans, Latinos, American Indians) lead immigrants and their children to be perceived – and to begin perceiving themselves as – 'Latinos', 'Asians', and so on. (Schmidt 2000: 188)

The voluntary/involuntary distinction turns out, then, to be questionable, though it does potentially have a bearing on the moral claims of minorities to have their languages and cultures supported by the state.

More significant as regards school achievement is persisting social stratification among racialised ethnolinguistic minorities in the United States, and the processes of exclusion and discrimination they continue to endure. Figures cited by Schmidt (2000: 93) are indicative here.[7] In 1989 the median household income of the white Euro-American population was $31,400 and that of Asian Americans $34,800. African Americans and Latinos fell behind somewhat at $19,800 and $24,200 respectively. Census Bureau statistics (1996) on poverty, cited by Schmidt (2000: 92), show an equally sharp contrast between Euro-Americans (a 8.6 per cent poverty rate) and Asian Americans (a 14.5 per cent poverty rate) on the one hand, and African Americans, Latinos and Native Americans on the other, whose poverty rates were 28.4 per cent, 30.3 per cent, and 31.2 per cent respectively. These tendencies are broadly corroborated by August and Hakuta (1997: 4), who report that 35 per cent of the families of LEP students speaking Asian/Pacific island languages had incomes under $20,000 as compared with 57 per cent of Spanish speakers.

Turning to educational outcomes, a similar picture of stratification emerges. Data from 1992 on high school graduation rates shows that whereas 91 per cent of Euro-Americans and 92 per cent of Asian Americans graduated from high school, the corresponding figure for Latinos was 60 per cent.[8] LEP students, the majority of whom are Spanish-speaking, receive on average lower grades and score lower on standardised reading and maths tests than their native English-speaking peers (Moss and Puma 1995).

Of note here is the relatively favourable educational performance of Asian Americans, a full explanation for which is beyond the scope of this chapter. All one can say here is that it seems plausible that part of the explanation lies in some combination of (a) cultural attitudes and practices within the home, which are relatively advantageous in socialising children toward academic achievement, and (b) a different history of incorporation into US society which, in turn, has influenced the degree of subordination and discrimination experienced by this group.

The implications of these differences between minority groups, however, are easier to discern. Most important is that they indicate the complexity of factors underlying minority pupils' school achievement, suggesting in particular that the language of instruction (the proportions of English and L1 used in instruction) cannot be the sole, or even the main, causal variable affecting educational outcomes. What needs to be taken into account additionally is the wider social context of schooling, including Mexican Americans' long experience of subordination and denigration, the influence of which on child development is widely acknowledged. Cummins (2000), for example, a leading figure in bilingual education research, now gives more emphasis to societal power relations, alongside more narrowly educational factors, as a significant determinant of minority students' academic outcomes:

> linguistic and psychological research provides few answers to questions regarding why some culturally diverse groups tend to experience persistent long-term underachievement, nor does it give us clear directions regarding the kind of educational interventions that will be effective in reversing this underachievement. For answers to these questions we need to shift to a sociological and socio-political orientation. (Cummins 2000: 34)

The social context of schooling for Mexican Americans, then, is one of inferior, truncated education, of disparagement of their languages and cultures and of exposure to an 'assimilationist' curriculum (Schmidt 2000: 109). August and Hakuta (1997) and Crawford (1997) note, meanwhile, that poverty, low social status and relative segregation[9] in underfunded urban schools staffed by inexperienced teachers are among the contemporary contextual features of many LEP students' schooling.

It is difficult, then, to be unsympathetic to Cummins's (2000: 44) argument that 'coercive relations of power', obliging minority students to 'acquiesce in the subordination of their identities', are an important contributor to their relative educational underperformance. For Cummins, these power relations operate on schooling by influencing educational structures (e.g. the level of parental involvement in schooling, the degree of recognition given to pupils' L1 in school) and the mindsets of educators, which, in turn, shape the micro-interactions between minority students and teachers. It is these, he argues, that most immediately determine how students' identities are negotiated and hence how well they perform in school.

The solution proposed (Cummins 1996, 2000) is a 'transformative pedagogy' in which teachers and administrators seek to change the nature of their micro-interactions with students, support the incorporation of subordinated languages and cultures into school life and encourage students to critically interrogate their life experiences in relation to existing power relations. In short, teachers are urged to adopt an explicitly political orientation and challenge the structures that impede educational progress for minorities.

One can only sympathise with Cummins's call for a 'transformative pedagogy', but there is less cause for optimism regarding its efficacy in bringing about the transformation desired – given the degree to which schooling processes are embedded in, and influenced by, the wider social context.

Two general points may be made by way of conclusion to this section. The first is to reiterate the significance of the wider out-of-school socio-political context, which, while it may be backgrounded as the discussion moves on to details of educational provision for minorities, should be kept in mind as a fundamental dimension of the bilingual education debate and as a critical influence on educational outcomes for language minority students. The second is that we have identified two salient features of contemporary US society: changing demographics wrought by large-scale recent immigration, and persisting ethnolinguistic stratification and inequality. It is the confluence of these two factors, argue some commentators (e.g. Schmidt 2000) that have fuelled recent US language policy conflict. On one hand, increased immigration from Latin America and Asia and the consequent rise in LEP enrolments have fed white Euro-American anxieties that English is losing ground, threatening national unity and identity. The growth of assimilationist lobby groups such as US English (see section 3.3), which currently claims 1.7 million members nationwide (US English 2003), is symptomatic here. On the other, the social injustices flowing from ethnolinguistic inequalities have given impetus to pluralist claims for their redress through policies that affirm and support minority languages and cultures.

We shall return later to the pluralist-assimilationist debate. For the present, we turn to the history of bilingual education and the types of educational program serving LEP students.

3.1.3 The legislative history of bilingual education in the United States since 1968

There is a wealth of high quality publications on the history of bilingual education in the United States, covering both the nineteenth and twentieth centuries and documenting fluctuations in policies and attitudes towards immigrants and their languages (e.g. Baker 2001; Crawford 1999, 2000; Lyons 1995; Ricento 1996, 1998; Arias and Casanova 1993; Schmid 2001; Fishman 1981; Ovando 2003, Gonzalez and Melis 2000). It would be inefficient, then, to narrate that history once more. All we shall do here, therefore, cutting a long story short, is single out a few key dates for brief comment, starting with the Bilingual Education Act of 1968.

The 1968 Bilingual Education Act (BEA)

Introduced by Senator Yarborough (D-Texas) as an amendment of the Elementary and Secondary Education Act (ESEA) of 1965 through the addition of Title VII, the BEA bill was originally conceived as a compensatory measure addressing the needs of poor pupils disadvantaged by weak English language skills. Initial funding ($7.5 million) was in fact very modest, so retrospectively the BEA is seen as having a primarily symbolic importance, legitimating – though not requiring – the use of home languages in the education of linguistic minority children.

1974 Lau v. Nichols

This famous case, a landmark in the modern history of US bilingual education, arose from a class action suit brought by Chinese-speaking parents against the San Francisco Unified School Board, alleging a breach of pupils' civil rights under Title VI of the Civil Rights Act of 1964 for not providing instruction in a language the children could understand. The Supreme Court found in favour of the plaintiffs ruling that:

> There is no equality of treatment merely by providing students with the same facilities, textbooks, teachers and curriculum; for students who do not understand English are effectively foreclosed from any meaningful education. (Cited in Lyons 1995: 4)

Subsequent to this decision, the Federal Department of Education drew up guidelines (known as the 'Lau Remedies') to assist school districts in receipt of federal funding to move into compliance with Title VI. Under these guidelines, schools were required to provide identified LEP pupils with ESL (English as a Second Language) teaching and academic subject instruction in the home language (L1) until they had attained sufficient English language proficiency to move to mainstream classes.

The wider historical significance of the Lau case and the ensuing Remedies, however, is that they established that 'sink or swim' submersion approaches (see section 3.1.4) to the education of LEP children constituted a breach of their civil rights.

1974–1994 Reauthorisations of the BEA, Title VII of ESEA

Between 1974 and 1994 there were five reauthorisations of the BEA. In the early reauthorisations of the 1970s (1974, 1978) the legislative tendency was towards increasing Title VII funding and extending the scope of bilingual programs through removal of eligibility restrictions, while at the same time defining bilingual education more restrictively in transitional terms. The native language (e.g. Spanish), for example, should only be used 'to the extent necessary to allow a child to achieve competence in English' Lyons 1995: 2).

By the 1980s and early 1990s, however, scepticism regarding bilingual education was on the rise both among the public and in the Federal Administration, especially in the Reagan years. Thus, in the reauthorisations of 1984 and 1988 the emphasis on the acquisition of English as the highest priority was reinforced. A further significant development was the extension of Title VII funding to 'special alternative instructional programs' (SAIPs), the majority of which were actually monolingual English-only programs.

In contrast with its immediate predecessors, and in an atmosphere of increasing hostility, the fifth BEA reauthorisation of 1994 strikes a relatively liberal note in explicitly recognising the value of bilingual programs ('especially those that aim to preserve and cultivate children's native language skills' (Crawford 1997: 3)) and in declaring equality of academic performance with majority English-speaking children a high priority goal.

1998 Proposition 227

Despite the more encouraging tone of the 1994 reauthorisation, public and political antagonism to bilingual education continued to grow throughout the 1990s, especially in states like California that were particularly impacted by increased immigration. An early sign of this was the 1994 adoption of Proposition 187, excluding 'undocumented' immigrants from most public services.

The most serious, specific setback to bilingual education came, however, in 1998 with the Californian electorate's adoption of Proposition 227, the so-called 'English for the Children' initiative, by a majority of 61 to 39 per cent. The Proposition, sponsored by the software millionaire and political activitist Ron Unz, replaces virtually all bilingual education[10] with 'sheltered English immersion' teaching during 'a temporary transition period not normally intended to exceed one year', after which the child would transfer to a mainstream classroom (Crawford 1999: 252).

Similar anti-bilingual education ballots, also financed by Unz, have been passed recently in Arizona in 2000 (Proposition 203) and in Massachusetts in 2002 with substantial majorities – 63 per cent in Arizona and 68 per cent in Massachusetts.

We discuss the arguments around Proposition 227 much more fully in section 3.2.3.

2002 The No Child Left Behind Act

Current federal education policy towards linguistic minority children is defined by the 'No Child Left Behind' Act (NCLBA) of 2002, a reauthorisation and major revision of the Elementary and Secondary Education Act (ESEA) of 1965 based on four key principles: increased accountability for results, emphasis on 'scientific' research guidance as to what works best, parental choice and local control and flexibility.

The following are among the more significant changes introduced under the Act:

1. Title VII funding for LEP students is replaced by Title III.
2. The Bilingual Education Act is retitled the English Language Acquisition Act.
3. In a major change to funding arrangements, a formula grant system allocating

monies to states replaces a system of competitive federal grants. One consequence is that state education agencies have greater control over disbursement decisions, meaning they can fund programs of their preference.

4. Funding for programs for LEP students is increased (to at least $650 million annually).[11]

5. Accountability provisions are tightened. Schools are assessed annually on the percentage of LEP students reclassified as 'English fluent'.

6. All education programs, including those for LEP students, should be informed by 'scientifically based' research.

7. A three-year time limit on enrolment in 'bilingual programs' is set, after which the child should transfer to a mainstream class.

8. The Federal Office of Bilingual Education and Minority Language Affairs (OBEMLA) is retitled the Office of English Language Acquisition, Language Enhancement and Academic Achievement for Limited English Proficient Students (OELA) (Crawford 2002).

A number of commentators (e.g. Crawford 2002, Evans and Hornberger 2005) see in these changes a retreat from the bilingual education provision made available under Title VII, and certainly it would appear that the Act does strengthen the emphasis on English language acquisition at the expense of the development of home language skills. That said, it is too early yet, perhaps, to assess its longer-term impact.

This brief overview has, of course, focused on federal policy and on legislation rather than implementation, both of which are significant restrictions in view of Ricento's (1998: 92) claim that there has been 'inadequate planning and allocation of resources to effectively implement legislative or judicial remedies'. The consequence has been hesitant and uncertain compliance with federal mandates.

A somewhat similar point is made by Macias (2000: 41), who points out that 'the language needs of many LEP students are not being addressed, most are taught entirely in English, and there are not enough qualified teachers for either bilingual or English as a second language instruction'. Federal funding for LEP students has certainly increased, but it has never kept pace with the growth in LEP enrolments, as confirmed by Gandara (1999), who reports from California that in 1997, contrary to the Lau ruling, between 20 and 25 per cent of LEP students received no special educational services. She also says that only around 30 per cent of LEP students were in a bilingual program, and that over the decade leading up to 1996 the ratio of bilingual teachers fell from 1:70 to 1:98. Related research (e.g. Gandara and Rumberger 2003) suggests meanwhile that underqualified teachers are much more likely to be found in schools serving poor or minority children.[12]

Such figures certainly undermine the assertions made by Proposition 227's supporters about the failure of bilingual education. Far from failing, it would seem that in California at least the majority of LEP learners have never experienced bilingual education.

By way of conclusion to this section, we highlight two general trends that seem to emerge out of the historical detail. First, notwithstanding the fluctuations between liberalism and restrictionism, the dominant tendency in US federal policy has been assimilationist. With the adoption of Propositions 227 and 203, and the enactment of the 'No Child Left Behind' Act, this seems to have become more pronounced: English language acquisition is the top priority, the development of native (home) language skills hardly features as an item of public debate.

A second trend, perhaps more positive, is that there have been moves recently towards a greater diversity of programs for linguistic minority children. Thus, alongside the growth in 'structured English immersion', there are increased numbers of dual language (or 'two-way bilingual') programs on offer. It is to a description of these program types, and to evaluation studies of their relative effectiveness, that we now turn.

3.1.4 Types of bilingual education

We outline below the main types of educational program provided for LEP students in the United States,[13] some of which are clearly bilingual and some quite evidently not, the aim again being to provide background contextual information for the discussion of bilingual education research in section 3.2.3.

Submersion ('sink or swim')
This approach can hardly be labelled a program type at all, for the LEP child is placed in a mainstream classroom alongside native English-speaking children but given no special assistance at all. Though this breaches the student's civil rights under the 1974 Lau ruling, it remains a not uncommon practice in the United States. Gandara (1999), for example, estimates that between 20–25 per cent of LEP students received in California this form of instruction in 1997, a statistic consistent with Crawford's (1997: 18) figures from 1994–95 showing 23 per cent of LEP pupils in 'sink or swim' classes.

ESL (English as a Second Language)
ESL provision comes in various forms, which for convenience we may divide into three categories: ESL pull-out, ESL-content, and 'Structured English Immersion'.

- ESL pull-out: In this program type LEP pupils attend mainstream content subject classes in English but are withdrawn for certain timetabled periods (of very variable length) to receive specialised English as a second language teaching from a trained instructor. Such programs are intended to offer temporary, short-term support prior to full integration into mainstream classes. August and Hakuta (1997) report that ESL and transitional bilingual education (see below) are the two most common program types serving LEP pupils, which is consistent with Crawford's (1997: 17) statement that 'ESL pull-out remains the program of choice for many school districts'. Thomas and Collier (1997) concur, stating that ESL pull-out was the most common program followed by students in their study (52 per cent of their sample).

- ESL-content ('sheltered English'): In this program type ESL lessons (focusing primarily on grammar and vocabulary) are combined with content subject classes taught in English but designed to be comprehensible to English language learners. The teaching is carried out by ESL qualified teachers. The focus is on acquiring English through content subject teaching as well as on learning content subject matter. Again, this program is usually conceived of as short term. In some cases, timetabled periods are set aside for native language arts instruction.

- Structured English Immersion: This program type is in fact very similar to the ESL-content type program outlined above. A defining characteristic is that academic content subjects are taught in English using specialised materials adapted to the student's developing proficiency in the language. Teachers tend to be proficient in the student's native language, unlike in ESL-content programs. The main reason for distinguishing Structured English Immersion (SEI) from ESL-content programs is their rather different rationale. Specifically, SEI draws inspiration, and justification, from the Canadian immersion model of bilingual education, despite the fact that it is actually quite different, as Thomas and Collier (1997: 57) point out. Canadian immersion models, for instance, have full bi-lingualism as their goal and seek to impart minority language skills (French) to majority English-speaking children using a methodology in which the students' home language retains a significant role. SEI programs, by contrast, teach the dominant majority language to linguistic minority pupils using a methodology that gives the students' L1 hardly any role. The number of structured English immersion programs is reported to have increased quite substantially since the passage of Proposition 227.

Transitional Bilingual Education (TBE)

TBE takes two distinct forms: early exit TBE and late exit TBE:

- Early exit TBE: Content subjects are taught in two languages: the pupil's L1 (e.g. Spanish) and English – along with ESL instruction. As the pupil's proficiency in English increases, the proportion of instruction delivered through their L1 diminishes. Federal (and state) regulations set a three-year time limit on the use of the L1 as an instruction medium, after which the pupil is expected to move into mainstream English-only classes. The student's L1 thus plays only a temporary supportive role, and for this reason early exit TBE has been seen as promoting subtractive rather than additive bilingualism.[14] It is also assimilationist in intent, the aim being to integrate pupils into an English-dominant education system.

- Late exit TBE: In this variant there is a more gradual transition to English-only instruction. Instruction in the pupil's L1 typically continues up to the sixth grade, though, again, the proportion of instruction through the L1 gradually diminishes. Throughout the pupil receives specialised ESL instruction. Late exit TBE is less prevalent than the much more common early exit TBE, though neither program serves anything approaching the majority of the LEP population. Gandara (1999), for example, estimates that in the period 1995–97 only about 30 per cent of

California's LEP pupils were enrolled in any form of bilingual education program, and that many of these pupils were not in fact taught by a fully credentialed bilingual teacher.

Developmental Bilingual Education (DBE)

DBE, or maintenance bilingual education, is a strong form of bilingual education (Baker 2001), which aims to maintain and enhance the pupil's L1 while they acquire the majority language (e.g. English), leading them to full bilingual proficiency and biliteracy.

A defining characteristic is the continued use of the L1 as a medium of instruction through elementary school for 50 per cent or more of the timetable. Teachers are usually bilingual and committed to supporting the pupil's L1 and its associated culture. A key justification for the prominence given to the minority language in school is that it is more likely to suffer attrition being not so well supported in the out-of-school environment

Though data is not easy to come by, DBE and the similar late-exit transitional bilingual education programs are thought to serve only a very small minority of LEP pupils. An illustrative statistic is that of Thomas and Collier (1997: 55), who report that only 7 per cent of students in their sample were enrolled in DBE.

Dual language (two-way bilingual education)

Majority and minority pupils attend this type of program in as close to equal proportions as possible. Both groups are integrated for most content subjects and are taught in two languages – for instance, Spanish and English. The overall program aim is the development of proficiency in two languages, satisfactory academic attainment at or above grade levels and positive cross-cultural attitudes.

Lindholm (1997, 2001) explains that there are two variants of the program: the 90:10 and the 50:50 model. In the former, 90 per cent of instruction in kindergarten and grade 1 is in the minority language (e.g. Spanish) and 10 per cent in English – making this effectively an immersion program for the majority language participants. However, the proportion of instructional time allocated to the minority language is progressively reduced so that by grade 5 or 6 instruction is equally divided between the two languages.

The 50:50 variant, by contrast, starts with an equal distribution of time between majority and minority language in kindergarten and continues with this proportion through elementary school. An important feature of the methodology is that language mixing (or concurrent language use) is discouraged. While teachers need to be bilingual, they separate their two languages: the separation is usually based on time of day, subject or occasionally by teacher – as, for example, in the team-teaching that sometimes occurs in the early grades. Throughout the program efforts are made to promote a bilingual/bicultural ethos and to encourage parental involvement (Guzman 2002).

Dual language programs first emerged in the 1960s: the Coral Way Elementary School of Dade County, Florida, is usually recognised as a pioneer. Another early example is the Oyster Elementary School program initiated in 1971. In the 1990s there has been a rapid expansion in the number of dual language programs – perhaps because of favourable evaluations. Crawford (1997) reports that by 1994–95 there were 182 program schools across ten states, still a small proportion relative to the total number of schools. Baker (2001) cites a figure of 200 dual language schools established by 2000.

Nearing the end of this overview, it needs to be said that the program types outlined above constitute only very loose categories. Not only is there considerable variation within each type but the generic labels given to particular programs may positively mislead as to their actual content and nature.

Willig and Ramirez (1993), for example, point out that some programs bearing the label 'transitional bilingual education' in fact provide very little instruction through the L1. Conversely, some SAIP programs that claim to instruct only in English, even those deemed exemplary (Lucas and Katz 1994), utilise the pupils' L1 for a variety of pedagogic purposes. Guzman (2002: 1) also warns that some dual language programs are incorrectly labelled as such: 'What school districts describe as dual language programs is not always clearly aligned with the technical definition'. And even when the label is correctly applied, there is 'variation in implementation'.

It is precisely this kind of variation, and mismatch between label and operationalisation, that has undermined the value of some of the research evaluations attempting to assess the relative effectiveness of program types. And it is this that prompts Willig and Ramirez (1993) to advise that any such research should document carefully the details of program implementation.

In conclusion to the section, then, we refer to some of the key parameters distinguishing programs and program types:

- *Proportion of instructional time in the L1*: The quantity of teaching in the L1 (relative to the L2), defined in terms of (a) the duration of L1 teaching in years and (b) the intensity of L1 use (that is, how much of the school week, and in how many subjects, instruction through L1 takes place) and its impact on educational outcomes for LEP pupils, has been a major focus of research, perhaps unduly so. As we shall see, there is a near consensus among bilingual education researchers that greater support for L1 development, and academic development in L1, is positively related to higher long-term academic attainment by LEP pupils.
- *Type of L2 support*: While all programs for LEP pupils provide ESL teaching, there is variation in the type of support offered. The main contrast is between ESL taught as a language arts subject, usually in ESL pull-out mode, with a focus on the grammar, vocabulary and phonology of the language, and ESL taught via content subject instruction by a qualified ESL teacher. Thomas and Collier (1997) claim that the latter is associated with higher long-term educational attainment.
- *Degree of integration with the mainstream*: In some program types (e.g. ESL pull-

out) pupils spend much of their time in mainstream classes but are withdrawn for part of the school day for separate ESL lessons, which may or may not be on the same school site. In others (e.g. 'sheltered English', Structured English Immersion and developmental bilingual education programs), pupils are often taught separately from the mainstream for substantial periods. In TBE programs, meanwhile, pupils are often taught some subjects in L1 during part of the school day but remain in mainstream classes for other portions of the day. Such variations are significant given that bilingual education is sometimes criticised for segregating LEP pupils from the mainstream with potentially undesirable social and pedagogic consequences. Isolation from English-speaking pupils may, for instance, limit opportunities for L2 input from this source and hence retard second language acquisition. Dual language programs, however, overcome this alleged disadvantage by integrating majority and minority pupils in the same classes, where they learn to value each others' language and culture.

3.2 BILINGUAL EDUCATION IN THE UNITED STATES: EDUCATIONAL RESEARCH AND PEDAGOGY

The bilingual education debate in the United States has an instrumental, pedagogic dimension and, more fundamentally, an ideological, political one. In this section, we focus on the former, where, as in the ideological domain, there are fundamental disagreements between two opposing camps, pluralists and assimilationists. Both camps' starting point, however, is common. Both accept that the United States is an English-dominant society and that therefore the acquisition of English is fundamental to securing equal opportunities for linguistic minority pupils. Both also accept that many LEP pupils, particularly those of Mexican descent, are over-represented among those performing poorly at school. Thereafter, however, the two sides part company to disagree fundamentally over the causes of, and remedies for, educational underperformance, as well as over the best means for promoting the acquisition of English.

Some of these disagreements have crystallised around the role of the native language (L1) in the educational process, and, in particular, around its use as a medium for teaching content subjects and for introducing literacy. Bilingual education (BE) opponents have tended to see L1 teaching as a distraction from, and even an impediment to, the important goal of acquiring English. Supporters of BE, on the other hand, backed by empirical evidence and theory, have tended to view support for the L1 as highly functional both in the mastery of academic content and in the acquisition of the L2. They also stress the potential cognitive advantages of full bilingualism.

One particular area of dispute is the research attempting to evaluate the comparative effectiveness of different types of educational program for LEP pupils. It is to this body of research literature that we now turn.

3.2.1 Research on the effectiveness of bilingual education programs

One of the most influential of the early program evaluations was the Baker and De Kanter (1981) study. Federally funded to inform policy decision-making, this, like other early studies, was narrowly focused on the comparative effectiveness of Transitional Bilingual Education (TBE) and English-only program models, and on a limited range of outcomes – specifically English language attainment and performance on certain non-language subjects tested in English.

Working within a positivist research paradigm, Baker and De Kanter (1981) reviewed well over 100 primary studies, identifying only 28 as methodologically sound on the basis of such criteria as the presence of a comparison group, random assignment between treatment and comparison groups and adjustment for pre-existing differences between groups. Having surveyed these 28, they concluded that there was no consistent evidence for the effectiveness of bilingual education and advised that 'exclusive reliance on this instructional method is clearly not justified' (Baker and De Kanter 1981: 1). They did, however, support experimentation with 'structured immersion' approaches.

Shortly after its publication, 23 of the 28 studies in the Baker and de Kanter (1981) review were reanalysed by Willig (1985),[15] employing the statistical technique of meta-analysis to measure and combine the size of program effects, even when these were not statistically significant, and to adjust for methodological flaws in some of the studies reviewed. She concluded, in sharp contrast to Baker and de Kanter, that there were 'positive effects for bilingual programs ... for all academic areas' (Willig 1985: 287), and that bilingual education using the native language was better than the alternative of no special treatment (that is, 'sink or swim').

Unsurprisingly, given the politicised climate of program evaluation, these contrasting findings have been strongly contested. Supporters of BE note the questionable 'vote counting' technique of the Baker and De Kanter study, the narrow range of outcomes it considers and the decisions to exclude certain studies. Opponents, meanwhile, point to the small number of studies reviewed by Willig (1985) and the mechanistic nature of the meta-analysis procedures.

The details of these criticisms need not detain us, however, as it may be more useful here to consider more recent studies in the same tradition, namely those by Ramirez et al. (1991), Rossell and Baker (1996) and Greene (1997).

3.2.1.1 *The Ramirez et al. study (1991)*

The Ramirez study is significant both for its quasi-experimental longitudinal design and for including – in a three-way comparison – the less commonly evaluated late exit bilingual program (bilingual instruction up to sixth grade).[16] A total of 2,300 Spanish-speaking pupils enrolled in English-only 'structured immersion', early exit TBE (65–75 per cent use of English) as well as late exit bilingual programs were followed at nine sites over four years. Efforts were made to match comparison groups for background characteristics, to establish fidelity of program implementation and to consider a range of outcomes. The findings, though broadly favourable to late exit bilingual programs making the most use of the native language, are not straightforward. They may be summarised as follows:

- After four years pupils enrolled in 'structured immersion' and early exit TBE programs performed at similar levels in English language, reading in English and mathematics when tested in English. Their growth in language and reading skills was as fast, or faster, than that of 'a norming population' receiving no special treatment. However, attainment in both groups settled at below national norms.
- There were different levels of attainment at the three late exit sites: at the two sites with the greater use of Spanish, pupil performance in mathematics at the end of grade 6 was better than that at the late exit site where pupils were '... abruptly transitioned into English instruction' (Ramirez et al. 1991: 2). Reading and English language attainment were similar at the three sites and showed sustained improvement between grades 3 and 6 in contrast with a decelerated growth rate in pupils in early exit and 'structured immersion'.
- Late exit programs appeared to encourage greater parental involvement in schooling.
- In all three program types the teaching methodology provided only a 'passive learning environment, limiting students' opportunities to develop complex language and critical thinking skills' (Ramirez 1991: 5).

There were two other conclusions of note. First, consistent with Cummins's linguistic interdependence hypothesis (Cummins 1979) (see below), substantial amounts of instruction in the pupils' L1 did not impede their acquisition of English or progress in content subjects. Second, consistent with other studies (e.g. Hakuta et al. 2000), LEP pupils appeared to take five years or longer to fully develop academic skills in English.

While these broad conclusions are reasonable inferences from the data, the Ramirez study is regarded as flawed, quite seriously, by its failure to achieve comparability between programs in different school sites. In particular, because the late exit programs were implemented at different sites from those of the early exit and 'structured immersion' programs, no legitimate direct comparison of outcomes is possible, and hence no clear evidence for the relative effectiveness of late exit bilingual education can be adduced. In this respect the Ramirez study illustrates some of the difficulties that beset quasi-experimental program evaluations. A National Research Council committee subsequently withheld its endorsement of the findings, concluding, in August and Hakuta's (1997: 11) words, that:

The formal designs of the Longitudinal and Immersion studies were ill-suited to answering the important policy questions that appear to have motivated them.

3.2.1.2 *The Rossell and Baker (1996) and Greene (1997) studies*

Focusing – somewhat narrowly – on a comparison of TBE with four other program types (submersion, ESL, 'structured immersion' and DBE) with respect to outcomes in English language, reading in English and mathematics, Rossell and Baker reviewed over 300 studies, identifying only 72 (25 per cent) as methodologically acceptable.[17] The key findings were:

- On standardised tests TBE proved superior to submersion in only 22 per cent of studies in the case of reading, 7 per cent in English language, and 9 per cent in mathematics.
- In none of the studies comparing TBE with 'structured immersion' (N=12) was there any advantage for TBE in reading, English language or mathematics.
- In the one study comparing TBE with maintenance bilingual education there was an advantage in reading skills for the TBE program.

Rossell and Baker (1996: 44) conclude that 'the case for transitional bilingual education is not based on the soundly derived research evidence that its supporters claim'. Their preferred program type is English-only 'structured immersion', 'modelled after the Canadian immersion programs', though they concede that that type of instructional program is only one of many factors influencing school achievement.

While these findings are at first sight very unfavourable to bilingual education, closer scrutiny of the Rossell and Baker (1996) methodology has revealed flaws that substantially undermine their validity. These include:

1. The use of narrative review, and in particular the raw, unsophisticated 'vote-counting' technique, which tallies studies for and against TBE. The problem here is that, given variations between studies in sample size, power and design, it is not at all clear that they should be equally weighted.
2. Programs are compared by label with little or no exploration of their actual operationalisation (e.g. Crawford 1997).[18]
3. Rossell and Baker (1996) appear to equate Canadian immersion programs with 'structured immersion' programs in the United States, drawing on one as evidence for the other, when in fact, as pointed out earlier, the two have quite different goals and serve quite different student populations (Cummins 1998, 2000).
4. Criteria for methodologically acceptable studies are applied inconsistently, resulting in the inclusion of some studies that should by these same criteria have been excluded (Greene 1997: 4).

There are good reasons, then, for concluding that the Rossell and Baker review is flawed, and cannot bear the weight placed on it by critics of BE in public discussion of Title VII programs.

In a curious parallel to Willig's re-analysis of the Baker and De Kanter (1981) review, Greene (1997) re-examined the 72 studies reviewed by Rossell and Baker, eventually identifying only 11 as methodologically acceptable. Excluded were studies that could not be located (5), that did not evaluate bilingual programs (3), that did not properly control for background differences between treatment and control groups (25), that did not compare programs taught entirely in English with those including some native language (L1) instruction (14), and that were re-analyses of the same program by the same authors (15). The remaining 11 were submitted to meta-analysis to take into account treatment effect sizes in each study, and on this basis Greene (1997: 6) concluded, contrary to Rossell and Baker, that native language instruction had positive effects on English test results and some less certain benefits for mathematics scores.

In acknowledgment of the limited number of high quality studies, Greene (1997: 11) makes a final plea for the commissioning of more 'random-assignment experiments … to compare different approaches to teaching LEP students'. However, for reasons we now come to, many commentators would be most reluctant to respond to this call.

3.2.2 Theory and the evaluation of bilingual education programs

Policy-makers who turn to formal evaluations of bilingual education (BE) programs for guidance are likely to experience disappointment. Filtered through the disputes of ideological adversaries, the findings appear to be, and are, inconclusive and inconsistent. In part, this is attributable to the formidable methodological obstacles to any quasi-experimental comparative evaluation of types of educational program, the most serious of which (see Willig and Ramirez 1993) is that the traditional best method of establishing true comparability between students in treatment and control groups, random allocation, is rarely feasible in the educational field. Other difficulties include changes in the composition of groups as pupils exit and join programs, and the ascertaining of a match between a program's label and its actual implementation. Program evaluations have also been criticised (Baker 2001) for focusing unduly on easily measurable attainments and overlooking less easy to ascertain but important outcomes such as individual self-esteem, emotional stability, parental involvement in schooling and future earnings.

Apart from the methodological concerns, the perception has also grown that program evaluations have been driven by the wrong kind of question. It is now widely acknowledged that programs are not single entities (see August and Hakuta 1997: 19) but complex constellations of interacting components, and that therefore the more productive question is not 'which program is best for LEP pupils?' but rather which program components and 'which sets of instructional practices allow identified groups of English learners (LEP pupils) to reach educational parity, across the curriculum, with the local or national group of native speakers of English?' (Thomas and Collier 1997: 19).

The consequence has been not so much an abandonment of comparative program evaluation (see Thomas and Collier 1997) but a reduced preoccupation with the single variable of language of instruction and a renewed emphasis on identifying effective programs at school level and on dissecting the factors that contribute to their effectiveness, a form of research sometimes labelled 'school effectiveness' research. And from this research, as summarised by August and Hakuta (1997: 75–82), comes the not unsurprising findings that among the attributes of effective schools are strong leadership by the principal, staff with high expectations of LEP pupils and a commitment to their achievement, instruction adapted to the needs of the pupils, systematic student assessment, a balanced curriculum, use of the pupils' native language, high levels of parental involvement and a gradual, well-organised transition from special language instruction to mainstream classes.

Implicit here throughout, of course, is the assumption, shared by Cummins (1998) that BE, specifically the use of the child's home language in school, is no panacea, no guarantor of success, and that bilingual programs of any type may be well or poorly implemented.

Another, more radical, response to the disappointing utility of program evaluations comes from Cummins (1988, 1999, 2000), who complains that the evaluative research has been inattentive to testing theoretical principles underlying bilingual education programs. Thus, he criticises August and Hakuta's (1997) research review for the National Research Council, favourable though it is to the benefits of L1 instruction for LEP pupils, for focusing unduly on research findings in isolation from the theory that provides a principled, sounder basis for their interpretation. In place of the unmediated interpretation of research findings, Cummins proposes an alternative paradigm for bilingual education research, labelled the 'research-theory-policy paradigm' (Cummins 2000: 213), in which theory has an expanded role.

A theoretical framework, Cummins points out, allows the generation of predictions about program outcomes under varying conditions. It allows us to integrate findings from studies conducted in different contexts and thereby to refine hypotheses from which further predictions can be deduced and tested. It also extends the scope of policy-relevant research beyond those studies with a matched treatment-control group design to, in principle, smaller-scale case studies reporting program outcomes against which the predictions of theory can be assessed.

One of the better known theoretical frameworks derives from Cummins's own work in which he proposes a set of theoretical principles to account for the outcomes of bilingual education in different settings. It is to these that we now turn, examining them through the prism of the debate over Proposition 227.

3.2.3 Proposition 227 and theories of bilingual education

Proposition 227, adopted by California voters in June 1998, states that:

> all children in California public schools shall be taught English by being taught in English. In particular, this shall require that all children be placed in English language classrooms. Children who are English learners shall be educated through sheltered English immersion during a temporary transition period not normally intended to exceed one year. (Cited in Crawford 1999: 302)

Underlying this mandate is an educational rationale based on three key principles, the first of which is the so-called 'time-on-task' principle, most explicitly propounded by Porter (1990), which claims a direct, positive correlation between the amount of time spent in learning a second language and proficiency in that language. Neatly dovetailing with popular intuition, the principle would suggest that if children need to learn English to access opportunities, then they should be given as much classroom instruction in, and through, English as possible. Instruction through the pupil's native language is nothing but an impediment to the acquisition of English, and thereby to LEP pupils' academic attainment.

The second principle, more a notion actually, and implied more than explicit, is that instruction in two languages unduly burdens pupils' cognitive capacities, especially average pupils, and can adversely affect educational performance. It would be more effective, then, to concentrate effort on developing pupils' skills in English, the language of opportunity.

The third principle is that younger children learn languages readily and rapidly, and, on the whole, are better learners than older children. The policy implication derived is that English teaching – in the form of structured English immersion – should start as early as possible. The point is made with unusual explicitness in Article 1 of Proposition 227:

(e) Whereas young immigrant children can easily acquire fluency in a new language, such as English, if they are heavily exposed to that language in the classroom at an early age.

(f) Therefore it is resolved that: all children in California public schools shall be taught English as rapidly and effectively as possible.

We now discuss each of these principles in reverse order.

3.2.3.1 Principles 3: 'The younger, the better'

Extended discussion of the third principle (the optimal age question in Second Language Acquisition (SLA)) lies beyond the scope of this chapter, so we confine ourselves to the straightforward point (Scovel 2000a, 2000b) that older learners may be advantaged in certain areas (e.g. vocabulary learning, pragmatics, literacy) and younger learners in others (e.g. pronunciation, syntax). In addition, age is not a 'stand-alone' factor but interacts with a range of other contextual and developmental factors jointly influencing second language acquisition. In a policy-relevant review, Johnstone (2002: 20) concludes on a positive note that:

given suitable teaching, motivation, and support, it is possible to make a success of language learning at any age and stage, though older learners are less likely to approximate to the levels of a native speaker.

The evidence for what Scovel (2000a: 114) calls 'the younger, the better myth' is thus more equivocal than the Proposition 227 drafters suggest.

3.2.3.2 Principle 2: bilingualism as cognitive burden

Less secure still is the second notion that bilingual instruction is cognitively burdensome for the LEP pupil. Implicit in this view is what Cummins (1980) has called the separate underlying proficiency model of bilingualism (SUP), which claims first that the two languages of the bilingual are stored and function separately, and second that they somehow compete over a finite cognitive space. Neither proposition, however, can be sustained. The available evidence suggests that the two languages interact, allowing the integration and transfer of cognitive material learnt in either language, an idea encapsulated in Cummins's proposal of a common underlying proficiency model of bilingualism (CUP), to which we return presently.

Moreover, ever since Peal and Lambert's (1962) watershed paper, there has been a steady accumulation of evidence that in certain circumstances the development of bilingual proficiency can procure particular, subtle, cognitive advantages: enhanced metalinguistic awareness, increased capacity for divergent thinking, heightened communicative sensitivity and greater field independence (see reviews of literature by Baker 2001; Cummins 1976, 2000).

The evidence is not wholly unequivocal, however, as there have been methodological problems with studies comparing the cognitive functioning of bilinguals against monolinguals, and questions may be asked regarding the persistence of cognitive benefits over time, the precise conditions under which bilingualism is cognitively beneficial, the mechanisms delivering these putative advantages and the direction of causality – from bilingualism to improved cognitive functioning, or the reverse. Additionally, there are studies reporting a neutral or negative relation between cognitive functioning and bilingualism (e.g. Torrance et al. 1970), particularly those conducted with language minority pupils acquiring an L2, which cannot be discounted purely on account of methodological flaws.

To reconcile these discrepant findings it has been suggested, following Lambert (1975), that positive cognitive effects are most likely to arise from conditions of 'additive' bilingualism, where the individual adds a second language at no cost to the maintenance of an L1, and negative or neutral effects from conditions of 'subtractive' bilingualism, where a minority language L1 is gradually replaced by a socially dominant L2.

Cummins's thresholds hypothesis

A rather different effort to resolve these inconsistencies, and to explain how a home-school language switch can be simultaneously associated with lowered academic achievement in language minority pupils in the United States and relatively high academic achievement in majority children in immersion programs in Canada, is represented by Cummins's thresholds hypothesis. First proposed in the 1970s (Cummins 1976, 1979), and subsequently modified and qualified, this, in its original version, claims that there are two thresholds of bilingual language competence that mediate the effects of bilingual learning experiences on cognitive functioning. The first threshold is reached once the individual has attained a sufficient competence in one or both languages to avoid potential cognitive disadvantage, but a second higher threshold of competence in both languages has to be attained before the potential cognitive benefits of bilingualism become accessible. An immediate policy implication is that these benefits cannot be realised unless cognitive-academic skills in the L1 are maintained and developed alongside skills in the L2, a goal that is, of course, best met by a maintenance BE program.

Faced with criticisms that the thresholds hypothesis rests on a weak conceptualisation of language proficiency, and is vague on the precise levels of language proficiency in L1 and L2 necessary to reach the first and second thresholds, Cummins has since downplayed its importance, referring to it as 'speculative' and 'not essential to the policy-making process' (Cummins 2000: 175). He remains committed, though, to a central practical implication, which is that continued development of academic proficiency in two languages is associated with specific enhancements in cognitive function, and in this he is broadly supported by other commentators who have surveyed the evidence. August and Hakuta (1997: 19), for example, in their National Research Council report conclude that:

> Bilingualism, far from impeding the child's overall cognitive or linguistic development, leads to positive growth in these areas. Programs whose goals are to promote bilingualism should do so without fear of negative consequences.

There are also educational and social arguments for promoting the minority child's L1 at school. For example, it communicates to the child and their family that their language and culture is valued, and thereby challenges the 'coercive relations of power', the subordination and denigration that Cummins (1996, 2000) convincingly proposes as a key contributory factor to the educational underperformance of certain minority groups. Additionally, there is evidence (see Ramirez et al. 1991) that it facilitates greater parental involvement in schooling, a factor accepted as associated with school effectiveness (August and Hakuta 1997).

Finally, the promotion of the minority child's L1 skills makes sense if, adopting a language-as-resource perspective, one sees the development of these skills as a contribution to the conservation of a national resource, a valuable economic and diplomatic asset. As commonly recognised, there is an unfortunate disjunction between the economic and social value attached to the development of the schooled bilingualism of majority pupils on the one hand, and the neglect of the home-based language skills of linguistic minorities on the other.

All considered, then, there seems little merit in the second notion underlying Proposition 227. The learning and use of two languages in school is not an obstacle to educational attainment

3.2.3.3 Principle 1: the 'time on task' principle

We turn now to the first key notion underlying Proposition 227, the 'time-on-task' principle, which, if valid, would considerably strengthen the case for Structured English Immersion (SEI). In fact, however, there is substantial evidence that time spent on developing literacy skills in the L1 does not detract from attainment in English. Indeed, the reverse may be true: the level of development of a pupil's L1, Cummins (2000, 2003) argues, is a strong predictor of their second language skills and of their eventual academic attainment. This position is supported by Thomas and Collier (1997: 15), whose data leads them to the strikingly strong conclusion that:

> The first predictor of long-term school success is cognitively complex on-grade level academic instruction through students' first language for as long as possible (at least through grade 5 or 6) and cognitively complex on-grade level academic instruction through the second language (English) for part of the day.

Evidence against the 'time-on-task' principle can be found in a range of studies. For example, the Ramirez study (1991), though flawed in several respects, is at least clear that pupils in early exit TBE programs and SEI programs performed comparably in English language and reading by the end of grade 3. This, of course, contradicts the 'time-on-task' principle's prediction that there is a direct relation between the amount of time allocated to instruction in and through English and level of skills in the language.

Meanwhile, from the quite different context of the Turkish community in the Netherlands, Verhoeven and Aarts (1998) report that the level of literacy attained in L1 Turkish by primary-age Turkish pupils correlates positively with the level of Dutch L2 literacy achieved, and that both are strongly related to 'home stimulation' (Verhoeven and Aarts 1998: 129).

Cummins's linguistic interdependence hypothesis

Such findings, and those of many other studies (e.g. Williams 1996), both support and are explained by the *linguistic interdependence hypothesis*, first proposed by Cummins in a 1979 paper. This holds that:

> to the extent that instruction through a minority language is effective in developing academic proficiency in the minority language, transfer of this proficiency to the majority language will occur given adequate exposure and motivation to learn the majority language. (Cummins 1986 reprinted in Baker and Hornberger 2001: 177)

A key underlying notion here, accounting for the transfer of academic literacy-related skills between languages, is the common underlying proficiency model of bilingualism (CUP), which – in direct contrast with the SUP model (see above) – postulates a 'central processing system' integrating and drawing on concepts and linguistic abilities learnt in either, or both, L1 and L2. Cummins's (2003: 63) helpful analogy is with learning to tell the time: once pupils have learnt to tell the time in their L1, they do not need to relearn the 'telling-the-time' concept in their second language, only the vocabulary and grammar for doing so in an L2. Similarly with academic-related literacy skills such as distinguishing the main idea from supporting details: once learnt in the L1, the skills can transfer to the L2, or indeed vice-versa.

The key policy implication of the linguistic interdependence hypothesis, then, is that time invested in developing pupils' academic literacy skills in their L1 does not adversely impact or retard the long-term growth of those same skills in the L2. Indeed, to the contrary, there is evidence (see Thomas and Collier 1997) that development of L1 skills provides a sound foundation for subsequent academic success in and through L2 English. Combined with other educational arguments for incorporating the child's home language into the schooling process (see above), a positive case thus emerges for bilingual education programs that promote additive forms of bilingualism. In short, data and theory combine to undermine the simplistic 'time-on-task' principle[19] underlying Proposition 227.

3.2.3.4 The 'how-long-does-it-take' issue

Proposition 227's problems do not end here, however. The requirement (Article 2) that LEP pupils undergo structured English immersion during 'a temporary transition period not normally intended to exceed one year' rests on assumptions about the rapidity of English language acquisition that have been described as 'wildly unrealistic' (Hakuta et al. 2000: 13). Just how unrealistic will be seen presently as we turn briefly to a body of research whose central question is: how long does it take for language minority pupils to acquire sufficient English language proficiency to attain parity in academic uses of English with native-speaking peers?

Answers have considerable significance for policy: they may help determine appropriate time limits for providing minority pupils with the special services now funded under Title III, and they may help avoid the situation of LEP pupils being prematurely classified English proficient on the basis of superficial oral proficiency, and subsequently transferred to mainstream classes where they underperform and get falsely labelled 'learning disabled'. 'How long' research may also allow a more realistic appraisal of the effectiveness of BE, often criticised for appearing not to develop pupils' English language sufficiently swiftly.

A prerequisite for satisfactory research on this matter is, of course, an adequate conceptualisation of the nature of second language proficiency, and so, before turning to what the data shows, it is worth commenting on Cummins's distinction between conversational and academic language proficiency (Cummins 2000).

Cummins's BISC/CALP distinction

The distinction derives from Cummins's (1981) analysis of data from the Toronto Board of Education, which appeared to show a time lag between the acquisition of oral fluency in the L2 and the attainment of 'grade norms in academic English' (Cummins 2000: 53). By way of explanation, Cummins (1984) proposed a distinction between BISC (basic interpersonal communicative skills) and CALP (cognitive-academic language proficiency), arguing that whereas minority pupils acquired L2 oral fluency relatively quickly, they took much longer to develop L2 academic-literacy skills.

The reason for this, according to Cummins (1984), is that CALP skills typically

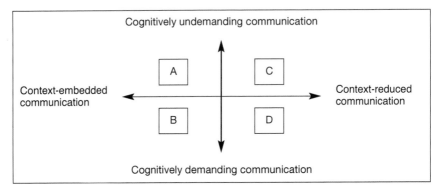

Figure 3.1   Two dimensions of communicative language use situations
(Cummins 2000: 68)

involve context-reduced, cognitively demanding situations of language, whereas BISC (conversational abilities) are typically deployed in cognitively undemanding, context-embedded situations supportive of easy communication. These two dimensions of communicative language use situations are depicted in Figure 3.1, where BISC would fall in quadrant A and CALP in quadrant D.

Over the years the BISC/CALP distinction has suffered considerable criticism on a variety of grounds. It is said, for example, to present an unduly simplified, dichotomous and static picture of the developing L2 language proficiency of the bilingual pupil. The terms themselves appear to suggest that CALP is a superior form of language proficiency, and encourage a 'deficit' view[20] of minority pupils' academic difficulties. The BISC/CALP constructs also seem to be constituted in such a way that they divorce language/literacy practices from their socio-cultural context.

Some of these criticisms have substance, some are unfair (see Baker 2001). Certainly, if intended as a complete theory of language proficiency, the distinction is inadequate, but, as Cummins (2000: 73) remarks, it was never intended as such. Rather it was an attempt to address specific issues in the language education of minority pupils, and in this light the figure above may more appropriately be regarded as a heuristic for analysing the cognitive-linguistic demands of certain types of school work.

Meanwhile, acknowledging that they are liable to misinterpretation, Cummins (2000: 75) has now dropped the terms BISC/CALP in favour of the less easily misconstrued, if less mnemonically useful, conversational and academic (language) proficiency. While theoretically imperfect, this distinction is similar to those of other researchers (e.g. Snow et al. 1991); it has established itself in the lexicon of educators; and it does, as Hakuta et al. (2000: 4) point out, 'make sense in the California context where very basic issues of English development still need to be resolved'.

A second conceptual issue, clearly central to the 'how long' research, is the criterion level of academic English proficiency at which LEP pupils may be deemed to be on an equal footing with native-speaking pupils. Discussion here is complicated by the fact that different studies employ different proficiency tests and utilise slightly different benchmarks. However, typical Californian practice, as reported by Hakuta et al. (2000: 3), is that pupils are reclassified as Fluent English Proficient (FEP) once they have passed an oral proficiency test and, additionally, scored above a designated level on an academic achievement test – usually 'a standardised English reading test' (e.g. SAT 9), which is 'norm-referenced to a national sample of English speakers'. The designated level is typically set at around the 36th percentile rank.

Both test and criterion have been criticised for two main reasons. First, it is widely recognised as problematic to assess minority language pupils against a criterion derived from a test norm-referenced to a different population. Second, the 36th percentile rank is by definition unattainable for at least one third of native English-speaking pupils, never mind minority language students.

There are, then, obvious limitations in the instrumentation used in reclassifying pupils as FEP, but, in the absence of more meaningful benchmarks (see Hakuta et al. 2000) and of useful normative developmental data, it seems for the present to be the accepted method.

Turning now to the 'how long' findings, caveated though they must be for the reasons just mentioned, we at least find that they display a persuasive consistency. Thus, Cummins's (1981) findings that immigrant children arriving in Canada after the age of six take between five and seven years on average to attain academic English proficiency but considerably less to develop high levels of oral proficiency are broadly consistent with those of later studies. Thomas and Collier (1997: 36), for example, conclude that it takes between four and ten years for minority language pupils to achieve 'on grade' levels of performance in reading in English. Progress, they say, is faster for those who receive L1 instruction and L1 support. Gandara (1999: 5) reports that by grade 3 LEP pupils' listening skills are at 80 per cent of native proficiency with reading and writing skills lagging behind, and Hakuta et al.'s (2000: 13) comprehensive review concludes that:

> in (school) districts that are considered the most successful in teaching English to EL students, oral proficiency takes 3 to 5 years to develop and academic English proficiency can take 4 to 7 years.

The reasons why academic English skills take this long to approach grade level norms are not, in fact, difficult to identify: acquiring English is difficult in itself, and LEP pupils are continuously striving to catch up with native-speaking peers whose own academic skills in English continue to advance.

It turns out, then, that Proposition 227's call for the mainstreaming of minority language pupils at the end of a transitional period 'not normally intended to exceed one year' is, on most evidence, unrealistic in what it assumes about the rate of acquisition of English academic skills. Too quick a shift to English-only instruction may, moreover, impede parental involvement with their child's schooling with the adverse consequences that typically follow.

There is, therefore, as Cummins (1998: 2) points out, no 'quick-fix' solution: indeed, Hakuta et al. (2000) propose the entire duration of elementary school as a realistic time span for the development of academic skills in English, during which time a pupil's other academic needs should receive attention, not least – given the accumulation of evidence about its positive influence on the child's future academic prospects – the continued development of the L1.

3.2.3.5 Conclusion: the educational arguments around Proposition 227

In the course of the preceding discussion we have seen that none of the educational assumptions underlying Proposition 227's provisions are supported by the research evidence. To summarise very briefly:

1. There is no backing for the 'time-on-task' principle. Time spent developing the literacy skills in the L1 need not detract from the development of those same skills in the L2.
2. There is no evidence that bilingual instruction is so burdensome that it impedes the pupil's acquisition of English. On the contrary, there is empirical and theoretical support for the cognitive benefits of the additive bilingualism that results when pupils continue to develop their L1 while learning an L2.
3. The idea that minority language pupils should be taught in English as early and quickly as possible because younger learners pick up second languages more readily is also not sustainable. First, the evidence on the age question is not clear-cut: younger learners may have an advantage but only in certain areas of second language acquisition. Second, there is a gap between premise and conclusion that needs to be bridged by further argument. There are grounds, in fact, for supposing that developing literacy skills in the L1 provides a good foundation for these same skills in the L2.
4. The time taken to acquire academic skills in English is considerably longer than that assumed in Proposition 227.

On the whole, then, theory and data point to the potential benefits of bilingual education (BE). They are only potential, however, because BE can be well or poorly delivered, and, as Cummins (1998: 3) has pointed out, it is no panacea for the relative educational underperformance of certain categories of minority pupils, some of whose complex causes may be found in the schooling process and others in a disempowering environment beyond the school.

Finally, the fact that Proposition 227 was so solidly endorsed in the face of unsupportive educational evidence leads one to suspect that the ideological and political dimensions of the BE debate carry as much, if not more, weight than the educational. It is, therefore, to these dimensions that we now turn.

3.3 THE POLITICS OF BILINGUAL EDUCATION IN THE UNITED STATES

The successful passage of California's Proposition 227 may be attributed, at least in part, to the importance that bilingual education (BE) now assumes as a symbolic issue in a wider language policy conflict. As already noted, this is sometimes presented – for convenience of exposition – as taking place between two opposing camps, assimilationists and pluralists (e.g. Schmidt 2000).

Institutionally, the assimilationist position is most obviously articulated by the lobby group US English, founded in 1983, which campaigns against bilingual education, against multilingual ballots and in favour of a federal constitutional amendment to make English the sole official language of the United States. Speaking for the pluralist position, meanwhile, is English Plus, an advocacy coalition founded to combat the successes of US English in the court of public opinion. Broadly, this supports genuinely bilingual education, the extension of the rights of ethnolinguistic minorities and the maintenance and learning of minority languages alongside English – hence 'English Plus'.

Our purpose here, however, is not to rehearse the origins and institutional history of these two movements (see Crawford 1999, 2000 for further detail) but to discuss the ideologies of assimilationism and pluralism that animate them. All that one might add here by way of historical analysis is that it is no accident that the rise of US English coincides with an era when mass immigration is reshaping the demographic structure of US society in such a way as to pose an apparent threat to the dominance of the English-speaking, Euro-American culture so long assumed to be the core of, if not coterminous with, the American national identity.

The mention here of identity signals what lies at the root of the conflict between assimilationists and pluralists. At one level, certainly, it is a dispute about the role of English and other languages in the civic realm, but, more fundamentally still, it is not about language per se but contrasting understandings of the nature of US society and its identity.

Thus, assimilationists, broadly speaking, adhere to a vision of the United States as a national community in which cohesion and social equality is best promoted by forsaking ethnolinguistic attachments in favour of allegiance to a single unifying language and culture. Traditionally encapsulated in the refrain *E pluribus unum* (one out of many) this solution is, assimilationists argue, the only one that can sustain the equitable, long-term functioning of a polyethnic society. Pluralists, on the other hand, emphasise ethnolinguistic diversity as inherent to the identity of the United States, point to a long and continuing history of racialised ethnolinguistic discrimination and argue that the goals of democracy and social justice, so conducive to national unity in the long term, are best served by policies (e.g. maintenance-oriented BE) that enhance the status of minority languages and cultures.

As the values of social justice and national unity are central to the arguments of both camps, with pluralists resting their case more heavily on the former, it may be convenient to organise our discussion around these two reference points.

First, however, following Schmidt (2000), we need to acknowledge the extent to which the arguments of either side are informed by quite different understandings of the origins of linguistic/cultural diversity in the United States. Thus, for assimilationists (Schmidt 2000: 119), the United States is – notwithstanding episodes of conquest and domination – first and foremost a nation of immigrants, willing to surrender old ethnic loyalties for integration into a society of opportunity, one in which parents positively encouraged their children to learn English. Now, however, these historic assimilative processes are seen as threatened by mass immigration and by the concentrations of non-English speakers in urban enclaves, where lack of incentive and the ideologies of pluralism articulated by ethnic spokespersons allegedly combine to encourage a reluctance to learn English.

Pluralists, by contrast, while recognising the contribution of immigration, emphasise a history of forcible incorporation through violence (e.g. African Americans), conquest (e.g. Native Americans) and annexation (e.g. the treaty of Guadeloupe-Hidalgo in 1848), and point to ongoing practices of racialised domination. A narrative of voluntary immigration and opportunity is thus replaced by one of involuntary incorporation and continuing discrimination.

Naturally enough, these two very different narratives lead to different conceptualisations of the relationship between minorities and the state, and hence of the level of rights to which minorities may be entitled: tolerance of the minority culture in the private domain only or its active promotion beyond this (see Kymlicka 1995, May 2001).

3.3.1 Bilingual education and social justice: the arguments of pluralists and assimilationists

Turning now to the social justice arguments, one finds on the assimilationist side a case that is as straightforward as it is flawed. Believing linguistic minorities to consist predominantly of immigrants, the assimilationist argues that not only are they morally contracted to limit the maintenance of their languages and cultures to the private domain but that it is actually in their interest to do so. This is because in an English-dominant society the surest path to socio-economic advancement is to integrate and to learn English. Pluralist policies, such as maintenance-oriented bilingual education, only encourage segregation, leave minorities suspended between two worlds and in the long term actually contribute to their subordination and marginalisation.

There are several problems with this argument, however. First, it misconceives bilingual education as somehow limiting, even denying, minority pupils' access to English. In fact, BE advocates accept that English is essential for social mobility but argue that the development of the pupil's L1 not only does not detract from acquiring English but is actually facilitative. Moreover, the incorporation of a pupil's home language into the schooling process may – in its affirmation of the value of the home language and culture – foster greater self-confidence and, hence, higher levels of eventual educational attainment. One might also mention that certain forms of BE – such as the increasingly popular dual language programs – promote integration and inter-group harmony.

A second difficulty with the assimilationist case, leaving aside the contested assumptions about the origins of US linguistic diversity, is that it is unduly optimistic both about the ease of assimilating and the socio-economic rewards for doing so. As Schmidt (2000: 188) has pointed out, to become an 'asimilado' is not only, or simply, a matter of self-ascription but depends crucially on how one is regarded by others; and in the United States – more often than not – minorities, whatever their personal wishes, are conscripted by public attitudes into pre-existing ethnic identities – Latino, Asian and so on. The not uncommon result, to use Parekh's (2000: 198) phrase, is that assimilation does not 'redeem its promise of ... full acceptance'.

As for rewards, it is clear that the acquisition of fluent English, does not necessarily of itself confer socio-economic advantage. Many African Americans, and Latinos, are long-standing speakers of English but, as we have seen, this does not prevent them from being over-represented among the lowest income groups.

A final point is that the assimilationist perhaps exaggerates the homogeneity of the society into which the minority person is supposed to assimilate, and in so doing offers an abridged version of national culture more or less identical with that of the dominant majority group.

Pluralists, obviously, have quite a different 'take' on social justice. Starting from a different understanding of the nature and history of US society, they call for state funding for the maintenance of minority languages and cultures, arguing that this is necessary not just to redress past injustices but to advance greater equality of opportunity and respect in a society marked by profound ethnolinguistic inequalities.

Invoked here also is the notion of collective (or group) rights to the maintenance of minority languages and cultures, extensively discussed by political theorists such as Kymlicka (1995), Parekh (2000), Raz (1994), Taylor (1994) and May (2001), particularly in respect of their contrast with the individual rights historically prioritised by liberals.

Discussion of normative theories of language rights lies beyond the scope of this chapter, however. All we can do in passing, then, is refer to Kymlicka (1995), who seeks to revise liberal political theory to render it more hospitable to cultural diversity and group-based rights. The barest nub of Kymlicka's (1995) argument is (a) that the well-being of individuals is entwined with the well-being of the cultural communities that shape them, and (b) that justice requires that ethnolinguistic minorities enjoy certain cultural rights, since withholding them would lead the state to fail in its moral obligation to represent all citizens fairly.

3.3.2 Bilingual education, national unity, the common good and social justice: the arguments of pluralists and assimilationists

We now come to the second key value in the assimilationist–pluralist debate, and the one most central to the assimilationist case; namely, national unity and the common good.

Pointing to ethnolinguistic tensions elsewhere (e.g. Quebec, Sri Lanka), assimilationists argue that bilingual education and other pluralist policies are deeply inimical to the unity of the nation. They encourage minority groups to identify interests distinct from, and often opposed to, those of the nation as a whole, and they increase the likelihood that competition for scarce resources will fracture along ethnic lines, feeding ethnic antagonism and hardening inter-group boundaries. Institutional bilingualism, in the words of the historian Arthur Schlesinger (1992: cited in May 2001: 99), 'nourishes self-ghettoisation, and ghettoisation nourishes racial antagonism'. In short, pluralist policies threaten the forging of a common American identity and thereby undermine national unity.

In a country as large and diverse as the United States, a single common language is, the assimilationist argues (see Schmidt 2000: 171), a necessary bond, an essential instrument for people to imagine themselves members of a unified society of equal individuals. It helps transcend ethnic divisions, facilitates communication and fosters an American consciousness.

It would not be too difficult at this point to disparage this assimilationist discourse as too obviously self-serving, as masking the dominant group's desire to preserve its hegemonic privilege, but to indulge this kind of ad hominem argument would be to miss the point that the assimilationist case emerges from a long tradition of liberal theory regarding the structure of the nation state. In the historically dominant conception, this is an homogenising institution composed not of groups but of individuals whose ethnic, religious or caste differences are abstracted away allowing them to be reunited 'in terms of their subscription to a common system of authority' (Parekh 2000: 181), to which they are expected to relate in a uniform, unmediated manner. To be a citizen is to be the possessor of identical individual rights and obligations in what Parekh (2000: 9) refers to as 'a homogenous legal space'; it is to transcend ethnic particularisms and give allegiance to a more impersonal authority. Thus, with 'several centuries of the cultural homogenising of the nation state' (Parekh 2000: 9) as background, it is unsurprising, perhaps, that assimilationists find it difficult not to equate unity with homogeneity.

The pluralist response to the arguments above operates on two levels: one practical and empirical, the other more theoretical. At the practical, empirical level, pluralists point out that multilingual states are not necessarily more prone to ethnolinguistic conflict than monolingual ones. After all, most states are multilingual, and while some have experienced ethnic conflict, many have not. And where ethnic conflict has arisen, it is not usually multilingualism or language per se that is the principal cause, rather material ethnic inequalities; though, in mobilising to secure redress for these, minority groups may seize on language, or language-based discrimination, as a symbol for their grievances and as a rallying point.

A related point is that coercive linguistic assimilation, unjust in itself, may actually provoke what it seeks to prevent. May (2001: 224), for instance, argues that the cause of many ethnolinguistic conflicts has not been the concession of minority language rights but their denial. In this view, the best way to defuse grievance and promote long-term stability is to display respect for the value of minority languages by granting them space in the civic realm.

But enhancing the position of minority languages is not just beneficial for those communities themselves. It also, pluralists argue, strengthens the nation as a whole. This is because a multilingual citizenry enriches cultural life, and is an invaluable asset in international trade and in matters of national security.

Meanwhile, the claims of US English that new immigrants, particularly Latinos, are less willing to learn English than previous generations are unsupported by empirical evidence. Indeed, the contrary may be true. On the basis of an extensive study drawing on recent census data, Veltman (2000: 90) concludes that:

> there is no evidence that continued immigration poses a threat to the linguistic integrity of the United States. The learning of English and its adoption as a personal, preferred language occur very rapidly in immigrant groups.

At the theoretical level, the pluralist response to assimilationist arguments drawing support from traditional conceptions of a culturally and socially homogenous nation state is more complicated. It involves acknowledging (a) that the nation state does have its advantages,[21] and (b) that it is not set to wither away; since, despite some attrition of its powers by globalisation from without and by more assertive minority populations from within, it remains the dominant form of political organisation, and one whose underlying ideology is still widely taken for granted.

That said, the traditional nation state has significant flaws, as pluralists point out: it is ill-equipped to respond equitably to the increased, more assertive multiculturalism of contemporary societies and tends, in May's words (2001: 104), to represent 'the particular communal interests and values of the dominant ethnie as if those values were held by all'. Moreover, in its individualist emphasis, it underestimates the cultural embeddedness of human individuals and, therefore, the degree to which respect for the individual requires an extension of respect to the language and culture that shapes them (see Parekh 2000).

Since the nation state is not set to wither away, and since its project of linguistic/cultural homogeneity is no longer feasible or valid, the best alternative, pluralists argue, is to rethink its nature, or, as May (2001: 17) puts it, 'reimagine [it] along more plural and inclusive lines'; this being in fact the current enterprise of political theorists such as Kymlicka (1995), Parekh (2000) and May (2001) himself.

Further discussion of this project is, however, neither feasible nor appropriate in the present chapter, focused as it is on bilingual education. All that one might add here is that such 're-imagining' is likely to involve acceptance of 'the legitimacy of some form of group-based rights' (May 2001: 17), a non-possessive, more inclusive re-definition of national identity, and, and at the most general level, some complex reconciliation of the demands of unity and diversity.

3.4 CONCLUSION

In this chapter we have surveyed the educational and ideological dimensions of recent US debate concerning the education of linguistic minority pupils. Inevitably, this has required locating the debate in its socio-historical context, one of the most salient features of which is the changes in US society wrought by recent large-scale immigration.

On the educational front, we have found no evidence that bilingual education (BE) is harmful. On the contrary, the considerable body of empirical evidence and theory that we have reviewed suggests that BE, understood as comprising the development of the pupil's L1 alongside the learning of English, is more likely than alternatives such as English-only 'structured immersion' to promote higher levels of educational attainment for linguistic minority pupils. That said, we recognise, with Cummins, that BE is no panacea for the educational underperformance of certain specific minority populations, the complex causes of which include the 'coercive relations of power' to which Cummins (2000) refers.

The weight of the educational evidence supportive of additive BE is such that it seems likely that at least some of the widespread opposition to it, evidenced in the adoption of Proposition 227, is ideologically rooted. In the latter part of the chapter we therefore explored the politics of BE, concluding that the dispute between pluralists and assimilationists is only partly about the role of non-English languages and cultures in the civic realm. At a more fundamental level, it is a struggle over how the national identity of the United States is to be understood and defined.

At this level of abstraction, the debate has clear relevance for other immigrant-receiving states such as Britain and France, since, despite obvious differences in the socio-political context and in their demography of ethnicity, they too are grappling with similar issues – how to accommodate linguistic and cultural difference within a nation-state framework biased towards homogeneity, how to re-imagine the state along more plural lines. And they too, like the United States,[22] are quite evidently multilingual and multicultural in a demographic sense, yet not, to employ Parekh's (2000) distinction, so convincingly multiculturalist in outlook, in habit of thought.

NOTES

1. Ruiz's much-cited three orientations are: *Language-as-problem* – an orientation that focuses on the difficulties sometimes attributed to multilingualism (e.g. alleged socio-economic costs and social divisions); *Language-as-right*, an orientation which focuses attention on the putative rights of linguistic minorities to enjoy education and access to other public services in the minority language; and *Language-as-resource*, an orientation which emphasises the social and personal value in developing minority language skills.

2. The national origins quota system derived from the 1921 Immigration Act, which limited admissions from each European country to 3 per cent of each foreign born nationality in 1910 (Schmid 2001). This tended to favour migrants from northern Europe.

3. The Spanish-speaking minority in the United States is heterogeneous, comprising sub-groups from Puerto Rico, Cuba, Mexico and other countries in Central/South America.

4. Some authors prefer the term 'English language learner' to the official term '*limited English proficient*' on the grounds that the latter suggests an unduly negative view of linguistic minority students, and fails to acknowledge their bilingualism and what they bring to schooling, namely knowledge of their L1.

5. Public discourse in the United States distinguishes five meta-ethnic groupings: Euro-Americans, African Americans, Native Americans, Latinos (or Hispanics) and Asian Americans. As note 3 above points out, there is considerable ethnic/cultural variation within these groupings.

6. 'Caste-like minorities', according to Ogbu (1978), are the most powerless and sub-ordinated of minorities, and frequently stigmatised by the dominant majority population. 'Immigrant minorities' (Ogbu 1978) are also subordinate and of low status but tend not to have internalised attributions of inferiority and have, as a result, greater self-confidence. 'Autonomous minorities', finally, have a well-developed sense of their cultural identity, and are not considered either by themselves or the dominant majority as a subordinate group.

7. Schmidt's source here is O'Hare, W. 1992 'America's minorities – The demographics of diversity'. *Population Bulletin* 47: 4 (December).

8. Again, this data derives from O'Hare, W. 1992.

9. Crawford (1997: 8) notes that in 1991–92, 55 per cent of LEP children attended schools with between 90–100 per cent minority enrolments as compared with 5 per cent of native English speakers. His data is from Bennici and Strang (1995).

10. Waivers to the provisions of Proposition 227 can be granted in some circumstances.

11. However, in view of increased LEP enrolments during the 1990s, Crawford (2002) estimates that this only amounts to only $149 worth of funding per eligible student.

12. According to Crawford (1997: 11), the shortage of qualified bilingual teachers has forced many schools into employing uncertified paraprofessionals whose 'only qualification in many cases is the ability to speak a language other than English'.

13. Information on the types of educational program provided is drawn from a variety of sources (e.g. August and Hakuta 1997; Rossell and Baker 1996; Thomas and Collier 1997; Faltis 1997).

14. The terms 'subtractive' and 'additive' bilingualism were first used by Lambert (1975). In subtractive bilingualism, skills in the first language are not consolidated while the second language is being acquired, with the result that they may eventually be lost through language shift. In additive bilingualism, by contrast, second language skills are developed, but not at the expense of the L1. Consequently, fully developed bilingual proficiency emerges. Lambert, and many other writers, associate additive bilingualism with positive cognitive consequences for the individual.

15. Willig (1985) excluded five of the 28 studies in the Baker and De Kanter review because they were carried out outside the United States.

16. Many commentators (e.g. Cummins 1998) regard late exit programs as sounder in theory than early exit TBE because, unlike the latter – which is monolingual in orientation – the former seek to develop, to the fullest extent possible, full literacy skills in the L1 and in the L2.

17. To qualify, studies had to: (1) compare students in a bilingual program to a control group of LEP students of similar ethnicity, (2) randomly assign students to treatment and control groups, or, where this was not possible, match the groups on factors influencing achievement, (3) base outcome measures on normal curve equivalents (NCEs), raw scores or percentiles, and not on grade equivalents, and (4) use appropriate statistical tests to measure differences between groups.

18. To be fair, Rossell and Baker (1996) acknowledge this problem and call for future research to take it into account.

19. It is referred to as 'simplistic' because, as Gandara (1999: 6) points out, one first needs to distinguish between time exposed to instruction and time actually attending to the instruction. Only the latter influences achievement levels.

20. A 'deficit' view is one that locates the educational problems of the minority language pupil in the child and his or her family rather than in the educational system that is supposed to serve them.

21. May (2001: 5) points out, for example, that that nation state 'liberates individuals from the tyranny of narrow communities', and offers an equal, common citizenship.

22. Of course, as the Latino population grows, it may acquire increased political influence, and be able therefore to negotiate an enhanced status for Spanish.

Chapter 4

Minority languages and language revitalisation

In this chapter our attention shifts from the United States to Europe, and from migrant, non-territorial linguistic minorities to autochthonous, regional minorities. These tend to have a more privileged position than the former in that their languages enjoy a greater degree of official protection – under the 1992 European Charter for Regional and Minority Languages,[1] for example. On the other hand, many of the regional autochthonous languages are endangered to a degree that the language of migrant communities patently are not, and language planning efforts on their behalf have, therefore, focused principally on language revitalisation, which is accordingly the main topic of this chapter. Bilingual education does receive some attention but primarily as an instrument of language transmission beyond the family rather than for the educational issues it raises.

The historical, socio-political and economic contexts of language revitalisation projects are, of course, critical not just to an understanding of their motivation but to their eventual success or failure, and for this reason we move in the latter part of this chapter to a comparative case study of Welsh and Breton. The two make an interesting pair for comparison in several respects: both are Celtic languages of the Brythonic or P-Celtic branch of that family; the speakers of both are located in westerly projections of the mainland territories of the founding European nation states of France and the United Kingdom; and both, exposed to competition from two prestigious, standard languages, have for some time been in decline. Their recent trajectories, however, are by no means identical. Welsh is a language whose decline has been, if not reversed, at least stemmed; Breton, on the other hand, is more seriously imperilled as a means of regular spoken communication within its historic territory.

By way of background to the case study, however, we first review the causes of language decline, theoretical frameworks for language revitalisation and the arguments commonly advanced for the undertaking of revitalisation in the first place.

4.1 LANGUAGE ENDANGERMENT: A BRIEF OVERVIEW

Over the last decade, following Krauss's 1992 paper on the crisis facing the world's languages, there has been a near flood of publications on the topic of language death and obsolescence (e.g. Dixon 1997, Grenoble and Whaley 1998, Nettle and Romaine 2000, Crystal 2000, Fishman 2001a and earlier, Dorian 1989). By now, therefore, the basic facts are reasonably well known: of the world's estimated 6,000 languages, only some 600 can be considered safe, or, conversely, 90 per cent of the less prestigious, less demographically strong of the world's languages may become extinct in the course of this century (Krauss 1992, Crystal 2000, Thomason 2001).

It would be unduly bold to claim that this literature offers a comprehensive theory of language death, but there is at least a considerable measure of agreement as to its general causes, the sociolinguistic processes that accompany it and the linguistic changes that dying languages typically undergo, which we now summarise briefly below.

4.1.1 Sociological and sociolinguistic factors in language death

The literature identifies two main routes to language death. In the less common, languages die with the relatively abrupt demise of their speakers, either through diseases introduced into indigenous communities by early European settlers – in the Americas, for example (see Crystal 2000), or through genocide (e.g. in Tasmania or El Salvador). In the more common route, by contrast, and the one we focus on here, language death is the outcome of gradual processes of language shift, taking place over a time span sufficient for the typical linguistic and sociolinguistic markers of decay to exhibit themselves.

The most immediate cause is a breakdown in the intergenerational transmission of the declining language within the family, indicated demographically by a preponderance of elderly speakers and a shortfall of speakers in younger age groups. With the death of the last of these elderly speakers, the language dies. Long before this, however, the language will have already entered a moribund, obsolescent state whose typical sociolinguistic markers are a retreat of the language from public into purely private domains – the family and neighbourhood, for example – leading to a loss of (linguistic) registers and a withdrawal into monostylism.

As obsolescence sets in, it is not uncommon for a cross-generational continuum of proficiency in the declining language to emerge, ranging from older speakers of considerable proficiency and fluency; through the middle-aged (the parents), bilingual in the dominant and the declining languages; to a younger generation with extremely limited proficiency in, or merely a passive knowledge of, the dying language. Through insufficient exposure, the speech of this latter group, labelled 'semi-speakers' by Dorian (1981), is typically marked by the frequent use of loan-words from the dominant language and by historically aberrant grammar and phonology. It is also halting, with normal conversation stressful.

Linguistic changes, then, are also accompaniments of obsolescence: most typically, (1) prolific and asymmetrical borrowing of vocabulary from the dominant language – a process of 'relexification' – and (2) simplification and reduction in the grammar and phonology.[2] Beyond the immediate causes of death, however, we also need to consider the often complex and subtle factors that lead minority language speakers to assess the opportunity costs of maintaining their language as greater than those involved in shifting to the dominant language.

A typical scenario is one in which a relatively isolated community is brought through processes of urbanisation, industrialisation or other forces of modernisation (e.g. education, media, tourism etc.) into increased contact with a more powerful, wealthier, possibly more numerous community. As the language of this dominant group is progressively associated in the minds of minority language speakers with wealth, power and opportunity, so it becomes more attractive, and often more necessary, to learn.

Conversely, the recessive language – as it loses speakers – comes to be associated with lack of opportunity, the elderly, the past, the rural and the backward. In these perceptions are mingled objectively accurate judgements as to the relative balance of economic opportunities, but also elements of self-denigration that are all too easily developed when the minority language is disparaged by members of the dominant group and marginalised by political arrangements denying it a role in the public realm – in state-funded education, for example. Matters are considerably worse if literacy in the declining language is restricted, if it lacks a literary tradition and if standardisation is incomplete or recent, for all these tend to weaken prestige.

Language shift in such circumstances is, of course, scarcely painless. Speakers are often deeply attached to the cultures, identities and histories embedded in their minority language, but they may nevertheless feel that for economic reasons they simply cannot afford to transmit the language to their offspring. Here, the problems of individual versus collective choices present themselves, and can be modelled psychologically as follows: if a speaker of a minority language decides for reasons of culture and identity to transmit that language to their children, while others of the same community transmit the dominant and more economically advantageous language, they risk ending up a double loser. First, they forgo the economic advantages available through the dominant language, and second, having done so, they may find that not enough speakers of the minority language remain for it to be viable. Anticipating others choices, they may reason that it is better to go with the flow and transmit the majority language in the first place.

4.1.2 The role of the nation state in minority language decline

Missing from the scenario sketched above, it may be argued, is any explicit mention of the nation state and nationalist ideology, which several writers have implicated in minority language marginalisation and loss. Dorian (1998: 18), for example, goes so far as to assert that:

> it is the concept of the nation state coupled with its official standard language, developed in Europe and extended to the many once-colonial territories of European states, that has in modern times posed the keenest threat to both the identities and the languages of small communities.

Grillo (1989: 173) talks, meanwhile, of a nation-state 'ideology of contempt' towards subordinated, minority languages; and May (2001: 75) too is similarly critical, arguing that the principal difficulty of the key nationalist principle of nation-state congruence, the idea that the civic culture of the state and that of the nation should be co-extensive and singular, lies 'in its inability to accommodate and/or recognise the legitimate claims of nations without states, or national minorities'. The weight and prevalence of these views is such that it seems useful to pause here to give them due consideration.

And, when one looks, there does indeed appear to be a considerable measure of scholarly agreement that the modern European nation state, since its emergence in the late eighteenth century, has been – to a degree far greater than the empires that preceded it (e.g. the Ottoman empire) – a homogenising institution. Homogenising because, through education and military conscription, it has promoted a common standardised language so as to fashion a national culture to which its citizens can give allegiance in the place of more primordial attachments (see May 2001: 54–6), and because it has been reluctant to concede status to regional languages lest this excite separatist tendencies. It has, moreover, not refrained from coercion in pursuit of these goals, as we see below.

4.1.2.1 The Jacobin project and the linguistic homogenisation of the nation state

This coercive dimension is perhaps most visible in the Jacobin project (see Grillo 1998), dating from the French Revolution of 1789–94, one of whose key objectives was to build a new republic of equality and fraternity around a single, unifying language. It is a project that has influenced the state's policies on French and the regional languages of France (Breton, Catalan, Corsican, Basque, Occitan, Flemish, Alsatian) right down to the very recent past. For the Jacobins, these regional languages ('patois') represented parochialism, feudalism, backwardness and the Ancien Regime, and they therefore merited eradication, as is made clear, famously, in Abbé Grégoire's report of 16th Prairal, Year II of the French Republic (6 June 1794) to the National Convention on 'The need and the means to eradicate the patois and to universalise the use of the French language'. Here, Grégoire states:

> Unity of language is an integral part of the Revolution. If we are ever to banish superstition and bring men closer to the truth, to develop talent and encourage virtue, to mould all citizens into a national whole, to simplify the mechanism of the political machine and make it run more smoothly, we must have a common language. (Cited in Grillo 1989: 24)

More explicitly hostile to linguistic difference still is Bertrand Barère's much-quoted speech to the National Convention of 8th Pluviôse (1794), in which he declares that:

> Le fédéralisme et la superstition parlent bas-breton; l'émigration et la haine de la République parlent allemand; la contre-révolution parle italien, et le fanatisme parle le basque. Cassons ces instruments de dommage et d'erreur. [Federalism and

superstition speak Breton, emigration and hatred of the Republic speak German, counter-revolution speaks Italian and fanaticism speaks Basque. Let us destroy these instruments of harm and error.] (Cited in May 2001: 159)

Admittedly, Barère's speech was made in a year of great external and internal danger to the Revolution (from, for example, the insurrection in the Vendée), but it nevertheless remains indicative of Jacobin ideology.

From a later period it is not difficult either to find evidence of the nation-state-inflicted marginalisation of minority languages of which May (2001), Grillo (1989) and others speak. Especially significant here, because of the delegitimation it implies, is the exclusion of minority languages (e.g. Breton, Welsh) from the public elementary school systems established in France, England and Wales in the late nineteenth century. Around this time, or not long after, there also occur such episodes as the use in some of Brittany's schools of '*le symbole*', a clog-like wooden object hung around the neck of children caught speaking Breton. Its counterpart in Wales was the 'Welsh Not', a kind of wooden placard worn by pupils discovered speaking Welsh (see Jones, M. 1998a; McDonald 1989, Press 1994).

Outside school, too, there is in official discourse a pattern of derogation of minority languages, a notorious instance of which is the episode of the 'Blue Books', one name for the 1847 Report of the Commissioners of Inquiry into the State of Education in Wales, which attributed the backwardness of Wales to the prevalence of the Welsh language, remarking that:

> The Welsh language is a vast drawback to Wales and a manifold barrier to the moral progress and commercial prosperity of the people. Because of their language the mass of the Welsh people are inferior to the English in every branch of practical knowledge and skill. He (the Welshman) is left to live in an underworld of his own and the march of society goes completely over his head. (Cited in Jones, R. 1993: 547)

Of course, policies and attitudes toward regional languages have been more vacillating, and not always so hostile as the above quotation might suggest. McDonald (1989: 47), for example, reports one general inspector of Brittany's schools, by the name of Carré, as firmly condemning the use of '*le symbole*'; and in the twentieth century the negatively charged remarks of Pompidou and other Gaullists[3] contrast with the more positive stance, at least rhetorically, of Mitterand and socialist governments post-1981 (see Safran 1999: 45). Overall, however, there is sufficient evidence that the European nation state has exhibited an endemic bias toward monolingualism in the dominant national language, or at best a 'benign neglect' of minority languages (Temple 1994: 194), sufficient for us to give qualified support to May (2001), Grillo (1989), Williams (1991a) and others' critiques.

4.1.2.2 Qualifying the thesis of nation-state culpability

Qualifications are necessary, however, lest we arraign the nation state too facilely. The first is that there are significant differences within and between the two main versions of the European nation state: the Romantic conception of the nation as a community based on kinship and consanguinity, '*Gemeinschaft*', and the nation conceived of as a voluntary association of citizens, '*Gesellschaft*' (see Chapter 3). Even within the latter, however, there are variations. In France, for example, language has traditionally had greater ideological significance than in Great Britain, as McDonald (1989: 5) points out:

> There is nothing in the British context to match the linguistic sensitivity of France. The French language and French national self-definition are deeply implicated, the one in the other, and linguistic self-consciousness and political centralism have been closely linked features of the French nation.

This greater linguistic sensitivity in concert with a pronounced tendency towards political centralism is probably, as we shall see, one of the reasons for the more retarded official status of Breton compared with Welsh.

A second qualification is that while linguistic homogenisation has indeed been an intermittent objective of European nation state policies, minority language decline has also occurred as a side effect of state polices that on other grounds might be considered beneficial. For example, if isolation is favourable to minority language maintenance, then the building of roads and railways, the construction of factories and the widening of leisure opportunities may all contribute to the undermining of those tightly knit social networks that help sustain the minority language.

A third point is that the nation state, and the identity associated with it, is not fixed and unalterable but an ongoing construction project, in which the historical tendency to marginalise minority languages has attenuated in recent years. Thus, throughout a range of European regions – Catalonia, the Basque country, the South Tyrol in Italy, and Wales – regional languages have been readmitted to the civic realm, and in some cases accorded co-equal status in their territories with the dominant majority language. Even France, along with Greece one of the states most suspicious of concessions to regional languages, has recently signed the European Charter for Regional and Minority Languages,[4] which requires signatory states to protect and promote these languages in such fields as education, public services, cultural activities and the media.[5] The reimagining of the nation state in the direction of greater ethnolinguistic democracy, for which May (2001: 311) calls, may, in short, have already commenced.

The case of Ireland shows, meanwhile, that official status and state support may not be sufficient to arrest language decline, for here Irish continues to succumb to socio-economic anglicising forces (see O'Riagain 2001) despite its formal status as a national language and despite extensive support through the state-funded education system.

Our conclusion, then, is equivocal. On the one hand, there is ample evidence that the processes of European nation-building have involved the institutionalisation of the languages of the powerful and dominant at the expense of minority languages, which have been excluded and subordinated. It is clear also that the sociolinguistic legacy of this history remains with us, taking the form of stigmatisation and occasional derogation, despite recent efforts at restitution. On the other hand, the causes of minority language decline are sufficiently complex for it to be an over-simplification to attribute sole agency to the 'philosophical matrix' of the nation state.

4.2 THE THEORY AND PRACTICE OF LANGUAGE REVITALISATION

Language revitalisation assumes different forms in different contexts, varying principally with the degree of endangerment of the particular language targeted and its cause. In the case of Catalan, for example, revival efforts have focused relatively successfully on the 'normalisation' of the language, that is, its rehabilitation from the suppression endured under the Franco regime and its reintroduction into such public domains as education, the media and administration.

In cases, however, where the language is substantially more endangered and literacy less established – one thinks here of the aboriginal languages of Australia, certain African languages or Amerindian languages – circumstances dictate more modest objectives and the employment of different means. Recording excerpts of the language from living speakers with a view to producing teaching materials and a dictionary, activities undertaken on behalf of the Gumbaynggin language in Australia (Lo Bianco and Rhydwen 2001: 406), may be all that is realistic, for example.

Whatever the circumstance, revitalisation evidently demands considerable ideo-logical commitment, which immediately raises the critical question posed by Fishman (1991: 2): why should such efforts should be undertaken in the first place? Answers can be found in Fishman (1991, 2001a), Dixon (1997), Crystal (2000) and Nettle and Romaine (2000), whose arguments we now review and assess.

4.2.1 Reviewing arguments for the preservation of global linguistic diversity

Arguments for the preservation of linguistic diversity divide roughly into two clusters that, for convenience of exposition, we can label the ecology of language cluster and the identity cluster.

4.2.1.1 Ecology of language arguments

The starting point here is Nettle and Romaine's observation (2000: 13) that linguistic diversity and biodiversity are closely correlated – so much so, indeed, that they speak of 'a common repository ... of biolinguistic diversity'. Both face analogous threats, and both can be defended on similar environmental grounds.

For example, the loss of small indigenous languages entails the loss of the knowledge embedded in them – specifically the 'detailed knowledge about local ecosystems encoded in indigenous languages' (Nettle and Romaine (2000: 166).

This is valuable not just because sustainable development is more likely where indigenous knowledge systems are utilised but because it adds to the total sum of human knowledge, making a contribution thence to human welfare by aiding, for example, the discovery of new medicines.

Also lost, Crystal (2000: 40) argues, are the histories of which languages are repositories, along with the worldviews they embody, and without these we are less capable of adapting and enriching our own. Diversity, he reminds us (2000: 33) is more propitious in evolutionary terms to the long-term survival of the species than uniformity. The strongest natural systems are those which are diverse. Combined here, then, are ecological arguments, suggesting that the reasons for preserving endangered languages are akin to those for protecting threatened species, and arguments from scientific advantage.

To these may be added arguments based on the intrinsic and aesthetic value of linguistic diversity. Particular languages, it is sometimes said (see Weinstock 2003: 254), are intrinsically valuable, independent of the utility they may have, because they represent unique human accomplishments, a singular way of conceptualising the world. They are, therefore, ends in themselves, and when a language is lost, something of intrinsic value goes with it.

Similar views are advanced by Crystal (2000: 54), who argues that linguistic diversity is worth protecting because 'languages are interesting in themselves', because in their variety they can tell us more about the nature of language and the human language faculty. An example would be the system of evidentiality, not found in most Western languages, but encoded in the grammar of the verb phrase in the Tuyuca language, where different verb forms signal different kinds of evidence for a proposition (Crystal 2000: 59).

Diversity, finally, confers broad aesthetic benefits; it just makes the world a more colourful, more stimulating place, affording more cultural choice and more resources for artistic expression.

4.2.1.2 Identity arguments

The initial premise here, now a commonplace, is that language is not just an instrument for communication but also – often – an important, even constitutive, feature of a community's identity. This being so, the loss of a language may do serious harm to the community's identity and culture, a viewpoint strongly articulated by Fishman, who proclaims that: 'the destruction of a language is the destruction of a rooted identity' (1991: 4).

For postmodernists, holding a view of identity as contingent, fluid, constructed, this particular claim will seem displeasingly essentialist (May 2001: 308). Fishman's overall position is subtler, however. He concedes that an ethnie's culture and identity may 'long outlast language maintenance' (1991: 17), just as an Irish identity has outlasted the decline of Irish as a language of regular spoken communication, or a Tlingit identity the loss of the Tlingit language (Dauenhauer and Dauenhauer 1998: 73), but insists that the culture and identity that endures is nonetheless changed.

This is because language and culture are linked indexically, symbolically and in part-whole fashion: indexically in that the language 'most historically and intimately associated with a given culture' is best attuned to 'express the artefacts and concerns of that culture' (Fishman 1991: 22); symbolically in that a community's language and culture come 'to stand for each other in the minds of insiders and outsiders' (1991: 24); in part-whole fashion in that parts of any culture (e.g. its songs, proverbs, blessings and curses) are 'verbally constituted'. It follows, then, that loss of a language may indeed produce cultural dislocation.

A not dissimilar point is made by May (2000: 373), who, adhering to a constructivist view of identity, nonetheless points out that 'in theory, language may well be just one of many markers of identity ... in practice, it is often more than that'. A few lines later, he adds:

> a detached scientific view of the link between language and identity may fail to capture the degree to which language is experienced as vital by those who speak it.

This leads us to a further, less commonly articulated, liberal reason for caring about the loss of languages, which is that if individuals take pride in the language of their community, if its fate matters deeply to them, then concern for the survival of that language, and for the possibility of its transmission to the next generation, is part of respecting what those individuals consider to be meaningful and worthwhile (see Boran 2003).

4.2.1.3 Assessing the arguments

Turning now to a brief assessment of these arguments, we can immediately concede that they are, in their totality, persuasive in putting across the view that the diminishment of global linguistic diversity is indeed a very serious matter requiring urgent action (see Crystal 2000: 166). This does not mean, however, that we need remain uncritical of particular arguments, or of how they hang together.

We may note straight away, therefore, that they have very different bases – some urging the preservation of linguistic diversity on instrumental or prudential grounds, others on grounds of the intrinsic value of particular languages or languages in general. Some treat global linguistic diversity as a 'public good', something of benefit to all mankind; others give more emphasis to the particular welfare of the speakers of endangered languages.

This last set, we believe, are the most persuasive, for they go to the heart of one of the greatest challenges to language revitalisation; namely, the choice made by some communities, or some of their members, to transmit only the dominant language because they see this as offering greater opportunities and greater social mobility to their offspring.

It is often pointed out, however (by Crystal 2000, May 2001, for example), that this 'choice' is not in fact freely made but is inflected rather by histories of discrimination, leaving speakers with feelings of inadequacy or shame, and by unjust institutional structures imposed by the nation state. Furthermore, as Crystal (2000:

109) points out, speakers of endangered languages are often not well-informed about the consequences of their abandoning their community language, and they may be insufficiently aware that learning the dominant language and maintaining the minority language need not necessarily be conflicting aspirations. Indeed, in much of the world people cope very happily with using two or more languages in their daily lives.[6]

These arguments are plausible, up to a certain point. It is probable that many, perhaps most, endangered languages become endangered precisely because of some injustice, historical or current, and there is a case in principle, therefore, for acting to protect these languages until such time as individual language choices can be assumed to be autonomous rather than the reflex of an internalised stigmatisation. That said, restitution of historic injustices may well not obliterate current disparities of opportunities available in the dominant and declining languages, which may be so marked as to lead some speakers to conclude that it is not in the best interest of their children for them to acquire the ancestral minority language.

Another reason for preferring arguments focusing on the welfare of speakers of endangered languages over those that highlight the 'public good' aspect of linguistic diversity is that the latter may, as Patten and Kymlicka (2003) suggest, overburden the speakers of endangered languages with unwanted responsibilities to maintain their languages for the sake of preserving linguistic diversity. It would be an unhappy situation, for example, if speakers of a small, threatened language, in the Amazon felt pressured against their inclinations to maintain their language in order to sustain a 'public good', whose benefits might mostly be enjoyed by populations in Europe, North America and Japan.

The environmentalist case for preserving linguistic diversity may also, Boran (2003: 108) argues, lead one to condone the coercive pressures that a minority group bent on language maintenance might apply to dissenting members for whom the language holds a different, lower identity value. The outcome could be a form of 'ethnic incarceration', a denial of a right that many liberal thinkers would wish to uphold – that of exit from one's ethnic group.

Space permits only two final observations here. The first is that, while the case for preserving global linguistic diversity is strong, it is not so well formulated as to render further conceptual and empirical work unnecessary. The second is that, as argued above, the most persuasive reasons for preserving linguistic diversity are to be found not in the environmentalist, prudential set of arguments but in those that give a central place to the interests and dispositions of speakers of endangered languages, many of whom for good reason will wish to maintain the language of their community, and should be helped to do so. Others, however, for varied reasons, may not, and though we may wish that they thought differently, we cannot and should not, if we wish to avoid the infringement of important liberal precepts, impose on them a duty to maintain the language for the sake of global linguistic diversity.

In short, the preservation of global linguistic diversity is certainly a worthy goal, but it is not obvious that it should be pursued in circumstances where 'it goes against the choices and preferences of significant numbers of people in the vulnerable language community or involves imposing significant restrictions on their opportunities or mobility' (Patten and Kymlicka 2003: 49).

4.2.2 Guiding frameworks for language revitalisation

Much of the language revitalisation literature consists of case studies, but there are also more theoretical contributions, two of which we single out for attention in this section: the GIDS scale of Fishman (1991, 2001b) and the model of ethnolinguistic vitality first proposed by Giles, Bourhis and Taylor (1977).

4.2.2.1 Fishman's GIDS Scale

Fishman's eight-stage Graded Intergenerational Disruption Scale (GIDS) (Fishman 1991: 87–109) has two main functions: first, it helps diagnose the extent to which a language is endangered, and, second, it helps guide revitalisation efforts, suggesting priorities for action and indicating how different restorative actions may be more effectively coordinated. Table 4.1 is an outline of its eight stages.

Table 4.1   The GIDS scale (after Fishman 1991, 2001b: 466)

Stage 8	Stage 8 lies at the most disrupted end of the scale, where the threatened language has undergone attrition to a point where only a few socially isolated, elderly speakers remain. Revitalisation efforts will involve work with informants directed at reassembling a grammar, a lexicon and a phonology, which can subsequently form the basis of teaching materials. This stage may also see efforts to instruct adults in the language.
Stage 7	At stage 7 the threatened language is spoken by the older generation but not the younger. These elderly speakers, in contrast with stage 8, are socially integrated – living in neighbourhoods and homes alongside other minority community members, many of whom may be monoglot speakers of the dominant majority language. The focus, and goal, of revitalisation at this stage is to re-establish knowledge of the threatened language in the younger generation so that they may be equipped to transmit the language to their children in due course.
Stage 6	Stage 6 is a key stage of the GIDS scale, for here the threatened language is transmitted intergenerationally within the family and is the normal language of informal spoken interaction across generations. Revitalisation efforts focus on consolidating the use of the threatened language in the family and on forming family-neighbourhood-community clusters of speakers, within which the language can be more effectively maintained as the principal medium of informal social interaction.
Stage 5	At stage 5 literacy in the threatened language is established. Literacy teaching – for adults and youngsters – is envisaged as taking place principally in institutions run and controlled by the minority community, for example in neighbourhood literacy centres. (Fishman's model here is the Basque *'ikastolas'*). The advantages of minority language literacy can be summarised as follows:

1. It extends the functional range of the language
2. It confers prestige, and reduces the minority community's dependence on the majority community's print media
3. It provides an alternative medium for communication across time and space.

Stage 4	At stage 4 the threatened language assumes a place in formal education – either in private schools maintained by the minority community or in state-funded public schools, where it is taught as a subject or else used as a joint medium along with the majority language. The attainment of stage 4 marks a significant break from the preceding stages in two main ways. First, the threatened minority language moves out of the informal, private domains to which it has largely been confined and into the public, formal domains hitherto reserved for the dominant majority language. Second, a measure of control is ceded to the majority community, on whose support further progress in revitalisation partly depends.
Stage 3	At stage 3 the threatened language reappears in the work domain outside the minority language community, principally in smaller enterprises, some of which will be catering to the minority community and others to the majority community. In some cases the enterprise will be mainly staffed by minority speakers with some in executive positions, in which case the focus of revitalisation efforts fall on ensuring that intra-company communication is carried out in the minority language and that a minority language ethos prevails. Where, however, the enterprise is controlled and run by majority language speakers, effort is directed towards ensuring that services are delivered to the minority community in their language.
State 2	At this stage, lower level state institutions (e.g. health and postal services, government-owned utilities, the police, courts etc.) begin to offer services in the minority language to those who request such provision. This represents a considerable advance for the minority language community, but Fishman (1991: 106) is wary that the resulting increased employability of minority language speakers may draw some of the more able into the ambit of the majority language community and away from their roots.
Stage 1	At this stage, the highest level of recovery on the GIDS scale, the minority language will be present in the mass media, higher levels of education and the upper reaches of state administration. It will have been accorded some degree of official status – perhaps to the level of co-official language within its territory (see, for example, the status of Welsh in Wales following the passage of the 1993 Welsh Language Act). The minority community will enjoy a degree of economic and cultural autonomy. Finally, although Fishman does not mention it explicitly, it seems likely that the state will have granted some minority language rights – either on a territorial or a personality principle.

For Fishman, stage 6 is pivotal since without intergenerational transmission the threatened language is merely 'biding its time'. Thus, actions undertaken at other stages are only truly productive to the extent that they link back and strengthen this process. He remains noticeably circumspect about the contribution of stages 1 to 4, seeing them as desirable but not central – as is evident in this comment on stage 3:

It is merely a highly desirable contributory stage, one that is usually at a considerable distance from the nexus of intergenerational mother tongue transmission and that is even indirectly tied back to that nexus only with considerable foresight and ingenuity. (Fishman 1991: 105)

Particular scepticism is also directed at the teaching of the minority language (stage 4). Mindful no doubt of the Irish situation, where the compulsory teaching of Irish did not stem its decline, Fishman's point is that while teaching the threatened minority language certainly makes a valuable contribution – by developing literacy, by extending the language's functional range, by conferring status, by raising awareness of its historical and ongoing cultural value, it does not always, or even often, feed into the intergenerational transmission process, and is therefore insufficient for the language's revival.

With this many writers would agree, including Baker (1993, 2001, 2002, 2003a), who points out, with respect to Welsh language schooling, that there is a danger that the language will become a school-only language divorced from the 'family-neighbourhood-community experience'. For long-term survival, Baker (2003a: 97) concludes, the language needs a range of support mechanisms operating before and after schooling: 'bilingual education cannot deliver language maintenance by itself'.

Yet Fishman may go too far in playing down the role of bilingual schooling. Welsh language teaching, for example, has made a substantial contribution to the revival of Welsh – disseminating knowledge of the language more widely, raising its status, changing perceptions and creating employment opportunities for Welsh speakers. It has also helped recruit new speakers to the language, and thereby enlarged the pool of speakers – native but also non-native – capable of passing the language on to their children. But, of course, as Jones (1998a: 353) points out, the crucial question remains of whether they will in fact choose to do so.

Similar remarks might be addressed to Fishman's pessimism regarding the impact of minority language broadcasting and media (stage 2): 'Xish media are really a weak reed … for RLS [reversing language shift] to lean upon substantially' (Fishman 1991: 107). True, they do not contribute directly to intergenerational transmission but they do bring the language to the attention of a wider audience, and help associate it with modernity. The impact, then, is almost entirely symbolic, but, where a language has previously been stigmatised, symbolic enhancement – in so far as it changes attitudes – is a useful contribution This is signalled by Moal (2000: 126), who acclaims the recent establishment of a private, Lorient-based digital TV channel broadcasting in Breton (TV-Breizh), and Williams (1995: 6), the former head of S4C programming (the publicly funded Welsh language TV channel), who points out that:

while the normalization of a language in its geographical area is of prime importance at this particular time, its acceptance by the people as part of living culture is crucial. This is why its representation in the audio-visual media as communicating a contemporary living culture is crucial to the act of survival.

Another aspect of the GIDS scale that has attracted comment is the relationship of the stages to each other. Fishman (1991) speaks of the scale as 'diachronic quasi-implicational', suggesting thereby, as O'Riagain (2001: 195) notes, a temporal sequencing such that certain stages are, or have to be, attained prior to others. In his 2001 volume, however, no doubt in response to misinterpretations, Fishman is more explicit, declaring that language revitalisation is not 'a step-by-step from the bottom upward effort', nor should it be worked on in 'a lock-step stage-by-stage progression' (2001: 467). He adds some lines later that 'multistage efforts ... are not contra-indicated', a clarification that brings his interpretation into line with revitalisation work carried out with Irish (O'Riagain 2001), Quechua (Hornberger and King 2001) and Welsh (Baker 2003b), in all of which cases a range of measures to promote the language (e.g. through the media, teaching, economic development etc.) have been implemented more or less contemporaneously.

Provided that the fundamental desideratum of intergenerational transmission is kept in mind, this seems sensible since in so difficult an endeavour as language revitalisation actions may well need to be taken simultaneously, in a mutually re-inforcing manner. It is difficult to disagree, then, with Hornberger and King's (2001) view that the GIDS stages are best seen as offering a useful heuristic for identifying priorities and links rather than as a detailed programme of action.

Moving on, we come to what is perhaps the GIDS framework's most notable omission – its inattention to the economic basis for language revival. One of the reasons for language shift in the first place is parents' perception that the threatened language no longer has sufficient labour market value to be worthwhile transmitting. It follows that revitalisation efforts need to strengthen the economic incentives for retaining the language – alongside cultural and integrative incentives. As Baker (2002: 231) says:

> The more a minority language can be tied in with employment, promotion in employment, and increasing affluence, the greater the perceived value of that language.

More than individual choices are involved, however. Languages exist in, and are sustained by, communities of speakers, and to the extent that communities and their social networks are affected by socio-economic and employment changes, so too is the vitality of its language. A good example might be the Gaeltacht areas of Ireland, whose small farm economy – up to the 1950s – supported localised social networks favourable to the maintenance of Irish (O'Riagain 2001: 208). Thereafter, however, socio-economic changes within the communities – a growth of non-agricultural employment opportunities, increased commuting to towns, changing recreational patterns – all contributed to a fundamental redrawing of social networks, which, in turn, impacted adversely on Irish maintenance.

The implications for language revitalisation planning seem clear: if a community's language use patterns have a socio-economic base, then revitalisation efforts need to tie in with other areas of social and economic policy whose focus may not be language but nevertheless affect it. Indeed, they cannot be kept separate, even from, say, town and country planning, for, as Aitchison and Carter (2000: 149) note, issues of housing and land use can have significant cultural and linguistic ramifications – as, for example, when a new housing estate, providing mainly for in-migrants, is erected in a rural Welsh-speaking area. No doubt it is considerations such as these that impel Williams, C. to assert that 'sound language planning is holistic in nature' (1991b: 315). In similar vein, both O'Riagain (2001: 213) and Baker (2001: 83) approvingly echo Bourdieu's (1991: 57) comment that:

> those who seek to defend a threatened language … are obliged to wage a total struggle. One cannot save the value of a competence unless one saves the market, in other words, the whole set of political and social conditions of production of the producers/consumers.

We conclude, then, that the GIDS scale has heuristic value, but gives insufficient weight to economic variables – to a 'linguistic market' affected by economic as well as political forces.

4.2.2.2 Ethnolinguistic vitality and language revitalisation

A second influential framework in the language revitalisation field, seen by some (e.g. Bourhis 2001) as complementary to the GIDS scale, is Giles, Bourhis and Taylor's 1977 model, or framework, of ethnolinguistic vitality; vitality being defined here as 'that which makes a group likely to behave as a distinct and collective entity within the intergroup setting'. Because groups with higher levels of ethnolinguistic vitality have better prospects of survival as a distinctive linguistic-cultural collectivity than those with lower levels, Giles et al.'s 1977 framework of structural variables affecting ethnolinguistic vitality assumes considerable significance, and is therefore, displayed in Figure 4.1.

On the left-hand side are demographic factors divided into two subcategories: numbers and distribution. The former encompasses the basic features of population change – growth or decline in absolute numbers as affected by birth rates, patterns of immigration/emigration and exogamous or endogamous marriages. The latter refers to the concentration and distribution of group members in particular geographical locales and their proportion relative to the entire population. Concentrations of speakers in an area where they constitute a high proportion of the population has long been acknowledged as one factor favourable to language maintenance.

Institutional support and control factors in the centre refer to the degree to which the ethnolinguistic group is represented in, and has control over, institutions at community, regional or even state level, for example in the media, civil administration, education, commerce and industry. 'Formal' here denotes the extent to which group members have decision-making powers within institutions, and 'informal' refers to the degree of lobby influence exercised by the group. Clearly, language groups with higher levels of institutional support and control have better prospects for enhancing their vitality.

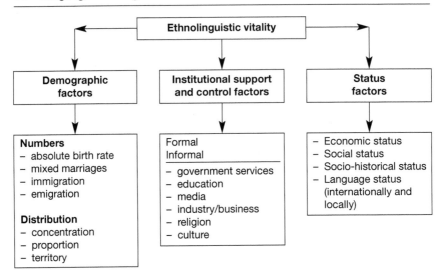

Figure 4.1 Structural variables affecting ethnolinguistic vitality
(after Giles, Bourhis and Taylor 1977)

Finally, on the right of the diagram are the status factors, which divide into economic status, the degree to which the group has influence in the economic life of the region or nation; social status, which refers to the prestige of the group and its associated language; socio-historical status, the prestige of the group over time; and language status within and outside the region, which refers to the degree of politico-legal recognition of the language of the group.

While the three clusters of factors are partially independent in that a group may be strong on, say, demographic factors but weak in status, Giles et al.'s (1977) essential point is that they combine to affect the overall level of ethnolinguistic vitality. As such, the framework makes a useful contribution to the diagnosis of the situation of linguistic minorities, and has been drawn on by various commentators – for example, Aitchison and Carter (2000), who exploit it to organise their discussion of the revival of Welsh in recent decades.

There are weaknesses, however. In particular, the framework seems more useful as a descriptive than as an explanatory device, as it does not indicate how the various factors may vary in weight in particular cases; nor does it inform us how they interact to produce particular language shift or maintenance outcomes in different settings. For this, we need more nuanced historical and sociological accounts. Furthermore, as Baker (2001: 72) points out, several of the factors (e.g. institutional control) do not admit easy measurement, and may be difficult to operationalise for purposes of empirical investigation.

We conclude, then, that while the ethnolinguistic vitality framework is a useful complement to the GIDS scale for describing the situation of linguistic minority groups and identifying areas of weakness, it does not by itself illuminate underlying processes or suggest a detailed programme for revitalisation efforts.

More useful, perhaps, as a guide to action are Crystal's (2000: 130–42) six propositions (or factors), presented below by way of conclusion to this section:

1. An endangered language will progress if its speakers increase their prestige within the dominant community.
2. An endangered language will progress if its speakers increase their wealth relative to the dominant community.
3. An endangered language will progress if its speakers increase their legitimate power in the eyes of the dominant community.
4. An endangered language will progress if its speakers have a strong presence in the educational system.
5. An endangered language will progress if its speakers can write their language down.
6. An endangered language will make progress if its speakers can make use of electronic technology.[7]

All the factors above, save perhaps the sixth, are likely to be familiar to readers of Fishman (1991, 2001) or Giles et al. (1977), but they nonetheless constitute a useful list because they reaffirm, and highlight, the central roles of prestige, power, economic incentives, education and institutional recognition in language revitalisation.

4.3 LANGUAGE PLANNING AND LANGUAGE REVITALISATION: A CASE STUDY OF WELSH AND BRETON

We now move to the main business of this chapter – a comparative case study of Welsh and Breton, covering their decline and contrasting trajectories of revival. Bringing them together in this contrastive fashion may help cast light on some of the factors that affect, and even determine, success or failure in language revitalisation more generally. Our starting point, however, is a historical overview of the slow decline of these two languages.

4.3.1 Welsh and Breton: a historical overview of language decline

We turn first to Welsh.

4.3.1.1 Welsh

The Acts of Union of 1536 and 1542, joining Wales with England and asserting English as the dominant language of law and governance, are a convenient starting point for an account of the decline of Welsh (*Cymraeg*), not because 1536 initiates the territorial contraction of Welsh, that having got underway much earlier with the Anglo-Norman invasions of around 1070, but because it marks the onset of the retreat of Welsh from public domains and its progressive inferiorisation relative to English. The Acts are seen as, if not triggering (see Jones, R. 1993), at least hastening the steady anglicisation of the Welsh gentry, who had little alternative but to acquire English if they wished to carve out a career in public life. Over time this process produced a linguistic-social correlation: English for the upper-class gentry, Welsh for the mass of the population. A secondary effect of the ousting of Welsh from the public domains of law and administration was a restriction in the register range of the language and, more tellingly, a loss of prestige. Welsh came to be associated with homeliness, rurality, farming and ultimately, by the mid-nineteenth century, economic backwardness.

Not every trend from this time was so negative, however. Into the late nineteenth century, Welsh remained the predominant language of the majority of the population, compelling its use in lower level administration. Meanwhile, the monolingual Welsh heartland (*y fro Gymraeg*) waxed strong, and the language retained a rich, prestigious literary heritage dating back to the medieval prose romances known as *Mabinogi* (Price 1984), and beyond.

William Morgan's 1588 translation of the Bible, employing a literary form of Welsh deriving from the bardic literature of previous centuries, not only added to this heritage but is seen by many writers (e.g. Jones, R. 1993; Jones, M. 1994, 1998a; Price 1984; Thorne 1994, Barbour 2000c) as an event of critical significance since it helped establish, disseminate and popularise a standard written Welsh, thereby averting the fragmentation of the language into mutually incomprehensible dialects, a fate not entirely avoided by Breton for instance. It also set in train a process of codification culminating in the 1928 publication of the report '*Orgraff yr Iaith Gymraeg*' (the Orthography of the Welsh Language), which laid down rules and principles for standard written Welsh. As Jones, M. (1994: 245) notes, this is an 'a-regional', common core variety arrived at by a standardising process different from the more typical elevation of a prestige dialect, and – perhaps for this very reason – it commanded widespread loyalty.

Another positive effect of the Welsh Bible, quite apart its enhancement of the language's prestige, is that it laid the basis for the use of Welsh in the religious domain, which is widely seen as playing a crucial role in the maintenance of Welsh, particularly in the eighteenth and nineteenth centuries. In particular, the Methodist revival of the eighteenth century and the growth of religious nonconformity (i.e. non-Anglican Protestantism) in the nineteenth century provided – through the chapel – not just a Welsh-oriented centre for social life but a formal domain in which Welsh held sway and from which it derived prestige. The use of the language in prayer meetings, Sunday schools, sermons and the like exposed a considerable swathe of the population to relatively formal models of spoken Welsh, and – no less importantly – the churches contributed to the spread of literacy in Welsh, and hence to increased book publication in the language. Particularly remarkable here is the work of Griffith Jones, vicar of Llanddowror, who in the 1730s established a system of 'circulating schools' staffed by itinerant teachers. By the time of his death in 1760 these had equipped no less than 160,000 children and adults in 3,325 schools with sufficient literacy to read the Bible in Welsh (Price 1984, Jones, R. 1993).

Placed alongside the revival of eisteddfodau,[8] and the growth of Welsh debating societies, it is perhaps tempting to view this extension of literacy as signalling something of a Welsh renaissance, but Aitchison and Carter's (2000: 31) assessment is more sober, and probably more realistic:

> The movements of the eighteenth century deepened and extended the domains in which Welsh was already used, and it conserved the language because of that; but it did not extend the domains and that was to be crucial in the next century.

One circumstance particularly unfavourable to the Welsh language was its exclusion from formal education for most of the nineteenth century, a situation formalised in the Elementary Education Act of 1870, which completely ignored the language. Only at the end of the century in limited ways did Welsh teaching reappear in schools, but by then a process of domain exclusion (from education, law, government and science), the anglicisation of the upper strata of society, and episodes such as the 1847 Education Report, known thereafter as the *Treason of the Blue Books*, had combined to undermine confidence in the relevance of the Welsh language to progress and modernity, leaving it, despite its apparent demographic strength, ill-equipped to resist the dislocation the twentieth century would bring.

Inward migration into Wales

For most commentators, the key factor in the decline of Welsh in the first half of the twentieth century is the industrialisation of Wales, a process already underway in the nineteenth century but whose effects on the language did not become apparent until considerably later. One of the early effects was migration from North to South Wales: in the period 1861–1911, for instance, no less than 160,000 people migrated to Glamorgan from other Welsh counties (Price 1984: 116). It might be thought that this internal migration, with its depopulating effect on the rural Welsh-speaking areas of the north, would have been highly detrimental (and it can hardly have been helpful), but there are some (e.g. Brindley Thomas 1987) who argue that the population redistribution increased the urban presence of the language, and that, had Wales remained largely agricultural and rural, like Ireland or northern Scotland, many, many more people would have emigrated and been lost to the language.

Whether or not this thesis is correct, there is little doubt that a second wave of industrialisation centred on the South Wales coalfields in the late nineteenth and early twentieth centuries had a dramatic anglicising effect, in as much as it produced high levels of in-migration from England and Ireland. Jones, R. (1993: 546) reports, for example, that in the years 1871–81, 57 per cent of incomers into Glamorgan came from England. The overall effect, in combination with the ensuing urbanisation, was to increase contact between Welsh and English speakers, to dilute the demographic concentration of the former and to extend a bilingual zone in which English speakers remained monoglot and Welsh speakers became bilingual. This, of course, was bilingualism in one direction, and it prepared the ground for subsequent language shift.

Other influential accompaniments of industrialisation should be mentioned here as well. First among these was the advent of new railway systems, ending the relative isolation that in so many areas and so many different respects had helped sustain the Welsh language. Second was the transforming effect of industrialisation on cultural and political life. Increased class consciousness, exacerbated by economic depression, found more apt expression in Labour socialism than in Liberal Nonconformity; and as Welsh life became more secular, working men's clubs and other English-oriented leisure outlets progressively displaced the chapels as centres for social life. The overall effect was to diminish the significance of a religious-social domain that had for long been the bastion of the language. And yet another anglicising influence was in the offing – the development and spread of a pervasive English language mass media.

Language demography
If the paragraphs above suggest causes for the decline of Welsh, the full extent of the decline is best illustrated by turning to demographic data. Table 4.2 displays the numbers of Welsh speakers as proportions of the total population from the beginning of the twentieth century, when census figures first become available, up to the most recent census of 2001.

Table 4.2   The Welsh-speaking population of Wales, 1901–2001 (in percentages)

	1901	1911	1921	1931	1951	1961	1971	1981	1991	2001
Wales	**49.9**	**43.5**	**37.1**	**36.8**	**28.9**	**26.0**	**20.8**	**19.0**	**18.7**	**20.8**
Clwyd			41.7	41.3	30.2	27.3	21.4	18.7	18.2	
Dyfed			67.8	69.1	63.3	60.1	52.5	46.3	43.7	
Gwent			5.0	4.7	2.8	2.9	1.9	2.5	2.4	
Gwynedd			78.7	82.5	74.2	71.4	64.7	61.2	61.0	
M. Glamorgan			38.4	37.1	22.8	18.5	10.5	8.4	8.5	
Powys			35.1	34.6	29.6	27.8	23.7	20.2	20.2	
S. Glamorgan			6.3	6.1	4.7	5.2	5.0	5.8	6.5	
W. Glamorgan			41.3	40.5	31.6	27.5	20.3	16.4	15.0	

(Sources: HM Census and Welsh Language Board for 2001 figures)

Immediately apparent is the very considerable decrease in the proportions of Welsh speakers from 1901 up to about 1971. Thereafter, the rate of decline abates, and, in fact, the most recent census of 2001 shows a small increase to 20.8% of the population (582,400 persons over the age of three), a development closely linked, as we shall see, to the spread of Welsh-medium schooling.

Also evident is the unevenness of the distribution by county of Welsh speakers. Not unexpectedly, Gwynedd and Dyfed, the traditional mainly rural Welsh heartlands, are the counties with the highest proportion of Welsh speakers – in 1991 61 per cent and about 44 per cent respectively, figures that contrast sharply with the low percentages recorded in the south-easterly counties of Gwent, Mid and South Glamorgan.

What is obscured in this data but revealed by the maps in Figure 4.2, however, is the degree (and rate) of territorial contraction of the north-westerly heartlands, which are progressively fragmenting – a process likened by one writer to the drying-

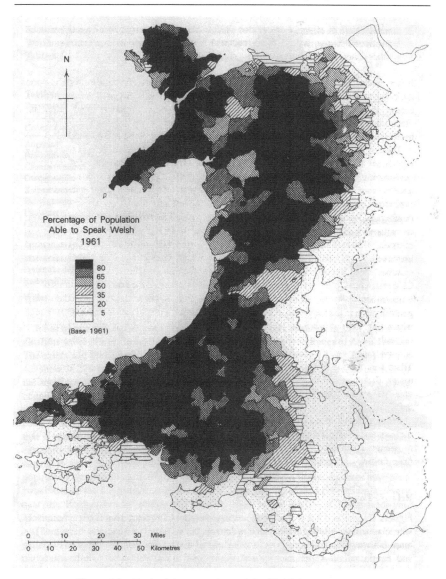

Figure 4.2   Territorial contractions of the Welsh language, 1961

(Source: Aitchison and Carter 2000)

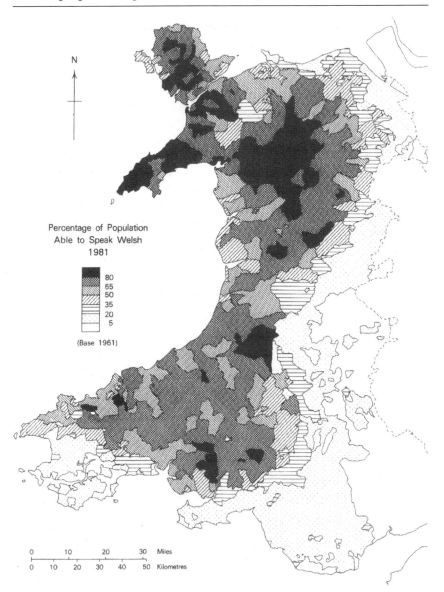

Figure 4.2   Territorial contractions of the Welsh language, 1981
(Source: Aitchison and Carter 2000)

out of a puddle, and attributed by Jones, R. (1983) to suburbanisation, second home purchases, and retirement settlement.

If traditional 'Welsh Wales' has been losing speakers, a feature of the recent revival has been an increase in the proportions, and numbers, of Welsh speakers in the urban south. The 2001 census, for example, records a 7.7 per cent gain in the proportion of Welsh speakers in Newport between 1991and 2001, and a 4.4 per cent gain in Cardiff as against a 3 per cent fall in Gwynedd. As Aitchison and Carter (2000: 134) remark, Welsh has been, for sometime, a predominantly urban language.

4.3.1.2 Breton

The dukedom of Brittany, an area originally colonised by Brythonic-speaking peoples from southern Britain, was incorporated into the French state under the Edict of Union of 1532. As a province, it held on to a measure of autonomy in ecclesiastical, judicial and fiscal matters, but this status, along with the associated privileges, was lost when, following the French Revolution of 1789, all provinces were abolished and replaced by *départements* supervised directly from Paris. As an administrative unit, Brittany only re-emerged in 1972, when it became one of 22 French *régions*, comprising the *départements* of Finistère, Morbihan, Côtes d'Armor and Ille-et-Vilaine.

The geographical and administrative region does not, however, have a singular linguistic-cultural identity, for, as is well known, it is divided into *Haute Bretagne* (Upper Brittany), which has since the thirteenth century been Romance rather than Breton-speaking, and *Basse Bretagne*, or *Breizh-Izel* (Lower Brittany), the traditional Breton heartland lying to the west of a line running roughly from Saint-Brieuc in the north to Vannes in the south, as indicated in Figure 4.3. This is not to say, however, that any contemporary casual visitor would be aware of any such divide, since, as Timm (1980), Humphreys (1993) and Price (2000) all observe, the last fifty years have witnessed a radical collapse of the heartland, leaving extensive areas from which Breton has largely disappeared. The towns of Lower Brittany, meanwhile, have been predominantly French-speaking for centuries.

If the linguistic division of the Brittany region has impeded the development of a pan-Breton sense of identity, an additional contributory factor is the fragmentation of the Breton language into four main dialects (there are sub-dialects) known as the Kerne, Leon, Treger and Gwened after the four ancient dioceses with which they are, or have been, very roughly coextensive (see Figure 4.4). Jones (1998b: 131) claims that these are only partly mutually intelligible, and, while this is disputed by some, there is evidence that many native Bretons are very conscious of linguistic differentiation, hence the common refrain – 'Ils ne parlent pas le même breton'.

Kuter (1989: 84), meanwhile, emphasises the local parochial nature of the identity of many Breton-speakers, suggesting that they identify most strongly with their *'pays'*, their *'commune'* and its distinctive features of dialect, of costumes, and even of the particular *coiffes* worn by the women. At regional, or subregional, level French remains the unifying language, the instrument for communication with outsiders –

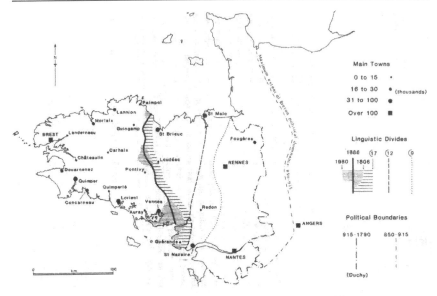

Figure 4.3   Map of Brittany showing westward retreat of Breton
(Source: Humphreys 1993: 622)

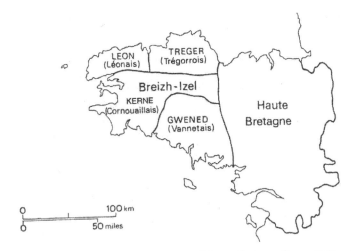

Figure 4.4   Map of traditional dioceses of Basse-Bretagne (Lower Brittany)
(Source: Kuter 1989: 83)

whether from outside Brittany or simply from other Breton-speaking communes, and the resulting very attenuated sense of a wider Breton identity, realised through the language, certainly appears to be one of the factors contributing to its decline, whose course we now turn to examine in a little further detail.

Charting the decline of Breton

For many commentators (e.g. Press 1992, Moal 2000, Texier and O'Neill 2000), the decline of Breton is traceable back to the Duchy period of the late Middle Ages, when the upper strata of Breton society – the aristocracy and higher clergy – adopted French in recognition of its greater prestige and power, leaving Breton to the lower social orders – the peasantry, the workers, the fishermen and craftsmen. Around the same time French established itself in the towns, there developing an ascendancy that over time restricted Breton mainly to the countryside and to rural life.

The French Revolution of 1789 marks a further stage in Breton's decline, for, from this period on, the Jacobin legacy of a centralised state unified around the French language cast a dark shadow over regional languages, which were viewed as a potential threat to the integrity of France and to the ideal of one state, one nation, one language (see Judge 2000). One expression of this ideology was the exclusion of Breton from the domains of education, law and administration; another, in its most malign form, was its denigration by public authorities. We have already provided examples of this, but it is not difficult to find others: for example, as late as 1927 we find the National Minister for Education, de Monzie, declaring that:

> Pour l'unité de la France, la langue bretonne doit disparaître. [For the linguistic unity of France, the Breton language must disappear] (Kuter 1989: 78)

Not surprisingly, such hostility, combined with domain restriction, encumbered Breton with a negative symbolism, which was eventually internalised by its speakers. It came to be seen – by outsiders and Bretons themselves – as a social handicap, as a marker of a backward peasant identity and as a 'barbarous relic' (Timm 1980: 33), and it was this as much as any other factor that prepared the way for the later collapse of intergenerational transmission.

The introduction of free, compulsory and secular elementary education under the Jules Ferry laws of 1882 to 1887, the establishment of universal military conscription in 1889 and the development of the railways, which reached Brest in 1864, all also played a part in undermining Breton: the first two because they were instrumental in disseminating French–Breton bilingualism, a necessary condition, of course, for bringing up the next generation as French speakers, and the last because it paved the way for an increased out-migration of young Bretons to the Paris region in search of employment opportunities.

To these may be added the First World War, which drew a large proportion of the Breton male population into the French-speaking military, and during which an estimated 120,000 Bretons were killed (Press 1994: 217). In their absence, the women assumed a greater role in the management of farm businesses, bringing them into contact with a French-speaking world and further introducing bilingualism into what had hitherto been a monoglot-predominant group.

Language demography

It might be supposed that the confluence of these various factors would have suppressed the numbers of Breton speakers but, in fact, what statistics there are – and there are few because French censuses have traditionally not sought information on language – show that at the beginning of the twentieth century there were probably around 1,400,000 Breton speakers (Humphreys 1993: 628). By the time of the most recent reliable survey in 1997, however, conducted by the French daily newspaper of Brest, *Le Télégramme*, there were only an estimated 240,000 fluent speakers with a further 125,000 semi-speakers. Their age distribution, moreover, points unambiguously to obsolescence, for, while 45 per cent of those over 75 could speak Breton well, the corresponding figures for those aged 20–39 were 5 per cent and for those under 20 years 1 per cent (Moal 2000: 119). The intergenerational transmission of the language has practically ceased, as is confirmed by a 1998 INED survey (National Institute of Demographic Studies) reporting an intergenerational transmission rate of close to 0 per cent and a Euromosaic report ranking Breton 32nd out of 48 communities for language reproduction).

It seems clear, then, that while the ground had long been prepared, the twentieth century, and especially the middle period from roughly 1950 to 1970, saw the most marked decrease in the number of speakers and in the vitality of the language. Again, various factors have played their part. One might note here, for instance, that the Catholic Church, along with its schools, a traditional bastion of the language, had by the 1950s largely completed its gradual shift from Breton to French – even in such auxiliary areas as catechism classes and private pastoral work.

Urbanisation and migration

More significant, however, are two broad socio-economic forces: urbanisation, which in comparison with Britain came relatively late to France, and out-migration. The former, fuelled partly by the mechanisation of agriculture from the 1950s, is linked closely with significant rural depopulation, a trend firmly evidenced by McDonald's (1989: 4) finding that the proportion of the Brittany population employed in agriculture declined from over 50 per cent in the 1950s to around 21 per cent in 1975. The effect, of course, was to weaken the rural basis of Breton. Out-migration, too, sapped the strength of the heartland by drawing away young Bretons to work in Paris and elsewhere: in the years 1954–62 alone, for example, an estimated 100,000 Bretons under the age of 30 emigrated out of the region (Oakey 2000: 644).

Adding the above to other aspects of modernisation – the growth of tourism, the mobility brought by the motor car, the reluctance of young women to tie themselves to a life of rurality and the ensuing rise of exogamy, and the decline of economic incentives – takes us a considerable distance towards an explanation of the swift collapse of intergenerational transmission.

Linguistic factors

One should not forget, however, the role of linguistic influences alongside the more sociological. The dialectal fragmentation of Breton, mentioned earlier, and the absence until relatively recently of a widely accepted standard written Breton has not only hindered the language's incorporation into formal education but militated against its use as a regional lingua franca and as a symbol for a pan-Breton identity. As Jones (1998b: 138) points out, Breton native speakers see in their dialects only an emblem of a localised identity; for the realisation of a wider identity, they seem content to rely on French, and it is this, in combination with the perception that Breton is but a hindrance to progress and to modernity, that constitutes the core of their psychological representation of the language, a representation that is at the root of the recent collapse of intergenerational transmission.

It is perhaps ironic, then, that the current demographic weakness of Breton and its near demise as a language of home and community should coincide with a period when the French state, as evidenced by its 1999 signing of the European Charter for Regional and Minority Languages, is at last displaying signs of conceding space to Breton in the civic realm and of supporting the teaching of the language. Though belated, this will support the efforts of those activists who have working – for some time now – for the revitalisation of Breton, a story to which we come presently. First, however, we return to Welsh and its revitalisation.

4.3.2 The revitalisation of Welsh

For convenience, we divide this brief overview of the revitalisation of Welsh into two categories: language status planning and institutional support, and language acquisition planning.

4.3.2.1 Status planning and institutional support

A remarkable feature of the late twentieth century revival of Welsh has been its transformation from a marginal language restricted to low status domains to a language that now enjoys official recognition and that has become institutionalised and legitimised to a degree scarcely imaginable only sixty years ago. Accompanying this rise in status has been a revalorisation of the language in the public's eyes: 88 per cent of respondents in a 1995 opinion survey, for example, agreed that Welsh was 'something to be proud of' (May 2000b: 158). Speaking Welsh has acquired something of a social cachet, especially in middle-class circles, and, as partly evidenced by the growing willingness of English-speaking parents to enrol their children in Welsh-medium schools, there is an increased awareness of the advantages of a knowledge of Welsh for careers in the public sector, in education and in the regional media (Aitchison and Carter 2000: 138).

A convenient starting point for an account of the revival of Welsh, but an arbitrary one given the prior foundation of the Welsh Nationalist Party (*Plaid Cymru*) in

1925, is the 1962 public lecture delivered on BBC Radio Cymru by Saunders Lewis, former president of *Plaid Cymru* (1926–39), entitled '*Tynged yr Iaith*' (the Fate of the Language), which called for constitutional and unconstitutional direct action on behalf of the threatened Welsh language (see Williams 1994, 2000a). An almost immediate response was the formation – some six months later – of the Welsh Language Society (*Cymdeithas yr Iaith Gymraeg*), a pressure group whose non-violent (or mainly non-violent) direct action campaigns were instrumental in forcing the pace of Welsh language promotion, leading, for example, to the introduction of bilingual road signs (1969), the issuing of bilingual road-fund licences (1970) and an enlargement in the range of bilingual services offered by local authorities.

Around this time, meanwhile, in response to earlier nationalist campaigns – but reflecting also a more sympathetic stance to the Welsh language, the British government in 1963 set up a committee to enquire into the legal status of the Welsh language. This duly delivered a sympathetic report in 1965, paving the way for the passage of the Welsh Language Act 1967, which established the principle of 'equal validity' for documents in either Welsh or English in public administration, and removed restrictions on the use of Welsh in the court system (Price 1984). Deeply disappointing though these limited measures were to the nationalist lobby, they nonetheless can be seen as a significant early step in the legitimation of Welsh in the civic realm, and a herald of further hard-won promotion successes.

Among the most significant of these, given its role in enhancing the visibility of the language, and in expanding the range of topics publicly discussed in Welsh (e.g. sport), was the establishment in 1982 of the Welsh-medium television channel *Sianel Pedwar Cymru*, otherwise known as S4C.[9] A commissioning rather than a production organisation, this has over the years considerably boosted the status of the language – not least economically, as it has contributed to the emergence of Cardiff as a significant media production centre and to a growth in Welsh media employment opportunities (Williams 2000a, 2001).

Continuing pressure from dissatisfied language activists, and a more amenable approach to national minority issues by the British government, eventually produced a further enhancement of the status of Welsh in the Welsh Language Act 1993, which sets out a statutory framework for treating Welsh and English on the basis of equality. Probably the most significant provision of the Act, however, was the statutory recognition awarded to the Welsh Language Board (*Bwrdd yr Iaith Gymraeg*), which has become, as Baker (2003b: 98) points out, the principal agency of formal Welsh language planning.

One of its main tasks is overseeing the implementation of Welsh Language Schemes, a scheme being the plan that every public sector organisation is required to produce, detailing how language equality and the right of members of the public to services in their preferred language will be implemented. By 1998 some 67 schemes, including those of local authorities, had been approved, and a further 58 public bodies had been instructed to prepare schemes. Additional activities of the Board include the distribution of grants to Welsh organisations, the development of Welsh electronic resources (e.g. spell-checkers and grammar-checkers) and promotional work to persuade private businesses to use Welsh in their communications with Welsh speakers.

There are limitations, however, both in the reach of the 1993 Act and in the remit of the Welsh Language Board, that have displeased activists. The Act, for example, stops short of conferring official language status on Welsh; private businesses are not bound to its central provisions on language equality; and the Board has powers to 'recommend' but not to compel compliance with its demands (Williams and Morris 2000).

That said, many commentators have seen the 1993 Act and the establishment of a statutory Welsh Language Board as significant institutional developments – boosting the status of Welsh, furthering its use in the public sector and signalling an advance towards a bilingual Wales. As Jones (1998a: 17) remarks, with its present degree of institutional support and its more positive image, Welsh has departed from the typical path of decline and obsolescence: it is now in some respects, as we see below, an expanding language.

4.3.2.2 Language acquisition planning

Given the importance of school as an agency for language socialisation and acquisition, it is unsurprising that Welsh-medium education has engaged so much of the energies of those working for Welsh revitalisation. Their efforts have been rewarded in that, over the sixty-five years since the opening of the first bilingual Welsh school in Aberystwyth in 1939, there has been a remarkable expansion in bilingual and Welsh-medium schooling, contributing to the recent rise in the number of Welsh speakers detected by the 2001 census (see above), and to the perception that bilingual education is a central pillar of the current Welsh revival.

The extent of this expansion is indicated in Tables 4.3 and 4.4, which show the numbers of primary and secondary pupils respectively studying through Welsh or studying Welsh as a second language. For purposes of comparison, the figures from 1992/93 are set alongside the most recent statistics for 2001/2002.

One of the more interesting features of these tables, apart from the impressive numbers studying Welsh or through Welsh, is the sharp fall over the last decade in the numbers of pupils not taught Welsh. This reflects the transforming effect on Welsh language education of the 1988 Education Act, which for the first time gave the teaching of Welsh a statutory basis, and under whose provisions Welsh became a core, hence compulsory, curricular subject in Welsh-medium schools and a foundation subject in all other schools throughout Key Stages 1–4. The effect has been to extend teaching of the language into the anglicised areas of the south and north-east.

Meanwhile, an increasing proportion of those entering Welsh-medium education come from English-speaking homes, up to 58 per cent according to May (1999: 162), and even higher in some of the more intensely anglicised areas (Jones 1998a); a situation reflecting the reputation for high-quality education enjoyed by Welsh bilingual schools (see Baker 1993: 23), the improved status of the language and

Table 4.3   Welsh teaching in maintained primary schools

	1992/93		2001/2002	
	Numbers of pupils	*% of pupils*	*Numbers of pupils*	*% of pupils*
Pupils in classes where Welsh is the sole or main medium of instruction	46,088	16.6	51,344	18.2
Pupils in classes where Welsh is the medium for part of the curriculum	8,986	3.2	5,034	1.8
Pupils in classes where Welsh is taught as a second language	175,323	63.3	222,337	78.7
Pupils not being taught Welsh	46,684	16.9	3,861	1.4
Total	277,081	100	282,576	100

In 2000 there were 445 primary schools with Welsh as the sole or main medium of education (26.8% of all primary schools), educating approximately 20% of all primary school pupils.

(Sources: National Assembly for Wales 2003, *Digest of Welsh Statistics 2002*. Cardiff: Wales; Welsh Language Board 1999, *Continuity in Welsh language Education*. Cardiff: Wales)

Table 4.4   Welsh teaching in maintained secondary schools (in year groups 7 to 11)

	1992/93		2001/2002	
	Numbers of pupils	*% of pupils*	*Numbers of pupils*	*% of pupils*
Pupils taught Welsh as a first language	20,552	12.1	26, 967	14.4
Pupils taught Welsh as a second language	94,663	55.9	158,185	84.5
Not taught Welsh	54,195	32.0	1,960	1.0
Total	169,410	100	186,081	100

In 2001 there were 53 'Welsh-speaking' secondary schools, defined as schools where half the curriculum is delivered in Welsh (around 23% of all secondary schools). These schools were attended by approximately 18% of secondary pupils.

(Sources: National Assembly for Wales 2003, *Digest of Welsh Statistics 2002*. Cardiff: Wales. National Assembly for Wales 2002, Our Language, its Future: Policy Review of the Welsh Language. Cardiff: Wales)

a growing perception that knowledge of Welsh enhances employability – a consequence itself of the stronger presence of Welsh in the public sector and the service and leisure economy (e.g. in retailing, media, public relations, etc.).

Alongside the contribution of primary and secondary education, one should also mention *Mudiad Ysgolion Meithrin* (the Welsh-medium nursery school movement), established in 1971, which in 1998 comprised 570 nursery groups and 386 toddler groups ('*cylchoedd ti a fi*') catering to some 13,500 children of whom no less than 61 per cent came from non-Welsh-speaking homes (Aitchison and Carter 2000:

140). These play an important role in consolidating L1 Welsh language skills and in raising the linguistic awareness of L2 Welsh learners, laying thereby a sound foundation for language work in the primary curriculum.

Not indicated in the tables above, but significant enough to mention, is the considerable variation in the nature of bilingual education provision across Wales, a variability conditioned principally by the demography of school catchment areas (see Baker 1993, 1997). Thus, whereas in the anglicised areas of the south, Welsh-medium schools cater principally to English L1 speakers, in the north and west the clientele consists predominantly of Welsh L1 speakers. But there are also mixed catchment areas producing school classes in which Welsh L1 speakers sit alongside L2 Welsh learners. The latter are in effect experiencing a form of Welsh immersion education on a Canadian model and the former a form of heritage or developmental bilingual education (see Chapter 3). There are, again, schools that only teach Welsh as an L2 subject, schools that teach almost all subjects in Welsh and schools that employ mixed-medium teaching, which is variously interpreted either as teaching some subjects in Welsh and others in English, or as teaching bilingually, that is using two language concurrently in the same lesson. This complex patterning of bilingual instruction is certainly interesting but space forbids any further discussion here. All one can say here is that it constitutes a potentially profitable area for bilingual education research.

Looking at the overall impact of Welsh language education on the fortunes of the language, we can summarise the principal contributions as follows:

- As activists had hoped, the education system in Wales has recruited new speakers to the language, compensating thereby for the shortfall in family-based repro-duction of the language. Evidence for this effect lies in the census returns of 1981, 1991 and 2001, which show an increase in the number of Welsh speakers between the ages of three and fifteen. And evidence for the effect of schooling independent of the family can be found in the 1991 census data showing that no less than 36.1 per cent of all Welsh-speaking children come from homes where neither parent speaks Welsh (Welsh Language Board 1999). This does not mean, however, that Welsh language planners, ignoring Fishman (1991), seek to underplay the importance of family-based transmission. Rather they emphasise the comple-mentary role of school-based language production in the maintenance of the language. And, of course, if language maintenance were the sole purpose of bilingual education, its justification would be weak. But, as we have seen in the previous chapter, there are independent grounds for supposing that bilingual education, properly implemented, can benefit the child educationally and psychologically as much as, or more than, monolingual schooling.
- Welsh-medium education has helped consolidate the language skills of L1 speakers, especially literacy skills, whose positive influence on language main-tenance is generally well attested. That it is now possible to study through Welsh from nursery up to postgraduate level is also in itself a considerable achievement.
- Finally, as Williams (2000a: 670) points out, the growth of bilingual education

has 'legitimised the status of Welsh in society', and its success now serves as an 'additional marker of Welsh (national) distinctiveness'.

Thus far, the tone of the last two subsections has been upbeat, so it may be appropriate to qualify this picture with a conclusion summarising the challenges that still confront the revitalisation project. Perhaps the most serious of these is the ongoing contraction of the Welsh native-speaking heartland, and the ageing of its inhabitants. It is true that the shortfall in family transmission of the language is partly compensated by increased school-based language production, but it is unclear whether these Welsh learners, many of whom are L2 speakers, will keep using the language throughout their lifetime, and still less clear whether they will in due course transmit it to the next generation. The question has particular pertinence for the new generation of young speakers in south-east Wales, for here a substantially anglicised urban environment makes it that bit more difficult to resist the perception that Welsh is principally a language of the school.

A second area of concern is the extent to which census figures reflect language acquisition. On the surface, certainly, they show a rise in the numbers of those able to speak Welsh, but a slightly different picture emerges if one examines the fluency levels of these speakers. Aitchison and Carter (2000: 141), for example, report headteachers' assessments from 1996/97, showing that, despite curriculum exposure, around 55 per cent of primary pupils had limited or no fluency in Welsh, and 30 per cent partial fluency. On the more positive side, by 1998/9 around 16 per cent of primary pupils spoke Welsh fluently, up from 13.1 per cent in 1986/87 (Williams 2001: 77).

A related issue is the variety of Welsh spoken by immersion learners attending Welsh-medium schools in the strongly anglicised areas of South Wales. Here, there are limited opportunities for practising Welsh outside school or for native-speaker monitoring, and a consequence, Jones (1998a: 258) argues, is that learners emerge speaking a 'school dialect' characterised by an absence of idiomatic constructions and a proportion of historically inappropriate forms, all of which adds weight to Fishman's (1991) key point that educational institutions cannot bear the entire burden of revitalisation. They need to be supported by, and linked to, a family-community base.

4.3.2.3 Concluding remarks on the future of Welsh revitalisation

Turning for a moment, finally, to status matters, it might be argued that the establishment in 1999 of a National Assembly pledged to treating English and Welsh on the basis of equality signals a further advance in the reincorporation of Welsh into the civic realm. There are some, however, who see this new level of political autonomy as an insidious, long-term threat to the language, because, in so far as it enhances the vitality of civic Welsh institutions – an assembly, university, national museum, opera, and so on, it also creates an option for these to become over time a new locus for the expression of Welsh identity, relegating language to a secondary, even anachronistic role (Aitchison and Carter 2000: 156). Unlikely though this seems at present, there are Irish and Scottish parallels, and there are some observers who would not be averse to such a development, for they see a Welsh language spoken by 20 per cent of the population as, ultimately, a divisive rather than a unifying force in the construction of a Welsh national identity.[10] Our concluding point here, therefore, is that while Welsh revitalisation has made great progress, its trajectory is not complete, and neither is it uncontested.

4.3.3 Efforts to revitalise Breton

Alongside Welsh, Breton revitalisation is very fragile, but this is not to deny the fact of progress in some areas. In education, for example, the Diwan organisation, a voluntary association of activist parents and teachers founded in 1977, has successfully established a network of private Breton-medium schools operating at nursery, primary and secondary levels. These are now complemented by bilingual streams at officially designated French–Breton bilingual schools in the public and Catholic sectors. Enrolment figures for 2002/03 are shown in Table 4.5.

Table 4.5   Enrolments of Pupils in bilingual medium and immersion classes at pre-primary, primary and secondary levels in 2002/2003

Pre-primary schools 2002/2003	Diwan		1,054
	Public bilingual		1,525
	Catholic bilingual		1,250
	Total		3,829
Primary schools 2002/2003	Diwan		1,073
	Public bilingual		1,073
	Catholic bilingual		1,053
	Total		3,199
Secondary schools 2002/2003	Diwan		
		collège level	504
		lycée level	137
	Public Bilingual		
		collège level	268
		lycée level	78
	Catholic bilingual		
		collège level	156
		lycée level	0
	Total		1143
	Grand Total		**8,171**

(Source: Mercator-Education 2003)

The figure of 8,171 above represents just under 1 per cent of the total school population of Brittany (Mercator-Education 2003: 30); certainly a very small proportion but not an insignificant one, considering that Breton only re-entered the public schools curriculum in 1951 under the Loi Deixonne.

One should not overlook, moreover, increased provision of Breton teaching at the universities of Brittany – Rennes, Brest, Lorient, Nantes, Université Catholique de l'Ouest (UCO) – where in 2003 an estimated 769 students were enrolled on single or dual degree courses, or, indeed, on courses for adults more generally. Enrolment on the latter, principally evening classes, stood at around 5,400 individuals, and further numbers participated in summer camps for learners and Breton enthusiasts, the best known of which are those run by the KEAV organisation (*Kamp Etrekeltiek ar Vrezhonegerien*).

Beyond the education domain, Breton has extended its presence in the broadcast media with the arrival on air in September 2000 of a new, privately funded digital TV channel, TV-Breizh, which now provides competition for the very limited Breton-language output (four hours weekly) of the existing terrestrial channel, France-Ouest (Moal 2000). On radio, meanwhile, France-Bleu Breiz-Izel, part of the national network, broadcasts two hours of Breton programmes daily, adding to the output of four independent local radio stations. In the print media, there are a variety of weekly, monthly and quarterly Breton-language publications, all with restricted circulations, but no daily Breton newspaper. The two regional dailies – *Le Télégramme* and *Ouest-France* – are almost entirely in French, though they do carry weekly Breton-language columns, focusing mainly on language learning issues (Texier and O'Neill 2000). Another development worth mentioning is the establishment in 1999 of a language promotion agency, the Office of the Breton Language (*Ofis ar Brezhoneg*), but as its powers and remit are still uncertain, it is difficult to gauge its eventual impact.

4.3.3.1 *Weaknesses in Breton revitalisation*

There is progress to report, then, but there are also weaknesses, one of the most significant of which is the division within the Breton-speaking community between native speakers and *néo-bretonnants*, the principal activists of the revitalisation movement (McDonald 1989; Jones 1998a, 1998b). The latter, like some other minority language movements (e.g. the Irish case), has a membership that is predominantly middle class, educated and politically mobilised, and this sets it apart socially and politically from the mainly elderly, country-dwelling native speakers, who tend to be illiterate in Breton and inclined – after decades of state-led marginalisation of the language – to regard it negatively.

The social meanings attached to the Breton language by the two groups are, therefore, quite different. For the native speakers, Breton is, as suggested earlier, an expression of a local, parochial identity, one that they are not unhappy to leave behind: '*tout ça* [Breton], *c'est le passé*' (all that's in the past) was the comment of one of Jones's informants (1998b: 135). The *néo-bretonnants*, on the other hand, passionate in their support for Breton-medium education, see the language as an indispensable constituent of a regional pan-Breton identity.

Reinforcing, and perhaps underpinning, these contrasting outlooks are differences in the kind of Breton used. Native *bretonnants* mainly speak a home-transmitted dialectal Breton, one whose grammar is distinctly Celtic but whose vocabulary, particularly for modern concepts, is heavily infiltrated by French borrowings. *Néo-bretonnants*, by contrast, are predominantly second language acquirers of a standardised, literary variety of Breton, and consequently their speech is French-influenced in its grammar while 'pure' in its lexicon (Jones 1998a: 322). Standard Breton, it may be added, is a synthesis of dialects and the comparatively recent product of a long struggle to establish a pre-eminent unified orthography suitable for use in school textbooks and the like.[11] As such, and because it is largely the creation of experts and committees, it has – from the point of view of the native *bretonnant* – a strained, artificial, even alien quality.

It is, therefore, not just attitudes to the language that separate native speakers from *néo-bretonnants*, but also the linguistic character of the varieties they characteristically speak. The consequences for revitalisation are, of course, unfavourable, for without native speaker backing, or indeed wholehearted state support, revivalist activity becomes very much the preoccupation and private enterprise of a somewhat narrow constituency. Small in numbers as this group is, it seems unlikely that they will be able to overcome the very serious shortfall in the intergenerational transmission of Breton as a native language. As second language speakers predominantly, they may, however, be able to transmit their 'new' (as opposed to 'old') Breton to their children, in whose mouths it will become what Jones (1998a: 323) refers to as a 'xenolect'.[12]

4.3.4 Comparing Welsh and Breton

As languages of Celtic minorities long since incorporated into the nation states of Britain and France, it would not be unreasonable to expect Welsh and Breton to have certain sociolinguistic similarities, and, looking at the patterns of their decline, this does indeed seem to be the case. The decline of both, for example, appears to have been accelerated by the nation-state formation processes of Britain and France and the accompanying allocation of resources and prestige to the dominant language of the state; both have – for varying periods – suffered exclusion from public, official arenas such as administration and education, finding succour only in the religious domain; the speakers of both have been led to regard their language as backward and of little economic value; both have been exposed to the homogenising forces of modernisation, which tend to privilege already dominant languages; and both, finally, have been undermined – to an extent – by economically driven demographic changes – outmigration and rural depopulation in the case of Brittany and in-migration in the case of Wales.

At a certain point, however, the parallels break down, for it is quite evident that Welsh is now in an incomparably stronger position – institutionally and in other respects – than Breton. We turn finally, therefore, to a brief examination of the factors that have helped Welsh and impeded Breton.

Principal among these is the roles played by the British and French states. The latter – for many historical reasons – is particularly sensitive to the French language as a unifying national symbol, and this, in combination with a tradition of political centralism, helps explain why regional languages, Breton included, are experienced as greater threats to the integrity of the state than those in Britain, where language is considered less of a central state interest and where, as a result, approaches to linguistic difference have been marked by greater pragmatism.

The ramifications are felt in language policy. The French state has consistently, sometimes aggressively, excluded Breton from public functions, contributing thereby to the devaluing of the language by its own speakers. The British state, by contrast, has felt able to respond more sympathetically to Welsh nationalist claims, as is reflected in the passage of the 1993 Welsh Language Act, institutionalising the use of Welsh in public domains across the country. Of course, it is true that the French state has in recent years adopted a somewhat more conciliatory posture, signalled, for example, by President François Mitterrand's 1981 promise of 'le droit à la différence', but a certain ambivalence remains, as indicated in the recent 2002 decision of the Conseil d'État not to admit Diwan schools to the public education sector after all (Mercator-Education 2003: 5).

Also distinguishing Welsh and Breton are the different identities available in, and constructed from, these languages. As we have already noted, native bretonnants identify with their 'pays' rather than with a larger Breton-speaking community, and see the Breton language as an expression of this localised identity. They do not conceive of Brittany as a nation: a region within France, yes perhaps; a nation, no. Welsh speakers, by contrast, do feel that they belong to a nation, and, though they have attachments to regions, these are overlaid by a greater affinity with a national Welsh identity and a greater loyalty to the national language (Jones 1998a). This sense of belonging to a national unit has, moreover, been encouraged by the recent establishment of national institutions – a National Assembly, a Welsh Language Board and so forth. In Brittany there are no institutions of corresponding status, and fewer opportunities, therefore, to realise an identity above that of the 'commune' or 'pays' and below that of the French nation. A consequence has been that Breton native speakers are generally resistant to the pan-Breton 'national' identity that the néo-bretonnants have sought to project. In Wales, however, there is less divisiveness: native speakers and language activists are far from co-extensive categories, but they are not antagonistic – something that is not generally the case in Brittany.

Linked to identity and language maintenance is language standardisation, which is generally thought to assist language revival by enhancing prestige and by permitting wider dissemination of the language through education and literacy. Jones (1998a) points out, however, that the manner of standardisation must also be considered, and she draws here a useful distinction between 'standardisation from below' and 'standardisation from above'. Welsh belongs to the former category in that a standard literary form of the language evolved over time from the medieval bardic schools and from the translation of the Bible, and it was this already prestigious variety that was readily adopted when the need for a modern standard Welsh arose. Standard Breton, by contrast, is a variety many native Bretons have difficulties identifying with, an important reason for this being that it is a relatively recent cross-dialectal hybrid, a creation of experts and committees long divided among themselves (see Jones 1998b). Standardised thus 'from above' it has not had time to evolve or to win the acceptance of a reluctant speech community, a situation which is clearly inimical to engagement in revival work.

A final factor distinguishing Welsh and Breton is one of timing. Welsh revitalisation, dating from the early twentieth century, got underway when family transmission of the language was still not uncommon and when there was a reasonably large constituency of younger native speakers, willing and able to mobilise on behalf of the language. Breton revitalisation, on the other hand, coming later, was confronted with a situation where family transmission had already all but collapsed, and thus it has had to cope not only with a divided speech community but with the absence of a solid base of younger native speakers.

For all these reasons, then, the fortunes of the two languages have diverged very considerably over recent decades, and it is perhaps true to say that in terms of vitality Breton now has more in common with Irish than it does with Welsh. Of all the Celtic languages, Welsh is the best placed socio-politically, demographically and institutionally to survive through the twenty-first century. One cannot express the same degree of optimism for Breton, however.

4.4. CONCLUSION: IMPLICATIONS OF THE WELSH/BRETON CASE STUDY

The forces affecting Welsh and Breton enter into distinct and individual configurations, but this does not mean these forces are in themselves unique. In many other situations of language decline and revitalisation in Europe one tends to encounter similar agents: the nation state whose resources are mainly channelled towards the favoured official language; a dominant standard language spoken by the more powerful members of society, which as a result comes to be associated over time with social mobility; minority language speakers with strong attachments to the ancestral language and who are on that account willing to mobilise in its support; other minority speakers whose sense of identity is less strongly bound to the ancestral language and who, therefore, are more predisposed to shift to what is perceived to be a more advantageous language; an educational system that may in one period be exploited to disseminate the official state language but in another used to teach and transmit the minority language; and, more nebulously, modernising forces (e.g. industrialisation, urbanisation), which tend to undermine the social networks sustaining minority language communities.

From this enumeration it is plain that it is primarily socio-political and economic factors that influence the fate of languages. But our previous discussion makes it equally clear that the interplay between them is complex and variable in different situations, and in such complex processes no one single variable is predictive of successful revitalisation or failure. Nationalist mobilisation, for example, appears to have been helpful to Welsh but much less so to Irish.

Slightly firmer conclusions are possible, however, with respect to the roles of education and economic incentives. Most commentators (e.g. Fishman 1991, 2001a; Baker 2002), on the basis of sound evidence, agree that bilingual education is of value in revitalisation, most specifically for increasing prestige, spreading literacy and recruiting speakers to the language. It is not sufficient to guarantee revival, however, especially if schooling is not linked back to what Fishman (1991) rightly identifies as the crucial nexus of family–home transmission, and to other uses of the language in the community beyond the schools.

This leads us to the role of economic incentives. It is increasingly recognised, through the work of O'Riagain (1997, 2001) and others, that, as language groups are simultaneously social and economic groups, language planning for revitalisation cannot afford to be autonomous from social and economic planning. Indeed, to have any chance of success, it needs, in Williams's words (1991b: 315), to be 'holistic in nature', to encompass even such apparently mundane yet important domains as town and country planning (see Aitchison and Carter 2000: 152). This also entails, as Baker (2002) suggests, giving thought to the economic foundations of minority language communities, and it is interesting therefore to observe in this connection that the Welsh Language Board, in a recent declaration of priorities, proposes 'to integrate the promotion of language use with economic principles of community development' (Williams, G., and Morris 2000: 188).

A final factor, believed by some to be ultimately decisive in revitalisation, is the attitude of a language's speakers. Ideological commitment and positive choices to use and transmit the language are clearly essential to language survival, but perhaps not sufficient. Much depends also on the number of speakers who are of the same persuasion, and on whether these speakers can find the political space and control necessary to translate aspirations into practice. In some cases (e.g. Wales and Catalonia), this has been possible because the state has been prepared to cede some control, even autonomy, to minority language communities. In other cases, the state has – for ideological reasons – shown greater reluctance to concede political space for the flourishing of linguistic diversity. However, with a growing awareness of minority language rights at national and supranational levels, and an increased pragmatic recognition of the cultural, even economic, value of linguistic diversity, there are realistic prospects of more accommodating policies. Whether or not these will take effect in time to save particular minority languages remains very uncertain.

NOTES

1. Article 1 of the Charter defines regional and minority languages as ones 'traditionally used within the given territory of a State by nationals who form a group numerically smaller than the rest of the State's population'. Excluded are 'dialects of the official language(s) of the State or the languages of migrants'.

2. Interesting though they are, exemplification and discussion of the details of these changes are beyond the scope of this chapter. For further detail see McMahon 1994; Jones, M. 1998a; Dorian 1981, 1989.

3. As late as 1972 Pompidou is reported to have declared:

'Il n'y a pas de place pour les langues minoritaires dans une France destinée à marquer L'Europe de son sceau.' [There is no place for regional languages in a France destined to make its mark in Europe]. (Cited in Temple 1994: 194)

4. France signed the Charter in 1999.

5. The state may grant minority language rights according to either a territorial or a personality principle. Under the territorial principle, the minority rights are only exercised within the defined territory of the minority language (as in Belgium). Under the personality principle, by contrast, language rights are more portable in that they attach to the individual speaker irrespective of his geographical location. There are fewer examples of states that grant rights on a personality principle, though Canada and Finland are sometimes cited here.

6. This is in fact a crucial point, and we shall return later to a discussion of the advantages/ disadvantages of the bilingual/multilingual solution, only noting here that much of the world's population is fact individually bilingual or multilingual. Monolingualism is a relatively unusual condition worldwide.

7. The last proposition here draws attention to the potential of technology in language revitalisation. The Internet, for example, may help minority language speakers build up a 'virtual community', thereby partially overcoming the problems of geographical dispersion. Technology also creates possibilities for distance and on-line language learning.

8. An eisteddfod is a festival of Welsh music, song and poetry recitation. Mitchell (personal communication), recalling the situation in the 1940s when every small town had its local eisteddfod and every young person (including himself) competed, makes the point that the importance of eisteddfodau to the maintenance of Welsh should not be underrated. He draws attention also to the supportive role of the Urdd Gobaith Cymru (the Welsh League of Youth).

9. It was in fact only a threat by Gwynfor Evans, former Plaid Cymru president, to fast to the death that finally convinced the London government to discharge its promise to establish a publicly funded Welsh-medium TV channel.

10. Davies, A. (personal communication) observes that the forceful promotion of Welsh could provoke a backlash from elements of the English-speaking Welsh population, especially if they felt disadvantaged in the labour market.

11. Jones (1998a: 305) provides a fascinating account of the Breton 'orthography wars'.

12. A xenolect has been defined as 'a foreignised variety spoken natively', but not a creole since it has not undergone significant restructuring (Jones 1998a: 323 after Holm 1998).

Chapter 5

The global spread of English: cause, agency, effects and policy responses

The global spread of English has been thoroughly documented in a range of well-known publications: for example, those by Cheshire (1991), Crystal (1995, 1997), McArthur (1998), Graddol (1997) and Ammon (2001a). By now, therefore, the dominance of English as a global lingua franca, or 'hypercentral language' (de Swaan 2001a), is hardly disputed empirically, even by those most critical of this state of affairs such as Phillipson (1992, 2000a, 2003), Phillipson and Skuttnab-Kangas (1995, 1996, 1999), Pennycook (1994, 1995, 2001) and Tollefson (1991, 2002a).

It would be uneconomical, therefore, to reiterate other than in the briefest manner the statistical and factual basis for the claims made to global dominance. Instead, our main focus is on the causes, effects and implications of the global spread of English and how these have been variously interpreted, bearing in mind Spolsky's observation (2004: 91) that 'English as a global language is now a factor that needs to be taken into account in its language policy by any nation state'.

In the present chapter, then, we focus on the socio-political and ideological dimensions of English spread, paying attention to implications for English language teaching. It need hardly be said that the implications of the global dominance of English for social justice, equality within and between nations, linguistic and cultural diversity and economic development are complex and contested. It may be helpful, therefore, to consider the debate over cause and agency in the spread of English before moving on to an examination of the various effects of the dominance of English.

5.1 CAUSE AND AGENCY IN THE GLOBAL SPREAD OF ENGLISH

It is widely accepted, with good reason, that the spread and decline of languages is causally linked to the power and the fortunes of their speakers rather than to any properties of the language code. Standard explanations of the spread of English have, therefore, emphasised firstly the role of the British empire and secondly the growing economic, military and political dominance of the United States in the later twentieth century as key factors (Crystal 1997; Graddol 1997).

The British colonial empire is seen as creating the necessary initial conditions for the emergence of English as a global language in two main ways: firstly, through the export of speakers to territories in Australasia and North America, where they established permanent settlements and subjugated indigenous populations, forming in due course new communities of native speakers; and secondly, through the colonisation of territories in Asia, Africa and Oceania, where indigenous populations – or at least an elite sector of them – learnt English not so much because they were compelled but mainly because they perceived its acquisition as socially and economically advantageous. In so doing, they became bilingual speakers of English, maintaining the use of indigenous languages in informal domains but resorting to English for inter-ethnic and for public, more formal communication. This Brutt-Griffler (2002: 138) refers to as spread by 'macro-acquisition', in contrast with the former process which she terms 'spread by speaker migration'.

Since the formal end of British rule in the non-settler colonies, English has largely maintained, and in some cases actually extended, its range of societal uses (see Fishman et al. 1996a). In part this is attributable to country-internal factors (see Chapter 7), but account must also be taken of external pressures, specifically the second major factor in the spread of English, the rise of the United States to a position of global dominance – economically, militarily and politically – in the twentieth century. Recent indicators show, for instance that the United States is comfortably the largest economy in the world with a GDP of some $10,383 billion (constituting 36 per cent of the OECD countries' economic output), roughly three times the size of the next largest economy, that of Japan (OECD 2003). Its share of the world's military expenditure, at 43 per cent, is many times larger than the next largest spender (SIPRI 2003).

Other indicators tell a similar tale: the scientific research output of the United States substantially exceeds that of any other single nation, while the country headquarters some of the world's best known, and iconic, multinational corporations (e.g. McDonald's, Microsoft, Time Warner, Disney, AT&T). It has substantial voting influence in the agencies of global financial governance established at the end of the Second World War – the IMF and the World Bank, for example – and, armed with this influence, it has been able to steer IMF policy towards its favoured nostrums of market liberalisation, privatisation and fiscal austerity, the central pillars of the neo-liberal 'Washington consensus' that so informed unsuccessful agency support to developing countries in the 1980s and 1990s (see Stiglitz 2002).

There is no shortage of evidence, then, for American economic and political influence, and it seems reasonable therefore to assent to the linkage Graddol (1997), Crystal (1997) and Phillipson (2003) propose between the dominance of the United States and the increased use of English not only in former colonies but as an international lingua franca in countries where there was no British colonial presence – in Europe, for example. Some of these accounts, however, leave opaque the precise mechanisms by which power is transmuted into the increased use of English, and this is a matter we shall return to. In the meantime, it may be useful to exemplify the impact of US influence by referring, albeit briefly, to an important domain that English has come to dominate – scientific publication.

5.1.1 English in scientific publication: an indicator of language spread

Up to the First World War, German was an international language of science of an importance equal to, or greater than, English, but thereafter entered into decline, an immediate trigger for which was its banishment post-war from international scientific conferences (Ammon 2001b). A more profound long-term cause, however, can be found in the expanding scientific research base of the United States, a resource left largely untouched by the destruction that the Second World War inflicted on the scientific communities of Germany and France, and enhanced by the immigration of important scientific figures, seeking refuge from the National Socialist regime.

The Cold War stimulus to US scientific research, the development of computer-based technology and the resourcing of large, research-oriented universities all contributed to an expansion in the United States' share of the world's scientific research output, and in due course this precipitated a switch from German to English as the principal medium of scientific discourse in some of the smaller European countries. Haarman and Holman (2001: 231), for example, date the reorientation of Finnish scientific and academic life to English to the 1950s, highlighting the significance of academic exchange programmes initiated in 1953 that gave Finnish academics the opportunity to spend substantial periods researching and teaching at US universities.

The more such switches to English occurred,[1] the more incentives grew for yet other researchers to read and publish in English, and so it is not difficult to see the expansion of English as a language of science as assuming a self-perpetuating dynamic of its own. The resulting current dominance of English as a language of science is well attested in statistics provided by Ammon (2003: 244), who – drawing on Anglo-Saxon bibliographic databases – shows that by 1995 English accounted for 87.2 per cent of publications in the natural sciences (biology, chemistry, physics, medicine, mathematics) and for 82.5 per cent of publications in the social sciences (sociology, history, philosophy).

A remarkable feature of this trend is the inroads English has made into the formerly strong and relatively self-sufficient German scientific research community. Graddol (1997: 9), for instance, produces data showing that as many as 76 per cent of German academics in the earth sciences claim English as their main working language. Comparable figures for physics, chemistry and biology are 98 per cent, 83 per cent and 81 per cent respectively. Ammon (2001b: 353) notes, meanwhile, how the microeconomics of journal publication have in several cases pushed German publishers into a change of language of publication and of journal title. The *Angewandte Chemie* journal, for example, has become *Applied Chemistry*, and now requires contributions in English, and the *Psychologische Forschung* has been retitled *Psychological Research*.

The dominance of English in such an inherently international domain as science is significant in itself, but it also has wider side effects. For example, it furnishes governments with a strong motive for retaining a prominent place for English in school and university curricula, the rationale being straightforward: economic prosperity requires a strong research infrastructure, and this means a significant cadre of persons with the language skills to access English language scientific publications. This, no doubt, is one of the reasons for the entrenchment of English in so many education systems worldwide.

5.1.2 Linguistic imperialism as an explanation of spread

Thus far, the picture presented is unexceptional and does not depart from the widely accepted view (see Crystal 1995, 1997; Graddol 1997) that the historical context of the global spread of English is one where the legacy of empire is supplemented and reinforced by the rise in the twentieth century of the United States as a world power. However, as one seeks to effect a conceptual transition from the abstractions of power to actual decisions to acquire English, and as one enquires more closely into the precise agencies of spread, one enters more contested terrain.

One influential view that has strongly shaped academic discussion in this area over the past decade and which, therefore, we need to discuss, is that of Phillipson, who in a series of publications since 1992 (e.g. 1997, 2000, 2003) has proposed that the diffusion of English has been, and still is, substantially orchestrated, facilitated and led by what he refers to as the Centre; that is, the United States and Britain, whose commercial and political interests such diffusion serves.

In the core chapters of his 1992 book (chapters 5 and 6), Phillipson implicates a variety of agencies in the promotion and spread of English. These include the British colonial authorities, and in the post-colonial era the British Council, the British Foreign Office, the United States Information Agency, the Agency for International Development, the Ford Foundation, the State Department, complicitous local elites and – not least – the TESOL/ELT profession. And to bolster his claims of orchestration and promotion Phillipson adduces a version of the 'cui bono' argument (see Spolsky 2004: 79); that is, if we wish to know who is responsible for a situation, we should ask who benefits. Phillipson's answer is clear: it is the Centre, with English serving as one of the key vehicles for maintaining its dominance and perpetuating the dependence of the 'Periphery'.

This thesis of linguistic imperialism, as propounded by Phillipson, encompasses effects as well as causes – the alleged adverse impact of global English on other languages, for example – but, as it is most centrally and coherently a theory of cause and agency, it is from this angle that we make our first approach.

5.1.2.1 Critiquing linguistic imperialism

An initial point is that the coherence of linguistic imperialism as a causal hypothesis requires us to identify it as a distinct form of imperialism, distinguishable from but complementary to imperialism in general, and one which has conscious, coordinated efforts to diffuse English at its core. Otherwise it risks redundancy, for the spread of English could be viewed as a side effect, or epiphenomenon, of the power relations of colonialism. The very assumptions of the hypothesis, in other words, oblige us to look carefully into the colonial and post-colonial eras for evidence of policies and plans to impose English at the expense of other languages. We may also observe here that linguistic imperialism is a strongly top-down, as opposed to bottom-up, theory of language spread in that it appears to attribute remarkable potency to language policy/planning as an instrument for effecting change in language behaviour.

Colonial language policy

As evidence for his view that colonial language policy was a vector of linguistic imperialism, Phillipson (1992) places considerable emphasis on Macaulay, and specifically his famous Minute of 1835, which he sees as settling the Orientalist–Anglicist controversy over the content and medium of government education in India in favour of the Anglicist position that education was best conducted in English, the aim being to cultivate a cadre of persons 'Indian in blood and colour, but English in taste, in opinions, in morals, and in intellect' (cited in Phillipson 1992: 110), who might serve as intermediaries between the colonial rulers and the masses. Phillipson goes on to argue that Macaulay had a 'seminal influence' not just on later colonial policy in India but 'throughout the empire'.

> His strategy [Macaulay's] was endorsed at the Imperial Conferences of 1913 and 1923. … English was the master language of the empire. The job of education was to produce people with mastery of English. (Phillipson 1992: 111)

However, this interpretation of colonial language policy, and of Macaulay's role, is contested by Evans (2002), who discusses in considerable detail the antecedents of the Macaulay Minute and subsequent colonial despatches, making the following points:

1. Nineteenth-century colonial language policy in India was steered as much by financial parsimony as by language ideology.
2. Anglicists and Orientalists agreed on the objective of developing vernacular language education for the masses, but disagreed as to the best means for its attainment.
3. The Wood's Despatch of 1854, with an importance equal to the Macaulay Minute, envisaged the use of both English and vernacular languages for the diffusion of 'European knowledge'. ('We have declared that our object is to extend European knowledge throughout all classes of the people. We have shown that this object must be affected by means of the English language in the higher branches of institution, and by that of the vernacular languages of India to the great masses of the people' [cited in Evans 2002: 276 from Richey 1922: 392].)
4. The expansion of English language education in India in the late nineteenth century reflected the growing urban demand for English, a language popularly seen as opening doors to employment in government service.
5. Colonial language policies were reappraised at the beginning of the twentieth century in the light of concerns that the spread of English-medium education

had created a class of disaffected, alienated Indians, the Babus, who posed a potential threat to the stability of the colonial regime.

6. Thereafter, colonial language policy sought to limit the teaching of English and expand the role of the vernaculars, a tendency given formal expression in the 1927 Report of the Advisory Committee on Education in the Colonies (Evans 2002: 279). The aim, however, was not so much the promotion of vernacular languages as the perpetuation of colonial rule over docile, submissive subjects.

This portrait of a reactive self-interested colonial language policy, conditioned by economic considerations, which sought to limit English language education to a narrow elite and to promote vernacular language education for the masses, often against the desires of native subjects, is entirely consistent with other detailed studies of colonial language polices; for example, that of Brutt-Griffler (2002: 78), who – in a key passage of a prolonged discussion – observes that:

> A close examination of the history of education policy in the British empire does not show any concerted, consistent attempt to spread English on a wide basis. On the contrary, it indicates a concern to limit the spread of English as much as was consonant with the purposes of a colonial empire as part of the reactive policy of containment, the effort to counteract the transformation of the colonizer's language into a 'language of liberation'.

This interpretation is, of course, considerably removed from that proposed by the linguistic imperialism hypothesis.

Post-colonial language promotion

Another event to which Phillipson (1992: 183) gives considerable attention in support of his linguistic imperialism postulate is the Makerere Conference of 1961, which, he argues, established a doctrine for ELT work in newly independent African countries, privileging English over other languages:

> There was an almost exclusive concentration on English at the Makerere itself. The same was true of the teacher training and curriculum activities which sprang from it. The conference did not look at the overall needs of periphery-English children, or even their overall linguistic development, but at English and ways of strengthening English. (Phillipson 1992: 216)

At first sight, the extracts from the Makerere report that Phillipson (1992) quotes appear to support his case. However, as Davies (1996: 492) suggests, once the broader context is considered, a more complex picture emerges. The conference was not, as Phillipson (1992) suggests, about 'strengthening English' but rather finding 'a means of increasing the efficiency of the teaching of English at all levels' (Makerere 1961:20), something quite different. Also, it did not focus 'almost exclusively on English', for, as Davies (1996: 492) again shows, the report does raise the matter of the linguistic and cultural background of the learner, and calls – among other things – for 'research into the needs and demands of the learner and the community from the point of view of practical bilingualism' (Makerere 1961: 492).

Phillipson (1992) is on potentially stronger ground when discussing the Anglo-American post-colonial promotion of English through such agencies as the British Council and the United States Information Agency (USIA), and through ELT aid projects in developing countries. That such promotion has indeed occurred and in a variety of forms – subsidised English language lessons, scholarships for ELT professionals, direct English language teaching operations, teacher-training programmes – is indisputable. This author, for example, was personally involved in the early and mid-1990s in the British Council-funded Service English Project in Hungary, whose main aim was to improve the quality of ESP/EAP teaching in selected Hungarian universities. One cannot easily dissent either from Phillipson's (1992) point that support for ELT is not disinterested, coinciding as it frequently does with the foreign policy goals of extending British and United States political and diplomatic influence and of gaining commercial advantage. Indeed, this much is on occasion openly avowed.

What we need to consider, then, is not so much the factual evidence for the promotion, or export, of English by these agencies as its interpretation, and whether or not it is most appropriately conceptualised as linguistic imperialism. On this matter we make three main points.

The first is that it is somewhat surprising that Phillipson seems surprised, or affronted, by the self-interested nature of support for English language learning, which he ipso facto adduces as evidence for linguistic imperialism. The foreign policies of most nation states – Japan, Britain, China, Germany, France – have long been recognised as animated principally by national self-interest. Indeed, extending influence and gaining a competitive advantage economically is largely what foreign policy is for; to the point, in fact, that failure to prosecute what is believed to be in the national interest might elicit charges of incompetence.

A second point, related to the first, is that nearly all of the major nations of the OECD – Germany, Japan, USA, Britain, France, Spain – invest considerable sums in exporting their national language. Kaiser (2003: 199) reports, for example, that the Japan Foundation, an agency of the Ministry of Foreign Affairs, has established language centres around the world – in Bangkok, Jakarta, Cologne, Los Angeles, Sao Paulo, Sydney and elsewhere – whose main function is to teach Japanese and support Japanese language teaching in local schools. MacLean (1999: 94), meanwhile, notes that the German government gives substantial support to the teaching of German abroad through such agencies as the Goethe Institut, the DAAD (*Deutscher Akademischer Austauschdienst*) and the Carl Duisberg Gesellschaft. In 1989, for instance, the Goethe Institut, which then had 149 branches in 68 countries, received DM230 million from the public purse. And similar, even stronger, support from the French government could be shown for the international teaching of French. It would be consistent, then, if one applies the term 'linguistic imperialism' to Anglo-American efforts to promote the learning of English, to apply it also to Japan and Germany and speak of Japanese or German linguistic imperialism; an extension too far one feels.

The third point is that promotion is not the same as, nor does it entail, the uptake of that which is promoted. For successful promotion, leading to diffusion, a reciprocal is needed; specifically, acceptance of English by those at whom the promotional efforts are directed. This much is evident from cases where the promotion, even imposition, of a language has not led to widespread use. One example might be the coercive introduction of Russian into the state school curricula of the former Soviet-controlled Eastern bloc countries, which cannot be said to have diffused Russian language proficiency very widely. Another might be Hindi in post-colonial India.[2]

It might be supposed, then, that among the necessary conditions for successful promotion of a lingua franca such as English are (1) the absence of ideological resistance to that which is promoted, and (2) the popular perception that there is some personal advantage to be gained from adoption. Phillipson (1992), and others of similar views, do, of course, have alternative explanations for the apparently ready acceptance of English, which we shall come to presently, but for the moment let us simply observe that the scale of the uptake of English is problematic for linguistic imperialism in its simplest top-down form.

The appropriation of English

By degrees, this leads us to what is perhaps the greatest single weakness of the linguistic imperialism hypothesis, one noted by a number of commentators (e.g. Bisong 1995; Pennycook 1994, 2001; Canagarajah 2000; Ridge 2000; Brutt-Griffler 2002), which is that it denies significant agency to speakers in the periphery, portraying them as passive recipients, or dupes, of imposition from the Centre. Such one-sided attribution of agency is, however, problematic, indeed erroneous, for several reasons.

First, there is a body of historical evidence (see Brutt-Griffler 2002) that colonial subjects often had to struggle for access to English language education against colonial authorities, who sought to withhold it. Moreover, once acquired, English eventually became a resource for mobilising colonial subjects in resistance against imperial rule. From Nyasaland (now Malawi) to the Gold Coast (now Ghana), and from Kenya to northern Rhodesia (now Zambia), nationalist leaders such as Banda, Nkrumah, Kenyatta and Kaunda used English alongside indigenous languages to draw linguistically and ethnically varied populations into a common struggle against colonial rule (see Mazrui and Mazrui 1998). There is, in short, sound evidence for Brutt-Griffler's (2002: 65) claim that:

> Africans and Asians under British rule deliberately took advantage of the imperial role of English … to undertake a policy of their own. They transformed English from a means of exploitation into a means of resistance. Through appropriating the language, they empowered themselves to resist colonialism at the most essential level.

One of her key conclusions, indeed, is that that the spread of English was as much a by-product of anti-colonial struggles as imperialism itself (Brutt-Griffler 2002: 111).

The wider point here is that because linguistic imperialism so strongly emphasises top-down processes of imposition, it neglects, or underplays, the possibility of the bottom-up planning mentioned above; that is, the ways in which English has been appropriated and turned to varying political purposes, often deeply uncongenial to the original imperial powers.

The role of English in anti-colonial resistance is certainly the key historical example of appropriation, but there are others closer to us in time. English, for instance, has become the lingua franca of the anti-globalisation movement. The *Guardian* newspaper (26 January 2004) reports that six of the nineteen hijackers involved in the attacks of 11 September 2001 entered the United States on the pretext of studying English as a foreign language. Canagarajah (2000: 128), meanwhile, outlines the role English has played in the local Tamil populace's resistance to the Tamil-only nationalism of groups who until recently waged an armed struggle for a separatist state on the island of Sri Lanka. The very variety of these instances, and their very different moral status, draws attention to the different political causes in which English has functioned as a resource, and underscores how its symbolic baggage is not a constant but varies with the local context in complex ways that the deterministic linguistic imperialism thesis is ill-equipped to explain.

Hegemony and English spread

An important explanatory concept invoked by Phillipson (1992) and indeed by other critical applied linguists (e.g. Pennycook 1995, 2001) to explain the wide-spread adoption of English is that of hegemony. This is not hegemony as straight-forward dominance, but hegemony in the Gramscian sense (Gramsci 1971); that is, a process by which ruling elites maintain their dominance not through overt coercion but by winning the consent of the mass of the population to their own domination and exploitation. They consent because the prestige of the ruling elite allied with dominant taken-for-granted discourses saturates their practical daily consciousness, communicating the idea that their subordination is an unavoidable given, part of the natural order. Similar hegemonic processes operate, so it is claimed, in the spread of English, particularly in the globalisation era: English is readily accepted – even by those whom it disadvantages – because people are seduced by dominant discourses that portray English as a beneficial language of modernisation and opportunity (see also Pennycook 1994).

This view is not, of course, wholly implausible. When one considers how parents in countries such as Zambia, Tanzania or Hong Kong demand education in English for their children, even though this often hinders rather than facilitates learning (see Chapter 7), one is tempted to postulate a hegemonic process.

There are, however, several problems that attach to the concept of hegemony when deployed as a causal explanation. One is that it is empirically difficult to falsify. What evidence can one produce to show that individual adoptions are not the product of hegemony but of rational choice, ill-informed though that may some-times be? Another, related problem is that by ruling out rational choice as a basis of individual action, the concept downplays critical reasoning capacities, and can end up on that account as ultimately patronising. A third is that some accounts of how hegemony operates tend to exaggerate the causal power of discourse. Pennycook (1994), for example, influenced heavily by Foucault, is one commentator who attributes considerable power to discourse, but in so doing underrates, as Holborow (1999) suggests, the material conditions of power as a more pressing constraint on individuals' decisions to acquire or reject English.

This is not to deny the existence of hegemonic processes, nor that there are some less than beneficent effects produced by the spread of English, as we shall see presently. It is rather to invite a recalibration of the relative contributions of hegemony and rational choice in favour of the latter, and to give weight to the role played by perceived economic advantages in individual language learning decisions.

We shall return to this theme shortly, but first, to conclude this discussion of linguistic imperialism as a theory of cause and agency, it seems opportune to mention Fishman et al.'s volume (1996a), in which contributors from a range of former British and United States colonies address empirically the question of whether linguistic imperialism is operative in a given context, an investigation that Phillipson (2000a: 93) himself has called for. Reflecting on the findings of the volume, Fishman (1996b: 639) concludes that, while British colonial history and linguistic diversity are among the significant correlates of degree of Anglification – as measured by the degree of penetration of English into such domains as education, government, commerce and print and broadcast media – the continuing spread of English is driven by forces that are both indigenous and external to the countries surveyed:

> the socioeconomic factors that are behind the spread of English are now in-digenous in most countries of the world and part and parcel of indigenous daily life and social stratification … Economically unifying and homogenous corporate and multinational forces are increasingly creating a single market into which all societies – former colonial and non-colonial states alike – can be and, indeed, for their own self-interests' sake usually seek to be, integrated. (Fishman 1996b: 639)

Although Fishman is not very precise about the exact nature of these impersonal forces, the evidence he summarises, added to the points made above and to Brutt-Griffler's (2002) historical evidence, tends to confirm that linguistic imperialism is an overly simple, hence unsatisfactory, explanation for the ongoing spread of English as a global lingua franca. An alternative is needed.

5.1.3 The spread of English: an alternative explanatory framework

Fortunately, in the work of de Swaan (1998, 2001a) there is an alternative framework at hand, which, incomplete though it is, offers a more plausible, more satisfying basis for understanding the spread of English as a global lingua franca. Among its attractive features is that it locates English within a global language constellation, which is itself an integral feature of an emergent global, transnational society. It shows how a multiplicity of individual choices, when aggregated, produce language spread or language shift at the macro-level; and, drawing on economic concepts embedded in a sociological framework, it also elucidates the factors that predispose individuals to acquire one language rather than another. Let us turn to a brief exposition.

5.1.3.1 The global language system

This is, in de Swaan's (2001a: 25) view, a hierarchical, coherent, 'strongly ordered' system held together by individual plurilingual speakers. At the base of the hierarchy are the majority of the world's languages, most of which are unwritten, remaining languages of memory and narration rather than record. The speakers of these 'peripheral' languages, as de Swaan (2001a: 4) calls them, tend to communicate with other peripheral groups through a common second language, which, because it plays this linking role, and is often official at a national or regional level, is termed a 'central' language. De Swaan (2001a) estimates that there may be around a hundred central languages spoken by 95 per cent of the world's population.

At the next higher level of the hierarchy are around twelve 'supercentral' languages, each of which – with the exception of Swahili – has a hundred million speakers or more: Arabic, Chinese (Mandarin), English, French, German, Hindi, Japanese, Malay, Portuguese, Russian, Spanish and Swahili. These are supercentral not just because they play important roles in administration, commerce and education within their respective spheres of influence, but because they link plurilingual speakers of a series of central languages both with each other and with the native speakers of the supercentral language. Thus, Malay (Bahasa Indonesia) is supercentral for the Indonesian language constellation because, among other things, it links plurilingual speakers of various Indonesian languages. For similar reasons French is supercentral in a constellation covering much of West and North Africa. The convergence of plurilingual speakers of a variety of central languages on a super-central language, acquired as a second language, is explained, de Swaan (2001a), argues, by a centripetal, upward tendency in language learning; that is, people usually prefer to learn a language at a higher level in the global hierarchy than one at the same or a lower level.

At the apex, finally, of the hierarchy is English, the hub of the world language system and the sole 'hypercentral' language that connects the speakers of the supercentral languages with one another.

De Swaan's account of the global language system is underspecified in some respects. It is unclear, for instance, where the boundaries of regional language constellations lie, or how exactly in an age of putative globalisation they may be drawn. The same language can, it seems, appear at different levels in the hierarchy: English, for example, is hypercentral in the world system, but also supercentral in relation to its own constellation. And French too is supercentral in relation to West and North Africa, but also central with respect to the regional languages of France. It would appear the hierarchy has two levels in Europe and three levels in the more multilingual states of Africa and Asia. Finally, one might also ask why Russian is identified as a current supercentral language: it may once have been with respect to the former Soviet Union and Eastern Europe, but is this still the case?

All that said, de Swaan's is a useful conceptualisation of the hierarchical ordering that characterises relationships between the world's languages. It highlights the evident inequalities between languages that track the material and political inequalities between regions and between countries, and it draws attention to the oligopolistic tendencies of the global language system that mirror oligopoly in the non-linguistic world.

However, to fully understand the architecture and dynamics of the global language system, we need, de Swaan argues (2001a), to take account of the special properties of language as an economic commodity

5.1.3.2 Languages as 'hypercollective' goods

Languages are special because, in economic parlance, they are not just collective but 'hypercollective goods', definable in terms of the following set of properties:

1. Like other collective goods, languages do not diminish in utility with use. Quite the opposite: the more speakers a language gains, the greater the number of potential interlocutors and the greater the production of texts, which, of course, boosts the utility of the language to all who are already proficient in it. The same is true of other kinds of networks – telecommunication networks, for instance: new subscribers increase the utility of the network for all existing subscribers by multiplying the number of potential connection points, a phenomenon economists refer to as 'external network effects'. One might add here that the choice of network to subscribe to, or language to acquire, is influenced by the individual's estimate as to which is most likely to retain an enduring utility in a competitive situation, a factor predisposing people to opt for the larger language, whose prestige tends to transfer to the acquirer, thereby further enhancing its attractiveness. And once acquired, people develop a vested interest in the language, or brand, they have invested in, which reduces the likelihood of transfer to an alternative.

2. Unlike telephone networks, which are 'excludable' in the sense that entry is usually dependent on payment of a toll or fee, languages are non-excludable, 'free' goods in the technical economic sense that they are open, in principle, to anyone willing to make the effort to learn them. In practice, however, there may be barriers: illiteracy or exclusion from education, for instance, and so 'non-excludability' here is a moot point.

3. As with other collective goods, the maintenance of language requires the collaboration of many persons.

4. The creation, or production, of a collective good requires the efforts of a community, not single individuals. The same is true of languages (see de Swaan 2001a: 31).

The hypercollective character of languages helps explain why language spread tends to acquire a self-reinforcing dynamic. To elaborate: since entry into a language is not easily controlled ('non-excludability'), and since the addition of each new speaker increases the utility of the language for all existing users ('external network effects'), there is an inbuilt propensity for further persons to acquire the language, and this potentially can escalate into a stampede toward it.

Rooted as it is in the behaviour of aggregates, the notion of hypercollectivity illuminates the dynamics of language spread but only partly explains why individuals elect to acquire one second language rather than another in the first place. This, de Swaan (2001a: 33) argues, is influenced by expectations regarding how others will act towards a language – whether they too will acquire it as a lingua franca, for example, and also by perceptions of the 'communication potential' of a language – its 'Q value' (de Swaan 2001a: 31).

The Q value of a language x is the product of its prevalence and its centrality. 'Prevalence' refers to the proportion of speakers of language x in a constellation, and 'centrality' to the proportion of plurilingual speakers of other languages in the constellation who may also be reached through language x – an indicator, therefore, of its connectedness. Centrality is important because a language x with a smaller number of speakers in a constellation than language y, hence less prevalence, may nonetheless end up with a higher Q value because it offers more connections to other plurilingual speakers.[3]

Q values, however, are, de Swaan (2001a) points out, most appropriately determined not by comparing single languages but language repertoires. Thus, a bilingual speaker of, say, German and Portuguese, faced with a choice between learning English or French as a third language, needs to ask (so to speak) how much the Q value of their entire repertoire will be enhanced by learning one of these languages rather than another.

To summarise, a language's Q value is an indicator of its communicative value in a particular language constellation, which is itself affected by the position of that language in the global language hierarchy outlined above. It represents – in formal fashion – the rough and ready intuitive estimations that guide individual choices as to which foreign language it is more advantageous to learn, and it is, therefore, not all that dissimilar in composition to the factors identified by Coulmas (1992) as making languages more or less attractive to learn: communicative range (the number of other persons one can communicate with using the language) and functional potential (what one can do with the language once it is acquired). The latter, Coulmas (1992) points out, is substantially determined by long-term historical processes, particularly investment in the language in the form of dictionaries, translations and the like. In one sense then, languages may be seen as long-term capital investment projects, with the quantity of investment affecting the functional potential of the language. And, at the individual level meanwhile, second language learning may be likened to capital formation, in this case the acquisition of symbolic and intellectual capital.

5.1.3.3 Assessing de Swaan's explanatory framework

In its emphasis on language spread as the aggregate product of many individual decisions guided by perceptions of what is personally advantageous, the explanatory framework outlined above is quite different from that of linguistic imperialism. This emphasises bottom-up processes; linguistic imperialism top-down processes of orchestration and promotion. As de Swaan (2001a: 186) puts it:

> The world language system was not designed for efficiency. It was never designed at all. It just happened, as the mostly unintended consequence of a myriad of individual decisions (and non-decisions, resignation and compliance) which completely ignored the aggregate consequences for the larger language constellation. (De Swaan 2001a: 186)

There is much to commend in this point of view and the framework underlying it. It shows how agency is present at the micro-level of individual decisions (or non-decisions), and how it becomes diluted, thus attenuated, over aggregations of individuals, often producing aggregate outcomes that are unforeseen, perhaps even undesirable to those same individuals. Also, in showing how agency is diffused and is often insensitive to aggregate outcomes (e.g. language decline) rather than concentrated in particular institutions, it serves to highlight the limited ability of language planning (LP) at state or even supranational level to contain the spread of English when this runs counter to popular perceptions of what enhances individuals' linguistic capital.

This is illustrated by the situation in the European Union, where, despite EU funding of programmes (e.g. Lingua, Erasmus) aimed at promoting a diversification in the foreign languages offered in the curriculum (see Wright 2004: 128), and despite a rhetorical climate supportive of linguistic diversification, there has been a continuing rise in the proportion of pupils studying English as their first (or only) foreign language. European Commission statistics (Eurydice 2002), for example, show that in 1999/2000 an average of 40 per cent of primary pupils across the EU learnt English, up from around 33 per cent in 1996/97 (Eurydice 2000), and that 87 per cent of general secondary school pupils studied English compared to 83 per cent in 1991/92.

A reasonable inference from these trends and from the limited uptake of other languages is that parents (and pupils) are reluctant to bear the considerable costs attaching to the acquisition of a second language unless they discern some tangible and likely benefits, and that English – given its position in the global hierarchy and its role as the lubricant of globalisation – fits the bill. Such perceptions of the economic value of English do not, moreover, seem to be obviously misplaced, for as Grin (2001: 73) shows, in the Swiss labour market English language skills are, independently of the effects of education, associated with significantly higher earnings; and it is possible that this is the case elsewhere in Europe.

The example above is supportive of de Swaan's (2001a) overall analysis of the bottom-up, demand-led, self-reinforcing nature of the spread of English, a spread that in democratic, non-autarkic societies LP is relatively powerless to reverse. That said, his framework, as remarked earlier, is incomplete, and it may be useful therefore to conclude this section with a brief discussion of some of its limitations.

Limitations of de Swaan's framework

The first of these limitations is that, if Phillipson's account is excessively top-down, de Swaan's is perhaps unduly bottom-up. That individual preferences between second languages are influenced by perceptions of their relative communicative value, and that spread, once initiated, has a self-accelerating propensity, are both convincing. But we should not overlook initial conditions or, to use a theological metaphor, a first cause. Thus, while not designed, the global language hierarchy did not 'just happen' either: it emerged from, and continues to reflect, the past imposition of British colonial rule on large areas of Africa and Asia and the present economic, military and political dominance of the United States.

Second, de Swaan's framework concentrates on, and explains, the demand for languages in general and English in particular, a demand intensified by globalisation. It has less to say, however, about supply; that is, decisions to expand or curtail school provision for the teaching of English. Clearly, this is highly responsive to demand, but such decisions are nevertheless at least partly autonomous and are taken by, or channelled through, institutions and powerful individuals within them, typically ministries of education. One thinks here of the Malaysian decision to curtail the role of English by switching to Bahasa Malaysia medium at secondary school, a decision partially retracted since, or the Tanzanian decision to continue with English as a medium of instruction at secondary school rather than switch to Swahili, and so forth.

The wider point here is that the linguistic market is not perfectly competitive, or untrammelled, but hedged by the powers that nation states still have, despite globalisation's attenuation of their freedom of action, to protect the market for their national languages through reserving certain public domains for their use. Thus, an analysis of spread with individual preferences as a key unit of that analysis is certainly illuminating, but one needs also to incorporate higher level units of decision-making, that is, national institutions and not just aggregates of individuals.

A similar point can be made in relation to globalisation, whose effects on the demand for English are analysable at the level of individual acquisition decisions. A broader analysis, however, might also encompass transnational corporations and their executives, who have played an agentive role in the diffusion of English. For example, when the Nissan-Renault partnership was established in 1999, the chief executive, Carlos Ghosn, decided to make English the working language of its mainly Japanese and French workforce, thus increasing the likelihood of other corporations doing likewise. The spread of lingua francas, then, is not only mediated by individual acquisition decisions but by the actions and decisions of higher level institutions such as transnational corporations and national governments.

A final limitation of de Swaan's framework is that it gives much more emphasis to language as an instrument of communication than to language as a marker of identity or repository of culture, and for this reason it is better adapted to explain the spread of lingua francas such as English, which are adopted principally for the instrumental, practical advantages they confer, than it is to explain the condition of lesser-used national languages, where identity considerations are more finely weighed against practical communicative benefits. The reason for this is that while external network effects operate relatively unimpeded in the case of spreading lingua francas, with lesser-used 'central' or 'periphery' languages, there are countervailing forces. First, linguistic protectionism: we have already referred to the powers states have to insist on the use of the national language in certain reserved public domains, policies that may be duplicated on a lesser scale by minority communities who take collective action, coercively or cooperatively, to maintain the community language and the cultural capital it represents. Second, identity considerations, and the emotional costs of deserting the ancestral language, are likely –even in these unequal conditions – to not so much prevent an eventual switch to the dominant language as to retard it, or – in the best circumstances – produce a more or less stable bilingualism.

These points are, however, minor qualifications to the value of de Swaan's (2001a) framework, which – drawing on well-founded social science concepts – does more to illuminate the dynamics of language spread than the hypothesis of linguistic imperialism. One of its principal contributions, particularly relevant in this context, is that it highlights the self-reinforcing nature of, and the very diffuse agency underlying, the spread of English, suggesting thereby that this spread is not under the control of any single collection of institutions, countries or individuals. This being so, calls by Phillipson (2000a: 102) and others for language policy/planning to restrain the spread of English and mitigate its effects, while well-intentioned, are overly optimistic about its potency. This is not to say that the unbridled spread of English is to be lauded. Far from it, as we see, as we now turn to the effects and implications of the global spread of English.

5.2 EFFECTS OF THE GLOBAL SPREAD OF ENGLISH

A benign view of the effects of the global spread of English, what Pennycook (2001, 2000: 108) calls the 'colonial-celebratory' and 'laissez-faire liberalism' positions, is sometimes portrayed as the dominant one. This is questionable, however, for recent publications (e.g. Pennycook 2001, 2000a, Skutnabb-Kangas 2000, Tollefson 2002a) have given greater prominence to critical views, which now tend, one might argue, to define the terms of the debate over global English. Because they problematise rather than accept the dominance of English, they are also more intellectually provocative, and for these reasons we now engage with them, albeit more briefly than is ideal.

Surveying the literature, there appear to be four main criticisms focused on the effects of the spread of English:

1. English as a global lingua franca produces inequalities in communication between native and non-native speakers of English, leading to inequity (e.g. Phillipson 1992, 2000b, 2003; Ammon 2000; Braine 1999).

2. English contributes to, and consolidates, socio-economic inequalities within and between societies, leading to inequity. Its spread is also implicated in manifest, and increasing, global inequality (e.g. Pennycook 1995, 2001; Tollefson 1991, 2002a; Ricento 2000a; Phillipson 2000a). A related criticism is that the use of English as a medium of instruction in many of the post-colonial countries of Africa and Asia is educationally ineffective, and thereby impedes rather than promotes human development (Williams and Cooke 2002).

3. The spread of English is a threat to global linguistic diversity. It disrupts linguistic ecologies, directly endangering some languages and marginalising others – principally by squeezing them from important public domains, such as scientific communication and higher education (e.g. Phillipson 1992; Phillipson and Skuttnab-Kangas 1996, 1997, 1999; Mühlhäusler 1996; Skuttnab-Kangas 2000).

4. English is implicated in processes of cultural homogenization. Specifically, it is a vector of 'Americanisation', what Phillipson and Skuttnab-Kangas (1997: 28) call 'McDonaldization' (see also Phillipson and Skuttnab-Kangas 1996, 1999; Pennycook 1995).

Two key notions – inequality and diversity – are central to these criticisms and it is useful, therefore, to structure our discussion around them, starting with the effects that the dominance of English has on linguistic and cultural diversity.

5.2.1 English as threat to linguistic diversity: assessing the claims

In discourses on language diversity and language endangerment one sometimes encounters the term 'killer languages' (e.g. Skuttnab-Kangas 2003: 33) applied to English and other dominant languages. This term, and other similar ones – linguicide, language murder and so on – are obviously metaphorical in that languages do not have an existence independent of their speakers, nor can they themselves act agentively. But while metaphors can illuminate, they can also obscure, as they do in this instance. They do so because they distract attention from more soundly founded explanations of language loss.

Fundamental among these, as discussed in Chapter 4, is a breakdown in the inter-generational transmission of the ancestral language, a process which typically sets in gradually as speakers of a less widely spoken, socio-economically marginal language come into contact with a more prestigious, more economically useful language that they choose, or feel economically obliged, to transmit to their offspring. As Mufwene (2002:12) argues:

> languages do not kill languages; their own speakers do, in giving them up, although they themselves are victims of changes in the socio-economic ecologies in which they evolve. Solutions that focus on the victims rather than on the causes of their plights are just as bad as environmental solutions that would focus on affected species rather than on the ecologies that affect the species.

There is still a case to answer, however, and a problem to address. Clearly, there are situations of contact with English where the consequences have been very adverse for indigenous vernaculars (e.g. Irish, Scots Gaelic, Australian aboriginal languages, etc.), but there are also others where the outcomes have been not at all threatening. So one wonders what the distinguishing circumstances are. Taking account of Mufwene's point above, it seems useful to start from an examination of the socio-economic circumstances of language contact, and identify those that seem more threatening.

The distinction drawn by Mufwene (2001, 2002) between settlement and exploitation colonies is helpful here.[4] It is predominantly in the former (e.g. in North America, Latin America, Australasia, Ireland, etc.) rather than the latter that European colonial languages – Spanish, Portuguese and French as well as English – have posed a threat to other languages. Mufwene (2002) attributes this to the socio-economic characteristics of settlement colonies: namely, the demographic pressures exerted by substantial European in-migration – leading eventually to demographic preponderance, the geographical displacement of indigenous peoples, their decimation through conflict and by infectious disease and the imposition of a new economic order to which indigenous peoples found it necessary to accommodate both socially and linguistically. The picture is one, then, of demographic, social and economic domination and eventual integration into a system of governance over which the language of the coloniser's nation held almost exclusive sway.

By contrast, in the exploitation colonies (e.g. Nigeria, the Gold Coast, the Congo, Senegal, Malaya, etc.), the key objectives were not settlement but control of raw materials and the opening of new markets for the manufactures of the metropole. Relative to the mass of the population, the European colonisers remained few in number, limited principally to civil servants, business people and missionaries, nearly all of whom looked forward to a retirement back in Europe. Under these circumstances a two-level economic system evolved: the mass of the population continued to function in indigenous lingua francas or ethnic vernaculars, while a small indigenous elite acquired English in their role as intermediaries between the masses and the colonial rulers (Mufwene 2002, Brutt-Griffler 2002).

In Africa then – as now – the language of (former) colonial powers have not so much displaced local languages from the repertoires of indigenous populations as added to them, a situation attributable to the clear functional demarcation between them: the former tend to be the languages of secondary and higher education, of higher public administration and of international commerce, spoken mainly by educated urban elites;[5] the latter the vernaculars of the majority of the population who work in lower economic sectors or live in rural areas, only partially touched by the apparatus of the state. Among a restricted elite, there are, it is true, signs that English is increasingly used in informal domains, but there are also, as Mufwene (2002: 10) suggests, countervailing pressures: elites retain competence in ethnic vernaculars to keep up links with relatives in rural areas.

Meanwhile, in the more affluent former colonies of Hong Kong, Malaysia and Singapore a similar situation obtains. English, to be sure, is an important language of transnational business networks, of education and of inter-ethnic communication beyond the home – at least in Malaysia and Singapore. But indigenous, non-European languages (Malay, Cantonese, Hokkien, etc.) remain the unmarked choice for most in-group communication.

All this is not to say that there is no threat to indigenous local languages in former exploitation colonies. On the contrary, ample evidence exists of ongoing language loss in Africa, South-east Asia and areas of the Pacific (see Grenoble and Whaley 1998, Nettle and Romaine 2000). Here, however, language shift is not towards English but to indigenous languages – some of which function as indigenous lingua francas – Swahili in East Africa, Hausa in Nigeria, Lingala in Congo-Zaire, Wolof in Senegal and Malay in Malaysia/Indonesia, for example. Moreover, with the increased urbanisation of many African societies, and the concomitant proletarianisation of significant numbers of people, many of these lingua francas are turning into urban vernaculars with sufficient economic allure to induce some rural populations to shift towards them and away from their ancestral languages.

Our conclusion, then, is that claims that former colonial languages, and English in particular, are endangering indigenous languages around the world are insufficiently nuanced. They have done so in former settlement colonies, but in the different language contact ecologies of former exploitation colonies the shift tends to be to other indigenous languages rather than English. The generalisation that best accounts for this contrast is that English tends to undermine indigenous local languages when it becomes a vernacular for a substantial segment of the population, as it has in most settlement colonies. Where, on the other hand, it is not a vernacular but a lingua franca, and a lingua franca for a minority at that, as appears to be the case in most former exploitation colonies, there is little threat to indigenous languages. As Mufwene (2002: 24) points out, 'languages or dialects can be a threat to each other only when they compete for the same functions. Languages ... that have separate communicative or social functions can coexist quite happily'. Thus far, there is little evidence to suggest that English is competing for vernacular functions with indigenous languages.

5.2.1.1 English as a lingua franca in Europe

Turning for a moment to Europe, where English has also been seen as a threat to other languages – as 'a kind of linguistic cuckoo, taking over where other breeds of language have historically nested' (Phillipson 2003: 4) – rather similar points can be made. There is little evidence that English is undermining the standardised national languages of European states, even the smaller ones (e.g. Norway). Certainly, it is in competition for, and displacing, other languages – most notably French – from lingua franca functions (see Wright 2004: 133), for example their roles in scientific communication, and it increasingly dominates the foreign language curricula of European schools and universities. But this does not mean that it poses a threat to the survival of other European languages. Any such suggestion is implausible for the following reasons: first, despite globalisation, most European states retain sufficient power to implement linguistic protectionist policies, reserving a privileged place for national languages in many public domains (e.g. education, administration, etc.); second, these languages index valued identities in a way that English as an instrumental lingua franca cannot, and this reduces considerably the likelihood of any wholesale shift to English.

But this does not, however, absolve English from all charges made by its critics, an unanswered one being that, even if English does not 'kill' other languages, it relegates them to a lesser role in an incipient global diglossia (Phillipson and Skuttnab-Kangas 1996: 446; Pennycook 2001: 58; Mühleisen 2003: 113), where indigenous languages are left, in Pennycook's words (2001: 57), as 'static markers of identity', as languages of informal, less prestigious domains, with English in control of the high prestige domains of higher education, scientific communication and transnational business.

Such points tend to be made most forcefully with respect to science, where English is clearly the dominant language (Ammon 2001a), and to higher education, where English plays an increasingly prominent role, most notably in such countries as Denmark, Sweden, Germany and Switzerland. The worry here is that this may lead in due course to register atrophy; that is, an impoverishment of a language's lexical and stylistic resources in the scientific domain through underuse (see Gunnarsson 2001: 306), just as a limb withers if it is not exercised.

Other concerns, perhaps more serious and to which we return later, are that higher education may become more isolated from the rest of society if it operates in a foreign language, and that researchers from non-English countries are placed at a significant communicative disadvantage relative to English native speakers when it comes to placing their research before an international audience (Ammon 2001b, 2003).

For the moment, however, let us concentrate on the question of register atrophy, and acknowledge Gunnarsson's point. Though clearly not yet moribund as a language of science, there is no guarantee that Swedish, and similar languages, will not eventually become so, this being one of the potential costs of the hegemony of English.

There are other authors, however, who take a more sanguine view. Writing in the same volume, Haarman and Holman (2001) acknowledge the influence of English on the structure of scientific Finnish but also argue that English has helped Finland become a leading player in its advance toward a 'network society':

Finland's decision to favour English as its primary vehicle for scientific research has enabled the country, perhaps unexpectedly, to assume a major role, both active and passive, in the process of globalisation. (Haarman and Holman 2001: 256)

Highlighted here are the opportunities English offers for transcending the limitations of a small national community and for interacting on a wider stage to the benefit of the economy and society. De Swaan (2001b: 74) observes, meanwhile, that the large number of technical and semi-technical terms that some languages have borrowed from English in no way threatens the integrity of those languages. As he puts it, 'the strong jaws of morphology chew loan-words with surprising ease into well-formed sentences.'

There are, then, contrasting views on English as a language of science, some giving greater prominence to the real disadvantages for indigenous languages of reduced use in such high status domains, others emphasising the advantages in a globalising world of an international vehicular language of science. That this language is English is, of course, a matter of historical contingency than of any intrinsic merit.

5.2.1.2 African languages and the role of English

There is less room, however, for such an ambivalent conclusion when it comes to Africa, where English, along with other former colonial languages, continues to dominate not just higher education but a range of other high status, formal domains – secondary education, government and administration. The inevitable effect has been to relegate indigenous African languages to lower status, informal domains, and thereby to deprive them of opportunities and resources for functional elaboration, for what Liddicoat and Bryant (2002: 10) refer to as 'intellectualisation'. Mazrui (2002: 275) highlights the problem by noting that *Das Kapital* cannot, even now, be read in any major African language, this very fact in his view (Mazrui 2002, 2004) indexing Africa's continuing, and debilitating, intellectual and epistemological dependency on the West.

For many African intellectuals, and others beside, redress of past neglect requires no less than a kind of linguistic decolonisation, this being achieved by promoting and developing African languages so that they attain a status equal to, or greater than, the former colonial language, losing in the process their stigma of inferiority. The principles, and rationale, for such a linguistic renaissance are set forth most clearly in the Asmara Declaration of January 2000 (reprinted in Mazrui 2004: 129), one of whose key clauses proclaims that African languages 'must take on the duty, the responsibility and the challenge of speaking for the continent'.

Given the persisting absence of indigenous African languages from high status domains and the often deleterious effects of the use of former colonial languages as media of instruction (see Chapter 7), it is difficult to feel anything but sympathetic to the aspirations underpinning the Declaration. At the same time, however, it raises issues of theory and practical implementation that merit closer scrutiny.

An initial point, made by Blommaert (2001: 137), is that rights-based discourse, of which the Asmara Declaration is one instance, tends to view problems of diversity and inequality as a matter of relationships between languages. Overlooked is the issue of diversity and equality within units defined as 'languages', which may actually have a more direct bearing on social mobility and equality:

> what counts is not the existence and distribution of languages, but the availability, accessibility and distribution of specific linguistic-communicative skills such as competence in standard and literate varieties of the languages. Granting a member of a minority group the right to speak his or her mother tongue in the public arena does not in itself empower him or her. (Blommaert 2001: 136)

Blommaert goes on to argue that the ideal of institutional equality between languages in a multilingual polity – each having a place in education, the media, administration and so on – is not just financially unfeasible but sociolinguistically impossible because this would involve the development of exclusive status varieties, which not all members of the group would control. The result, Blommaert (2001: 137) avers, is that 'inequality among language groups would be reduced, but inequality within languages would be increased'.

Another contentious aspect of the Asmara Declaration is the assertion in its tenth clause that 'African languages are essential for decolonisation of African minds and the African renaissance'. Informed, clearly, by Ngugi's (1986) ideas on 'decolonising the mind', this proposition more than bears a trace of Whorfianism; the notion that the language we speak organises and controls our conceptualisation/perception of the world. Such a deterministic outlook is widely disputed, however, most relevantly by such African writers as Mphahlele (1963) and Achebe (1976), the latter of whom has argued that English can be indigenised, that it can 'carry the weight of the African experience' and that it can become the medium for oppositional discourses. The existence of an indigenised literature in English, the emergence of African varieties of English and the fact that opposition to English as a global language tends overwhelmingly to be expressed in English are all supportive of Achebe's opinion that the appropriation of English is possible, a viewpoint many would endorse as a more accurate, less essentialised account of how language works.

There are also, of course, practical and socio-political impediments to the re-centring of indigenous African languages, as the recent experience of South Africa, one of Africa's richer states, illustrates. Here, the 1996 constitution commits the government to the development of the nine indigenous languages granted official status alongside English and Afrikaans, one aspect of which is their intellectualisation (Finlayson and Madiba 2002). Finlayson and Madiba report that, while progress has been made in terminology development and other technical areas through agencies like the Pan South African Language Board (PanSALB), there remain doubts as to whether the government has enough resources to support the simultaneous development of all nine languages[6] in the face of competing priorities – housing, electricity, health, water and so on.

More problematic than this, however – given that use in education is an important driver of intellectualisation[7] – is the resistance of the African population to the use of indigenous languages as instructional media, an attitude that most probably reflects both the past inferiorisation of the these languages under apartheid and current perceptions that English is more economically advantageous. Documenting this trend, Finlayson and Madiba (2002: 45) note that all fifteen universities responding to a questionnaire survey on language tuition report the continued use of English as the sole language of instruction. In secondary education a similar pattern prevails: English continues to be the favoured medium in African schools. Kamwangamalu (2003: 241) observes, meanwhile, that English takes up as much as 91 per cent of the available airtime on South African television and that, in 1994, 87 per cent of parliamentary speeches were delivered in English.

Such figures, and the testimony of observers (e.g. Ridge 2000), impel one to the conclusion that, despite the constitution, the dominance of English in contemporary South Africa is increasing rather than diminishing, a trend that gives weight to Maclean and McCormick's (1996: 329) suggestion that the official multilingualism of the constitution has a primarily symbolic purpose, and to the suspicion voiced by de Swaan (2001a: 140) that the current situation is not entirely displeasing to the country's leaders.

The wider lesson, however, is not that there is no problem: a greater public role for indigenous African languages would clearly be beneficial, and English does have an undue dominance in education. It is rather that solutions remain elusive. As we have seen, official recognition and official promotion top-down cannot of themselves improve a language's status if its speakers prefer to learn and use some other language to enhance their employment prospects. And calls for the revalorisation of indigenous African languages, as exemplified by the sociolinguistically flawed Asmara Declaration, may draw attention to an inequitable situation but do not of themselves provide the resources nor create the political will necessary for their implementation.

The South African situation also highlights, once again, the limited capacity language status planning has of itself to alter the sociolinguistic balance of power. To bring that about some more profound economic reconfiguration is needed that makes the other languages of South Africa equally attractive to the population. As Kamwangamalu (2003: 244) remarks, 'the masses need to know what an education in these languages [the nine indigenous official languages] would do for them in terms of upward social mobility'. Ridge (2000: 166) makes a similar point when he argues that:

> the dominant position of English in South Africa is … the choice of a non-English majority, who have real needs which they see as met through the language. … They deserve to be taken seriously.

It needs spelling out, perhaps, that these South African applied linguists are not arguing that the language provisions of the constitution[8] are unnecessary or misguided. Rather that – given the complex socio-economic and ideological forces currently operating in favour of English – they are not sufficient to reduce English to equality with the other official languages. Reconciling the popular demand for education in English with action to elevate the status of indigenous African languages is, thus, a more delicate and complex matter than some have supposed, not just in South Africa but even more so in the weaker states to the north. We return to this issue in a little more detail in Chapter 7, but for the present we move on to consider the impact of English spread on cultural diversity.

5.2.2 English as threat to cultural diversity: assessing the claims

In critical writings, English is often implicated in globalising processes of cultural homogenisation and Americanisation. One of the more 'up-front' assertions of this thesis can be found in Phillipson and Skuttnab-Kangas (1996: 439), who – drawing on Tsuda's (1994) work – state that:

> The projection of English as the 'world language' par excellence is symptomatic of globalisation processes. We live in a world characterized by ideological global-ization, transnationalization, and Americanization and the homogenization of world culture, … spearheaded by films, pop culture, and fast-food chains.

Claims of a similar kind appear in later publications. Phillipson (2000a: 90), for example, remarks that:

> you don't have to be a sociologist to register that our world is increasingly dominated by Coca Cola, CNN, Microsoft and the many transnational corporations for whom the key language is English, and who through processes of McDonaldization … are seeking to create and imagine, in Benedict Anderson's sense (1983), a global consumerist culture, a single market.

The deployment here of the McDonaldisation metaphor is a token of the influence of such sociologists of globalisation as Ritzer (1996) or Barber (1995), whose dystopic representations of the complex, contested phenomenon we know as globalisation conjure up visions of endless shopping malls, theme parks and fast-food outlets, or, as Block and Cameron (2002: 4) characterise it, a 'creeping uniformity' of taste, of work patterns, of entertainment preferences.

The portrait of globalisation painted by Phillipson and others is, then, relatively straightforward. Globalisation is seen as the globalisation of capitalism, a process facilitated by the spread of English and by complicitous, Western-dominated trans-national media corporations and which, in its cultural aspect, encroaches on and undermines local identities through the imposition of a market-driven, homogenised Western consumer culture. In short, alongside linguistic imperialism there is in globalisation a kind of cultural imperialism at work.

This story, one can agree, has a certain intuitive attractiveness, a prima facie plausibility. After all, almost everywhere one travels, at least in countries integrated into the global economy, the presence of Western, particularly American, cultural products and artefacts impress themselves on the senses: McDonald's, Starbucks, CNN, cinema multiplexes –predominately screening Hollywood films – and so on. There is, moreover, an asymmetry about these cultural flows, as data assembled by Phillipson (2003: 72) indicates. In 1998, US films, for example, accounted for 90 per cent of Dutch and German box office takings and for more than 80 per cent in the UK. The corresponding market share of EU-originated films in the United States was of the order of 2–3 per cent. Thompson (2003: 254) describes a similar scenario in the television market: the United States sells far more material abroad than it imports, and developing countries with few resources for programme production find the import of American TV serials, whose cost is depressed by economies of scale, a relatively inexpensive way of filling out broadcasting schedules.

Concern at these asymmetries has, one might add, reached the highest political levels: the French government, for example, imposes quotas on the distribution of

Hollywood products to protect the domestic film industry, and as Tomlinson (1997: 174) observes, disagreements about films and TV imports disrupted the 1993 GATT trade negotiations.

One other reason why one might wish to equate globalisation on the cultural plane with homogenisation and cultural imperialism is the close association, amply documented, of globalisation and transnational capitalism, whose expansionary dynamic and economic power pull many cultures into the ambit of a global capitalist culture. An illustration of how this process works out may be found in Machin and van Leeuwen's (2003) analysis of *Cosmopolitan*, an internationally popular women's magazine. Drawing on data from eight different national versions of the magazine they argue that, though each of these versions is published in a different language and represents different local cultural practices, there is an underlying sameness at the more abstract level of 'discourse schemas', of linguistic constructions of reality. Thus, the world – as discursively constructed in *Cosmopolitan* – is, according to Machin and van Leeuwen (2003: 505), one where:

> there is no solidarity with fellow human beings, no counsel from religious and cultural traditions, and there are no structural and political solutions by means of whatever form of collective action. It is all up to the individual, who must, alone, face the world using survival strategies in which traditional 'female wiles' continue to play a key role ... This 'survival of the fittest' and 'winner takes all' approach is the essential message of the discourse schema, its meaning, the way it interprets the social practices of work and the personal relationships it recontextualises. ... it is clearly an approach that suits the interests of the global neo-capitalist order of which *Cosmopolitan* forms part.

What is diffused, then, is no particular language, nor any particular set of solutions to the vicissitudes of life portrayed in *Cosmopolitan*, but something more abstract – values and life-worlds, that are particularly accommodating of global capitalism. Similar points, no doubt, might be made with regard to McDonald's, whose global outlets operate to a common template but one within which culinary products may be tailored to national tastes and served in a local lingua franca.

However plausible though all these accounts may be, there are reasons for resisting the assimilation of these phenomena to a cultural imperialism explanatory framework. First of all, it would be erroneous to read off from the ubiquity of Western cultural goods any profound and necessary cultural penetration, leading to Western-dominated cultural homogenisation. As Tomlinson (1997: 180) points out, global media markets, to take one economic sector, are more complex and pluralised than is sometimes supposed. TV Globo in Brazil, for example, not only dominates its domestic market but exports products to other Latin American countries. And local TV programmes, replete with local, culturally specific references, such as *Coronation Street* in the UK, typically and consistently attract more viewers than American imports.

The more serious problem, however, with the cultural imperialism thesis is that, rather like linguistic imperialism, it tends to portray the recipients of Western cultural goods as passive and unreflecting, and it represents cultural influence as moving in a single direction – from the centre to the periphery. This, Tomlinson (1997: 182) persuasively argues, misconceives the nature of cultural flows, which can more profitably be understood in dialectic terms as an interplay between external influence and local cultural forms, often producing mutation and hybridity. Tomlinson's (1997: 183) example of a hybrid form that has entered global popular culture is hip hop, not a Black American form as is commonly assumed but actually a 'hybrid mix of Afro-American and Caribbean musical cultures'.

This leads us to the further point that the notions of core and periphery, integral to the cultural imperialism thesis, are increasingly problematic in a contemporary world of migration and diasporas. The periphery, if by that that one means Asian, African and Latin American populations and cultures, has already irrupted into the core, as demographic statistics on Los Angeles, London or, for that matter, Leicester show[9] (see Chapter 3). The cultural consequences are complex and variable, ranging from the mundane commodification of 'ethnic' foods, clothing and artefacts visible to any casual observer of the urban British scene to more profound effects on Western cultural and national identities. For Tomlinson (1997: 185), the increased multiculturalism of European and North American societies in concert with declining Western self-confidence in cultural matters means that one needs to reach out for a more complex analytic framework than one in which a cohesive West imposes its cultural forms on a weak periphery.

Lending weight to this analysis is the increasingly common depiction of globalisation (Tomlinson 1997, Giddens 1999) as a 'decentred process'. That is, although there are blatant disparities of wealth and power between nations, with the United States, Japan and Europe having vastly more influence in world affairs than, say, the poorer states of Africa, it is difficult to argue that globalisation is under the control of any one set of countries or corporations.

Indeed, under globalisation complex patterns of advantage and disadvantage have emerged within and between countries, cutting across old dualities of North and South or core and periphery. Thus, the growing economic prosperity of formerly less developed countries such as China or South Korea, itself reflecting shifts in the balance of economic power, can be causally linked in complex ways to the economic decline, of, say, parts of the North-East of England, whose products have ceased to be competitive in world markets.[10] And through the same dense web of economic interconnections global capitalism also creates strange juxtapositions of pockets of affluence alongside, and adjacent to, pockets of poverty in the same society: a Hackney or Tower Hamlets, say, in close proximity to the finance houses of the City of London.

The general point emerging here is that there is no longer a monolithic cohesive core capable of dominating a weak periphery. The core-periphery model underpinning the cultural imperialism thesis cannot capture the complexities of the flows of cultural influence that characterise globalisation, and so a more nuanced account emphasising the interplay of the global and local is needed.

Our conclusion, then, is that although global media corporations (e.g. Time

Warner, Viacom, Bertelsmann, Sony, Disney, etc.) may be leading some uniform-isation of popular tastes in entertainment (McChesney 2003), there is no strong evidence that anything so simple as Western-dominated cultural homogenisation is taking place. National and local identities seem resilient, and, far from sweeping these away, globalisation may be bringing into existence new hybrid cultural forms, new identities and new cosmopolitan sensibilities, adding an additional layer of complexity to the multiplicity of identities already available.

The role of English in these processes can hardly be said to be central either. As Machin and van Leeuwen's (2003) work suggests, what is being diffused, if anything, is not so much the English language or any specific cultural practices, rather what they call 'discourse schemas' and values, that harmonise safely with capitalism. In fact, global capitalism has demonstrated a fair degree of nimbleness in customising its products, and the languages in which they are marketed, to the tastes of national markets. But this perhaps is not surprising, for the pursuit of profit is far more central to the purposes of global conglomerates than linguistic or cultural homogenisation.

5.2.3 English and inequality

In critical perspectives, the spread of English is frequently linked to two main forms of inequality: inequalities in communication between those with greater and lesser levels of proficiency in English or between native and non-native speakers, and social, economic and political inequalities within and between countries. It is to the former kind that we turn first.

5.2.3.1 Inequalities in communication

Many commentators (e.g. de Swaan 2001a: 52; Wright 2004: 174) acknowledge the undeserved advantages that accrue to native speakers from the global dominance of English. They are undeserved in that whereas native speakers acquire the language naturalistically in childhood,[11] second language users, and the societies they come from, incur the considerable costs of formal study, books, teachers and all the paraphernalia of learning, not to mention the costs of the time and effort expended. Through the operation of network effects, these second language learners also add to the utility of the language for all other users, including native speakers, who – in economic parlance – enjoy 'location rent' (de Swaan 2001a: 189) in as much as they draw benefits from a collective good, towards the cost of whose production they make comparatively little contribution.

Unsurprisingly, this asymmetry of costs often gives rise to feelings of unfairness and sometimes resentment, only partially assuaged by arguments that native speakers do in fact need to make a considerable effort to develop the skill of writing in the standard language, and that unfairnesses of this kind, arising from accidents of geography, climate or natural resources, are endemic to the human condition. They have also generated politically unrealistic but ethically very defensible proposals that native-speaking communities should make transfer payments to help defray the costs borne by other societies in teaching English as a second language.

In the literature, however, it is the disadvantage suffered by non-native speakers, particularly in scientific and academic communication, rather than the advantage of native speakers that attracts the most comment. Phillipson (2000a: 97), for example, draws an unfavourable comparison between an English-speaking conference, where some participants struggled to express their ideas in English, and a conference conducted in Esperanto, at which participants from a range of countries communicated on equal terms with ease and confidence.

Knapp (2002: 236–8), meanwhile, casts doubt on the belief that lingua franca interactions, whether between non-native speakers, or natives and non-natives, are almost invariably cooperative. Drawing on data from a week-long international student simulation in English of United Nations proceedings, he observes that this competitive situation not only produced low levels of participation by non-native speakers,[12] who subsequently complained of feeling excluded, but, worse, instances of discriminatory behaviour directed at non-natives whose linguistic limitations slowed the formulation of their contributions. Although, very significantly, the initiators of this uncooperative behaviour were what Knapp (2002: 224) refers to as 'quasi-native speakers', that is second language speakers of a near-native proficiency level rather than British or American native speakers, these instances, unrepresentative though they may be, do highlight the potential or actual communicative disadvantage that non-native users of English may experience at international conferences or similar events.

Inequalities in the domain of academic/scientific publication

Other writers focus more on inequalities in the domain of academic publication. There are claims, for example, that scholars from non-English-speaking backgrounds are disadvantaged when it comes to getting their work published in high prestige international journals that overwhelmingly publish in English (see Tardy 2004). And there are also arguments (de Swaan 2001b: 78) that, because these periodicals are typically British or American, it is British and American editors that assume important gatekeeping roles, exerting 'a major impact on the selection and promotion of academics in other countries who depend on these publications for their advancement'. Their gatekeeping practices also bolster, so it is argued, the dominance of Anglo-American discursive norms, styles and conceptions, to the disadvantage of third world scholars in particular (see Tardy 2004). Another common criticism is that work not published in English often tends to be undervalued or even ignored, thereby falling into the domain of lost science (Phillipson 2001: 9; Tardy 2004: 251).

Empirical evidence for these claims, as opposed to anecdote or assertion, is mixed, particularly with regard to the question of how difficult it is for non-native academics to get their work published in prestigious international journals. Tardy (2004) cites various authors such as Canagarajah (1996) who emphasise the difficulties, not all of them linguistic. Contrary evidence, however, is supplied by Wood (2001: 80), who concludes on the basis of a study of one year's issues (1997–98) of the journals *Science* and *Nature* that while there may be financial and physical impediments to third world scientists publishing their work, the barriers of language are not formidable:

> From the data here the linguistic barriers for NNS's [non-native speakers] to be published in even the most prestigious journal do not seem high.[13]

Of course, Wood's sample is limited, and it would require replication over a wider range of journals to convince one that non-native researchers are not disadvantaged in gaining access to international publication. Nonetheless, his findings provide grounds for suspending an automatic assumption of disadvantage.

If one turns to the different matter of perceptions of disadvantage, the evidence again is mixed. Tardy (2004) cites a number of authors who have found that non-native scholars do feel disadvantaged with respect to native English-speaking academics, yet the findings of her own survey of international graduate students' attitudes are more qualified. All questionnaire respondents (N=45) believed there were beneficial aspects to the use of English as an international language of science, but at the same time thirty-six of these same respondents identified disadvantageous aspects – the time needed to learn English to a high level, for example.

A similar qualified picture emerges from a survey of Swiss researchers' attitudes (n=250) to English in science, carried out by Murray and Dingwall (2001: 100). In the survey 41 per cent of respondents indicated that they thought the dominance of English was a slight disadvantage in their careers and 8 per cent thought it a major handicap, but 27 per cent believed it was actually a slight advantage with a further 24 per cent seeing it as having no effect either way. These findings are not dissimilar to Ammon's 1990 survey of German scientists' attitudes, where 55 per cent of the sample reported no sense of disadvantage in their ability to communicate in English. They contrast sharply, however, with Truchot (2001: 320), whose 1984 Strasbourg survey found that as many as 60 per cent of the French scientists in the sample considered themselves to be significantly disadvantaged relative to native English-speaking scientists.

Drawing any definitive conclusion from these various survey findings is, of course, very difficult. The questions and samples are very different, and the responses are clearly influenced by perceptions of who the respondents believe themselves to be in competition with, and by how good they believe their own English to be. Then there is the influence of national background: Swiss researchers from a relatively small and officially multilingual country may be more easily reconciled to the use of English to transcend the national science community than, say, French scientists, whose language has been in competition with English as an international language and whose government has enacted legislation (1994) to defend the use of French in scientific and academic domains.

What one can say, however, is that there is evidence of ambivalent attitudes towards the dominance of English, and that there is, as one would expect on a priori grounds, a widespread, though far from universal, sense that non-native researchers are indeed disadvantaged relative to native English-speaking scientists when it comes to international scientific communication.

Addressing inequalities in communication

Proposals to ameliorate, if not redress, these inequalities have been advanced by various parties, some more radical than others. Ammon (2000: 114), for example, in eminently reasonable fashion, calls for greater tolerance on the part of Anglo-American journal editors and reviewers towards deviations from native standards, and argues for the non-native writer's right to 'linguistic peculiarities'. He recognises, however, that without concerted institutional and political backing such pleas stand on weak ground, a point de Swaan (2001b: 79) implicitly concurs with when he says that 'more than good intentions are required'. Like Ammon, de Swaan (2001b) believes that the best way of mitigating inequality and Anglo-Saxon bias may be to pursue the long term 'de-anglicisation' of English, a process he hopes may be accomplished through the gradual emergence of a 'Euro-English' variety that in due course undergoes codification and ultimately receives official European Union (EU) endorsement (see Chapter 6). For the short term, he proposes limited practical measures such as the appointment in greater numbers of fluent non-native speakers of English to the editorial boards of international journals, and more careful monitoring of the proportions of submissions from non-native writers accepted for publication.

There are, of course, more radical solutions proposed, one of which involves the abandonment of English as the global lingua franca of science, and as the main de facto working language of EU institutions, and its replacement by some neutral, more equitable communication code such as Esperanto (Phillipson 2003: 121). Another, entertained as a possibility for EU-internal communication, involves the contrivance of situations of equal disadvantage – by insisting, for example, that in official discussions delegates speak a language other than their mother tongue. Neither of these latter suggestions is very persuasive, however; not so much for reasons of principle but because of the practical and political obstacles to their implementation. The first – to abandon English – is unworkable because, as de Swaan (2001b: 79) points out, there is no central institution sufficiently in control of global English to enforce such a decision. Besides, the advantages of English as the international language of science are widely appreciated, and those many scholars worldwide who have invested time in learning English are understandably likely to be resistant to its replacement. The second – equal disadvantage – also seems unlikely to gain acceptance precisely because of the contrivance involved, but also because political support from France and the UK, two of the more powerful EU member states, seems highly improbable.

In truth, resolving inequalities in communication between non-native and native speakers of English in academic and scientific domains is difficult, and it is hardly surprising, therefore, that convincing solutions – ones that do not have other un-desirable side effects – remain elusive. Changes in the way English is taught as a lingua franca (see Chapter 6) may make a very minor contribution to more equitable communication. That apart, one can only suggest that native speakers of English, particularly professional educators, would be well advised to keep in mind the fact that their privileged position as native speakers of a global language is accidental and unearned, and should be regarded circumspectly.

On this note, we turn to another form of inequality said to be associated with the global spread of English: socio-economic inequality.

5.2.3.2 English and socio-economic inequality[14]

One early articulation of the view that English sustains and reinforces socio-economic inequalities can be found in Tollefson (1991: 7), where he argues that English is not the neutral instrument for development that it is sometimes portrayed to be but a mechanism 'for creating and sustaining social and economic divisions'. A similar stance has since been taken by other authors such as Pennycook (1995: 54), who remarks that:

> English ... acts as a gatekeeper to positions of wealth and prestige both within and between nations, and is the language through which much of the unequal distribution of wealth, resources, and knowledge operates.

A particular focus for criticism, and a central mechanism mediating the production of inequality, so it is argued, is the continued use of English as a medium of instruction in primary and post-primary education in many post-colonial countries, a practice that is not only educationally inefficient (see Chapter 7) where the language is poorly understood, and therefore socially and economically costly (see Williams 1996, William and Cooke 2002), but also inequitable in that it privileges the relatively well-off urban-based elite and further marginalises the rural poor.

Many of these claims, we wish to argue, have substance – and not just those relating to educational inefficiency. There is considerable circumstantial evidence, for example, that English, or more exactly literacy skills in standard varieties, are a necessary, though not sufficient, resource for gaining access to better-paid white collar employment, to higher education, to global culture and to prestigious 'middle-class' identities. This, after all, is why English is in such demand, and it is for this reason that English skills may legitimately be regarded, in Pennycook's (1995: 54) terminology, as a gatekeeper to positions of status.

It is a resource that is very unequally distributed, however. Elite groups typically find it much easier to accumulate the capital that English represents either because their way of life (books, TV, travel, etc.) affords greater environmental exposure to the language or because, in societies where secondary education is often neither universal nor free, they are better placed to gain entry to higher quality secondary education, where the acquisition of English language literacy skills is a central priority. And, if the state school sector is felt to be inadequate at imparting these skills, wealthier parents, unlike their less well-off peers, often have the option of sending their offspring to private English-medium schools, or to institutions offering private supplementary instruction. Vavrus (2002: 377), for example, reports that, following the imposition of an IMF structural adjustment programme in the 1980s, there has been a rapid growth of private fee-paying English-medium schools in Tanzania. In India, meanwhile, there has also been a growth in the number of private

English-medium schools, institutions that cater primarily to the children of wealthier middle-class parents (Annamalai 2004: 187).

It is not difficult, therefore, to see English, and English-medium education, as assisting the reproduction of the elite's privileged position; this class-stratifying property serving, in the view of some commentators (e.g. de Swaan 2001a: 104), as one motive for the retention of colonial languages (e.g. English and French) as languages of governance and education. They function, in Myers-Scotton's (1990) phrase, as instruments of 'elite closure'; that is, the elite, who in part owe their privileged position to their control over high status varieties of English or French, see the continued official role of these languages as one means of excluding the masses from higher levels of the labour market and thereby as instrumental in consolidating their near monopolistic control over it.

If this analysis of the link between English and inequality is reasonably persuasive, the remedies often mooted carry less conviction. Replacing English as a medium of instruction with indigenous languages is one of the more obvious, but is problematic for a range of reasons (see Chapter 7), the most powerful of which is that it is usually opposed, paradoxically, by those who collectively lose most from the perpetuation of a foreign language medium of education.

Their behaviour cannot be seen as irrational, however, for at the individual level parents want their children to receive the education that best enhances their employment chances, and this usually means education in English. They may well realise that English skills do not guarantee a good job, and that chances of school failure are high. But they also understand that without English one is definitively excluded from the more desirable forms of employment. The trouble is, however, though rational at the individual level, these preferences, when aggregated, help collectively to maintain a system of education that may well disadvantage most of them.

Drastically curtailing the presence of English in the curriculum is also problematic, however, for reasons beyond those of democratic choice. With national economies increasingly in thrall to transnational corporations and globalising industries like tourism, it is increasingly difficult to gainsay the economic value of English language skills, a fact well understood by elite groups, who would very probably switch to private English-medium schooling if exposure to English was limited in the state education sector. The effect, surely, would be to exacerbate rather than reduce inequality.

The logic of this position appears to suggest an extension of English, making it more available to all. And for such democratisation of access there is definitely something to be said. After all, the more widely distributed English language skills are, the more likely they are to become a banal skill and the less likely they are to command a premium in the labour market (Grin 2001), or to serve as an instrument for 'elite closure'.

Democratisation of access can, however, take a variety of forms, one of the less desirable of which is an extension of English medium into the lower levels of primary education. The reasons why this is inadvisable have to do with both educational efficiency and economic and human development. As regards education, there is plenty of evidence, for instance (see Chapter 3), that second language skills are best developed subsequent to the consolidation of literacy skills in a language with which pupils are familiar, and that initial literacy, similarly, is usually best introduced in a familiar local language. There is evidence, too, that where governments have invested heavily in the early introduction of English, either as a subject or the medium of instruction, it has often been to little effect (see Nunan 2003), a significant reason for which is that resources of teachers and materials become overstretched leading to poor quality teaching in English, poor provision of materials and ineffective learning.[15]

The use of English as a medium of primary education also tends to contribute to the further marginalisation of indigenous local languages, which are, as several commentators persuasively argue (e.g. Stroud 2002, 2003, Bruthiaux 2002), valuable resources for development and empowerment. Extending their use would, for example, allow marginalised communities to participate more fully in development processes, leading to more sustainable and more relevant development. It would enhance the democratic process by facilitating the exchange of information between the political centre and local communities, and it would bind these communities more closely to their schools, making them less alien places (Stroud 2003: 23).

Local languages, and associated multilingual practices, are also important in the functioning of the informal economy, in which many of the poorest find their livelihoods. In similar vein, Bruthiaux (2002: 203) argues that for the poorest sectors of society basic literacy in local languages will make the most immediate contribution to development and poverty alleviation. English language education, for these groups, he adds, is largely an irrelevance, promising more than it can deliver, and should therefore be targeted to those specific populations who 'have a realistic chance of participating in international exchanges soon'.

Added together, these arguments do make a persuasive case for extending the use of local languages in education, and elsewhere. They do, however, have their limitations, one of these being that while local languages can, as suggested, empower and dignify, they can also constrain and limit. Another is that demand for English is strong, even in poorer communities, many of which persist in seeing education in local languages as an educational dead-end. Targeting English language education to those who are likely to participate in 'international exchanges' sounds technocratically reasonable but it leads to many further questions: Who is to do the targeting? On what politically acceptable basis are specific populations to be targeted and others not? How are those excluded going to be reconciled to the frustration of their aspirations? In what ways will such targeting reduce socio-economic inequalities?

The discussion appears to be leading towards the conclusion that any policy solutions that assume a necessary opposition between English and local languages and seek to promote one above the other are likely to be flawed. They are flawed because English and local languages are both valuable for different reasons: English because it offers employment opportunities in economies increasingly governed by global forces; local languages because they contribute to more effective learning, to greater participation in the political process and to more sustainable and more locally relevant development.

The best hope, then, may be to embrace complementarity as a policy principle and look to bilingual, or multilingual solutions. In education, this implies bilingual media of instruction operating in a framework of additive bilingualism, where literacy in a familiar language is consolidated prior to the introduction of English and where access to English is steadily democratised.

But, of course, these suggestions can only be offered tentatively as a set of general principles. It would be highly presumptuous to suppose, given the great variability between countries in labour markets, economies, sociolinguistic situations and education systems, that there is any one best solution to the difficult matter of reconciling efficiency, opportunity and equity. Besides, there is still a scarcity of the kinds of empirical data information that could inform language education policy-making. Detailed country-specific studies of how English and other languages perform economically for particular individuals are, for example, not abundant.

Two points may be added by way of conclusion to this section. The first is that that the marginalisation of indigenous local languages, a common feature of the political economy of many African countries, is probably more the consequence than the cause of the low status and limited power of their speakers. Empowering local languages, in the face of opposing ideological and economic forces, is likely therefore to make but a minor contribution to the empowerment of their speakers. For the latter to happen more profound economic and political changes would be needed, a point that is not always easily inferable from discourses on language and equality that attribute greater power to language policy than the evidence actually warrants.

Intimately related to this is the second point that inequality has a complex multi-factorial causation in which language probably plays a relatively minor role beside unequal economic and political relations. It would be very unrealistic, therefore, to suppose that the removal of English from the scene, even if possible, could eliminate inequality, of which there are many other sources, including, as Blommaert (2003: 136) notes, differential access to the power varieties of indigenous languages.

5.3 CONCLUSION: IMPLICATIONS OF THE GLOBAL SPREAD OF ENGLISH FOR ENGLISH LANGUAGE TEACHING

Critical perspectives on the global spread of English have gained considerable attention and influence over the last decade, and it is for this reason, as well as rhetorical convenience, that reflections on these have been an organising principle of much of the preceding review. For the most part, we have been unable to agree with the viewpoints expressed in the critical literature. We have argued, for instance, that the promotional efforts of the United States and Britain cannot convincingly be portrayed as the main cause of the spread of English. More plausible are accounts that assign a more diffuse agency to this process, and highlight bottom-up factors, in particular the demand for English arising from individual perceptions that its acquisition would be economically and educationally advantageous. Such explanations accept rather than deny the active agency of individuals in the 'periphery', and they also give proper recognition to the self-reinforcing nature of language spread, which springs from the operation of 'external network effects'; the tendency, that is, for language to gain in utility as new users join the communicative network.

The idea that English directly endangers other languages, and that as a vehicle of globalisation it plays a role in Western-dominated cultural homogenisation was also rejected as an unduly simple conceptualisation of complex processes. Small indigenous languages are being lost, but the shift is mostly to powerful regional languages rather than to English. Some homogenisation of taste does appear to be a concomitant of globalisation, but there is little evidence that globalisation is eradicating identities and local cultural practices. If anything, it makes possible new identities, adding an additional layer to what is already available.

Another focus of criticism has been the link between English and two main forms of inequality: inequality in communication between native and non-native speakers of English, and socio-economic inequalities arising from differential access to English. The first of these receives comment particularly with regard to English-dominated scientific communication, where native speakers are said to be unduly advantaged because of their greater proficiency in the language. An associated observation is that while the benefits of English as an international lingua franca accrue to all users, especially native speakers, the costs are disproportionately borne by non-native speakers who expend effort and money in learning the language formally, unlike English native speakers.

The second form of inequality is viewed as most prevalent in developing countries where English is a gatekeeper to educational opportunity and high-status employment, but where elite groups tend to be better positioned to acquire English, whether formally at school or informally. In such a situation English can become a barrier, an instrument even for the social and economic exclusion of the poorer sectors of the population.

As suggested earlier, these criticisms do seem to have more substance than many of the claims outlined above. But it is not very clear where they lead in terms of language policy. For example, it is difficult to deny the unearned advantages English native speakers have in a world dominated by English, and that in this sense inequality prevails. It is much more problematic, however, to see these advantages as arising from linguistic practices per se rather than from unequal economic and political power relations, which, because they are not fundamentally linguistically founded, are less amenable to language policy solutions.

This does not mean, however, that around the margins nothing can be done. Ammon (2000) and de Swaan (2001b) argue, for example, that some politically endorsed future codification of international lingua franca norms, distinct from present native-speaker-based standards, would contribute to the 'deanglicisation' of English and allow ELF (English as a lingua franca) users to assume an identity as competent, authoritative users of a distinct variety. The outcome, they believe, would be communication on more equal terms. There are obvious implications for the teaching of English here, but first we turn to the second form of inequality mentioned above.

For this, the remedy most commonly proposed, particularly for post-colonial Africa, involves circumscribing the role of English and elevating the status of indigenous local languages so as to empower hitherto excluded and marginalised groups. Given the long-standing neglect of local languages, and all too obvious current socio-economic inequalities, this proposal has, we argued, real merit. Yet it needs to take account of the reality that in societies tied into an increasingly globalised economy English is, and is seen to be, a language of mobility and opportunity, and that therefore any drastic curtailing of its educational position could be politically problematic. For this reason we argued that a policy of complementarity involving both an enhanced role for local languages and democratisation of access to English might be one of the more feasible ways of ameliorating language-related inequality.

Democratisation in this context positively does not mean, however, the ever earlier introduction of English into the curriculum, a policy response that is usually expensive and ineffective in equal measure (see Nunan 2003). It refers rather to the enhancement of access to English for disadvantaged groups in circumstances where the language is necessary for mobility and participation yet relatively inaccessible. Relevant here, and illustrative of what we mean by democratisation, are the criteria set out by Voluntary Service Overseas (VSO), a British aid agency, to guide their support to English language teaching (ELT) worldwide, which state that:

> VSO support (for ELT) should be for a clear time-bound period with clearly articulated outcomes for disadvantaged individuals and groups. (VSO 2002: 5)

Later in the same guidelines one finds the following distinction drawn:

> It is crucial to distinguish between the provision of English to those who already have access to it and to those for whom it is relatively inaccessible. So, it would not be appropriate to support ELT simply for 'national development' purposes, where English is accessed only by the more educated 'middle classes' on the assumption they will contribute to increasing economic growth, some benefits of which may 'trickle down' to the poorest people. Experience shows this does not necessarily happen. (VSO 2002: 5)

Applying these principles has meant that in China, for example, VSO support for ELT has been targeted primarily to the remoter, less developed provinces rather than to the more affluent, faster developing coastal regions, and to middle schools and teacher training rather than to high schools and universities (VSO 2001: 5). In these guidelines it is possible to detect one salutary influence of critical perspectives on global English: a greater sensitivity, namely, to the effects and socio-economic context of ELT, a sensitivity which one hopes will steadily diffuse more widely through the profession.

Another quite different kind of democratisation, to which we have already alluded, requires, so it is argued, the departure of British and North American native speakers from the centre stage of ELT, the key political argument being that English as a global language cannot remain the property of particular native speaker populations (see Widdowson 1994: 2001). It must become possible rather for non-native bilingual users of English to identify themselves, and be identified, as competent, authoritative users of their own variety as opposed to imperfect or deficient speakers of British or American standard English. Already widely debated in the applied linguistics literature, the implications of such a decentring of the native speaker for ELT are very considerable, and cut across a range of domains, including:

1. Employment practices: to what extent, if any, is it appropriate in an era of global English to count native speakerhood as in itself a significant qualification for teaching? (See Braine 1999)
2. Classroom pedagogy: McKay (2003: 17) is one of those who argue that communicative language teaching (CLT) is a culturally-influenced methodology that cannot be assumed to be the best globally applicable method of teaching English. What is required rather is a methodology that is sensitive to local cultures of teaching and learning and that has plausibility[16] for local teachers.
3. The learning goal: is native-like competence an appropriate goal for those learning English for lingua franca communication, and should the language of learners be assessed against metropolitan British/American native speaker standards? (See Davies 2003)
4. Norms and models for teaching: related to the above, should institutionalised second language varieties of English (e.g. Indian English) or an emergent ELF variety (English as a lingua franca) be recognised as appropriate, alternative models for English language teaching alongside British and American standard English?

Discussion of these various issues would take us well beyond the scope of this chapter, since each could be, and has been, the subject of book-length treatments. In the next chapter, however, we return to the fourth, perhaps most crucial, of the issues above and probe in a little more detail the cogency of arguments calling for the recognition in ELT of models and norms beyond those traditionally offered by British or American standard English.

NOTES

1. There is evidence of several similar switches elsewhere from German to English as a language of scientific discourse (see Gunnarsson 2001).

2. The position of Hindi in India has been most strongly contested by speakers of Dravidian languages from South India.

3. An example might be the relative positions of English and German in the European Union. German has more native speakers, hence greater prevalence, but English, with a smaller number of native speakers in the language constellation, has greater centrality because it offers more connections with plurilingual speakers of languages other than German or English.

4. Mufwene's (2002) typology of forms of colonisation is more refined than a dichotomy of settlement and exploitation colonies. He talks, for instance, of trade colonies, whose language contact ecology has been most favourable to the emergence of new language varieties (e.g. pidgins), and of plantation settlement colonies (e.g. Jamaica), where creoles have survived alongside the colonial language. He also stresses, crucially, that the vitality of indigenous languages, even in settlement colonies, has not been uniformly affected by colonisation, and this, he goes on to argue, 'makes it compelling for linguists to have to investigate and better understand the socio-economic factors that affect language vitality, favouring colonial language in some settings and indigenous ones in others'. (Mufwene 2002: 19)

5. There are, however, some countries (e.g. Nigeria, Cameroon, Papau New Guinea) where English-based pidgins have evolved and are used by relatively large sections of the population.

6. This is one of the reasons underlying Alexander's proposal (2000) that the Nguni and Sotho cluster of languages be harmonised to establish two strong African languages better equipped materially and demographically to compete with English in South Africa.

7. Finlayson and Madiba (2002: 46) observe that use as an instructional medium both creates a 'demand for new terms' and provides opportunities for using them.

8. The Bill of Rights, an integral part of the constitution, gives individual citizens the right to communicate with government departments in the language of their choice, to be tried in court in a language they understand and to receive education in an official language of their choice 'where that education is reasonably practical'.

9. Tomlinson (1997: 183) cites figures for Los Angeles showing that 40 per cent of the city's population is composed of Asians and Latinos, and is projected to rise still further. In Leicester the population of Asian descent is projected to rise above 50 per cent in the next thirty to forty years.

10. One thinks here, for example, of the shipbuilding industry, once strong in the North-East of England.

11. I am aware that the concept of native speakerness, which Davies's (1999b, 2003) work has done much to illuminate, is more complex and problematic than indicated here. However, for economy of presentation I adhere here to conventional understandings of the terms 'native speaker' and 'non-native speaker'.

12. Jenkins (2003: 83) argues, very reasonably, that a more appropriate designation for this category of speakers would be 'bilingual English speakers' (see Chapter 6 for a fuller discussion).

13. Woods (2001:79) reports that '45.9% of papers in Science and 40.6% of papers in Nature, or an average of 45.6% of RAs [research articles] in these two journals are written by NNSs'.

14. The main focus in this section is on the developing world.

15. When, however, this is pointed out by foreign advisers, and recommendations made to

curtail the teaching of English, it is not unheard of for these to be rejected, as Davies's (1996, 1999a) account of his experiences in Nepal in the 1980s illustrates.

16. The term 'plausibility' comes from Prabhu (1990), who argues that an appropriate methodology is one that local teachers feel is effective in their context, and one, therefore, that engages what he calls their sense of plausibility.

Chapter 6

New Englishes and teaching models: the continuing debate

We now turn, as indicated in the previous chapter, to another major effect of the global spread of English – one with significant implications for education, ELT and for social equity. This is the diversification in the language that global spread has induced, a phenomenon signalled by the increasingly widely accepted pluralisation of 'English' in, for example, the journal *World Englishes*, the phrase 'New Englishes', and in the arresting title of McArthur's (1998) book *The English Languages*.

There has, of course, always been variation and change in English from the Old English period on, but what is different now, and exceptional, is the scale of the proliferation of regional/national varieties, of newly standardising second language varieties (New Englishes) and of hybrid varieties, the latter referring to the mixed varieties created by English 'flowing into' (McArthur 1998: 15) local languages – Singlish, Spanglish, Japlish, Franglais, Chinglish, as they are sometimes, though not always felicitously, labelled. It is the luxuriance, then, as well as the fact of diversification that the plural connotes.

Accompanying, and causally linked to, this linguistic diversification is a demographic change in the users of English. No longer, according to various estimates (e.g. Graddol 1999: 62), are native speakers numerically the most populous group of users: they are about to be, or have already been, overtaken in number by L2 users, many of whom learn and use English not so much for communication with native speakers but with other bilingual L2 users either intranationally or as an international lingua franca.

Such changes in use, in form and in demography – in combination with the ideological and pedagogic challenges to the centrality of the native speaker mounted by commentators such as Cook (1999) and Seidlhofer (1999) – have brought into question the continued dominance of British and American standard varieties as the most appropriate models for teaching English, and as the most suitable target for learners to aim at. For how much longer, Graddol (1999: 68) and others ask, can, or should, native speaker varieties be the ultimate source for authoritative norms of usage?

This chapter addresses this question from a language education policy and planning perspective, but before we enter into the debate on norms and models, a brief outline of the sociolinguistic circumstances of the global use of English may be useful.

6.1 SOCIOLINGUISTIC CONTEXTS OF THE GLOBAL USE OF ENGLISH

One of the most widely cited representations of the macro-sociolinguistic contexts within which English is used is Kachru's (1985: 12) schema of the three circles of English (see Figure 6.1 below). Although certainly not unproblematic (see Bruthiaux 2003 for a critique), it is so widely known that it is a convenient entry point into the topic.

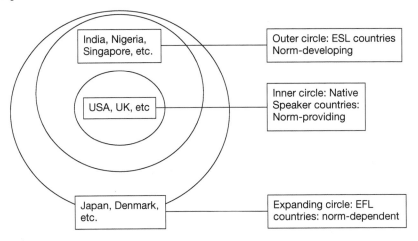

Figure 6.1   The three circles of English (after Kachru 1985: 12)

The inner circle above comprises the traditional native-speaking English countries – the United States, USA, the UK, Ireland, Canada, Australia and so on – that have historically been the norm-providing centres.

The outer circle – the focus until recently for much of the debate over norms and models – includes countries such as Singapore, India and Nigeria, where English is an official language, is of long standing, has a wide range of intranational functions and, crucially, is widely used as a medium of education. The resulting pervasiveness, and depth of use, of English has encouraged what Kachru (1985, 1992b) refers to as 'nativisation' or 'indigenisation', the evolution, that is, of usages that diverge from those found in the United States or Britain as a consequence of the distinctive communicative needs of speakers living in very different physical and cultural environments.

The expanding circle, outermost in the diagram, includes countries such as Japan, China, Spain, Austria and Egypt, where English has no official status, few internal functions and is learnt primarily for international communication or for academic study. Reflecting these more limited internal functions, these countries have traditionally been norm-dependent, or exonormative, in that they have looked to British or American standard English as the most appropriate model for the teaching of the language. This traditional normative orientation is, however, under increasing challenge from commentators such as Seidlhofer (2001, 2002a, 2004) and Jenkins (1998, 2000, 2002), who argue – with particular, though not exclusive, reference to Europe – that English is now so widely used as a lingua franca by and between high proficiency L2 users that it is evolving distinct de-anglicised features that can, and should, eventually be codified as a separate set of English Lingua Franca (ELF) norms.

We shall return to these arguments later, but this is a suitable juncture to note first that, though useful, the three circles schema has limitations. The principal one is that, for understandable summarising reasons, it takes the nation as the unit of categorisation, but in so doing masks, even obscures, important sociolinguistic complexities within these national units. In Singapore or Nigeria, for example, speakers of a variety close to British standard English coexist with native speakers of an educated local variety of English, speakers of pidgin or bazaar English, and non-speakers, in all of whose speech repertoires English may have quite different roles ranging from dominant to non-existent.

In the inner circle countries, meanwhile, there are communities whose members are predominantly bilingual second language users of English. Thus, the three circle schema only portrays a highly idealised dominant national pattern of English use, and not the more complex variation that actually obtains between speakers within these countries. As Gupta (2001: 365) points out, it is not countries that speak languages, but people.

A related difficulty is that drawing a distinction between the outer and expanding circles on the basis of the predominantly intranational functions of English in the former as compared with the predominance of international functions in the latter obscures the role of English as an international lingua franca, for speakers from all three circles, in the international and supranational spaces that globalisation has created. In the European bureaucracy and beyond, for instance, English has become a dominant lingua franca between Finns and Greeks or Portuguese and Germans, to take two of many possible pairings, and in the process there is developing a variety to which some (e.g. Jenkins, Modiano and Seidlhofer 2001: 13) give the label 'Euro-English'. Linguistically, this is characterised – according to Crystal (1999: 15) – by simpler sentence constructions, the avoidance of culturally loaded colloquial or idiomatic phraseology and slower speech with clearer articulation.

Another limitation of the typology is that, like other typologies, it does not cope well with change over time. An illustrative case might be Denmark, a country that one might once have confidently been placed in the expanding circle category. Now, however, the country's higher education sector is undergoing what Phillipson and Skuttnab-Kangas (1999: 25) call 'Englishisation', the steady accretion to the language of functions once served by Danish. English, for instance, is now the medium of instruction in some academic departments; students are increasingly expected not only to read but – in some cases – write in English; and Danish academic journals have shifted to publication in English. In short, it is no longer just a foreign language but one with significant internal uses, a situation usually diagnostic of membership of the outer circle.

This returns us to our original point: the three circles schema summarises the broad context of the use of English worldwide, but in so doing inevitably abstracts and simplifies a more complex reality. As long as we remain alert to this, it remains a useful device.

6.2 DEFINING THE NEW ENGLISHES

The term 'New Englishes' is usually understood to denote varieties of English from post-colonial societies (e.g. India, Pakistan, Malaysia, Ghana) whose formal properties – phonological, lexical, grammatical, discoursal – show a measure of divergence from British or American standard English. They are distinguished from what Kachru (1992b) calls 'performance varieties', spoken in expanding circle countries such as Japan, by the following sociolinguistic characteristics (Kachru 1992b: 55):

1. Length of time in use (New Englishes are of long standing, having developed in the colonial era);
2. Extension in use (In many post-colonial outer circle countries, English has attained a considerable level of penetration in terms of functions and numbers of users, for many of whom the localised English expresses a distinct, independent identity);
3. Emotional attachment of L2 users with the variety (see above);
4. Functional importance (see above);
5. Sociolinguistic status (see above. Also, English is an official language, or serves official functions, in many outer circle countries).

Relatively clear though this sociolinguistic specification may be, labels for New Englishes – 'Singapore English', 'Nigerian English', 'Indian English' and so forth – can mislead if they are taken to refer to homogenous, clear-cut and clearly individuated entities, for in fact the labels shelter considerable heterogeneity. Indigenisation has been accompanied by sociolinguistic variation – conditioned mainly, it appears, by education and occupational status – so that in Nigeria, for example, there is now a cline of varieties ranging from educated Nigerian English, which is relatively close to British standard English, to Nigerian Pidgin English, a linguistically more distinct variety. Similarly, in Singapore a cline of comparable subvarieties has long been recognised (see Gupta 1999; Platt, Weber and Ho 1989), ranging from Standard English, through educated Singapore English, to a contact variety, Colloquial Singapore English (SCE), also known as *Singlish*, which is acquired both as a first language and as a second language. Borrowing terminology from creole studies, some writers use the terms acrolect, mesolect and basilect to refer to the most educated, the middling and the most informal varieties respectively.

Individuals with higher levels of education usually control the full lectal range and can, therefore, style-shift – to a basilect when the social circumstances seem appropriate, as illustrated in the following extract from Chinua Achebe's novel *No Longer at Ease*, where Christopher, a senior Nigerian civil servant, is conversing with two friends Obi and Clara. At the end of the conversation, Achebe appends a brief sociolinguistic commentary for the benefit of the reader:

What can I offer you?
Champagne.
Ah? na Obi go buy you that-o. Me never reach that grade yet. Na squash me get.
They laughed.
Obi, what about some beer?
If you'll split a bottle with me.
Fine. What are you people doing this evening? Make we go dance somewhere?
Obi tried to make some excuses, but Clara cut him short. They would go she said.
Na film I wan' go, said Bisi.
Look here, Bisi, we are not interested in what you want to do. It's for me and Obi to decide. This na Africa, you know.

Whether Christopher spoke good or 'broken' English depended on what he was saying, where he was saying it, and how he wanted to say it. Of course, that was to some extent true of most educated people.

(Chinua Achebe 1987, *No Longer at Ease*)

Similar style-shifting is also common in other outer circle countries.

English is, of course, usually only one of the languages in individuals' multilingual speech repertoires, and a result, alongside style-shifting between subvarieties of indigenised English, one often also finds code-mixed speech, incorporating elements from two or more languages. This mixed speech is so common, in fact, that in some settings it is the normal, unmarked code of everyday encounters. The following extract from a conversation in a Malay-English mix (McArthur 1998: 13) is an apt illustration of the phenomenon; and, though often frowned on by purists and policy-makers, it is more appropriately regarded as a manifestation of bilingual creativity than of linguistic deficit.

Speaker 1: Apa ini? What happened to you pagi-tudi? I tunggu tunguu
          sampai dah fed up! Man you pergi, joker you!
Speaker 2: Nowhere lah! I was stuck in the computer room …

Though most commentators would not wish to bring such speech forms within the scope of New Englishes, they merit a mention here for pointing up the lived complexity of daily language practices in intensely multilingual societies, and for calling to account the top-down assumptions of those policy-makers for whom multilingualism is no more than the coexistence of diverse but clearly bounded language entities – English, Malay, Chinese, Swahili and so on.

6.2.1 An overview of linguistic characteristics of the New Englishes

Study of the linguistic features of the New Englishes dates back to the 1960s, and possibly earlier, and so a large body of descriptive literature has accumulated in journal and book form (see e.g. Burchfield 1994; Cheshire 1991; de Klerk 1996; Gorlach 1995, 2002; 1992a, 1994; McArthur 1998; Platt, Weber and Ho 1984; Pride 1986; Schmied 1991; Schneider 1997). It would be uneconomical, therefore, to attempt a summary of this large body of work, nor appropriate, as our focus here is on language education policy rather than linguistic description. That said, a brief review of some of the more prominent linguistic features of the New Englishes is useful to give a flavour of the nature of the divergence from British and American standard English and indicate what exactly it is that is at stake in debates over pedagogical models.

Because they are particularly well documented, we mainly draw our examples from Singapore English and Indian English, noting in passing by way of justification that Singapore English has been regarded (Platt and Weber 1980) as a classic case of 'indigenisation'. Divergence from British or American standard English takes place at various linguistic levels – phonological, grammatical, lexical and discoursal. Let us start, then, with phonology.

6.2.1.1 Phonology

Unlike British English, which is stress-timed,[1] Singapore English is syllable-timed, with a tendency to fewer intonational patterns – both characteristics reflecting transfer from the tone-based Chinese languages natively spoken by the majority of the population (Tay 1982: 65). At the segmental level, vowels tend to be shorter and less tense than in RP (received pronunciation) or GA (General American), and there are numerous consonantal differences, the most commonly cited being the realisation of /θ/ and /ð/ as [t] and [d]; the stereotypical lack of differentiation between /r/ as /l/; and the reduction of final consonant clusters to the first consonant of the cluster (see Gramley and Pätzold 1992: 449).

There are also significant phonological differences between Indian English on the one hand and British or American English on the other. Word stress, for example, tends to fall on the penultimate syllable – whatever its location in British English. At the segmental level, Indian English has a seventeen-vowel system consisting of eleven pure vowels and six dipthongs (Kachru 1994: 515), though, as Jenkins (2003: 24) observes, Indian English speakers, in common with those of other New Englishes varieties, tend to a minimal distinction between the short and long vowels /ɪ/ and /iː/ (the vowels in *sit* and *seat* being rendered by /ɪ/). The principal consonantal differences can be summarised as follows (see Kachru 1994: 514–15):

1. A tendency to retroflection of alveolar consonants (t, d);
2. The replacement of fricatives /θ/ and /ð/ by plosives [th], [d], or [dh];
3. No distinction between clear and dark /l/;
4. The modification of initial consonant clusters (not found in North Indian

languages such as Hindi) by the insertion of an epenthetic vowel. Thus, orthographic *school* might be realised as [isku:l].

6.2.1.2 Grammar

Grammatical divergence from British or American norms is evident in the more informal, colloquial subvarieties. For example, in Singapore Colloquial English (SCE), though not in the educated acrolectal variety, there is – under influence from the substrate languages[2] – a tendency to dispense with certain grammatical inflections and function words, including:

1. Articles (e.g. *you have book*);
2. Plural inflections (e.g. *I got three sister*);
3. Third person singular present tense '*s*' (e.g. *My mum, she come from China*);
4. Past tense inflection '*ed*' (e.g. *Yesterday, I work for seventeen hour*);
5. Copula *be* (e.g. *This dress very cheap*).

Other salient grammatical divergences include:

6. The use of invariant question tags (e.g. *you are busy now, isn't it?*);
7. The use of *already* as an aspectual marker to signal completion (e.g. *Eight years she work here already*);
8. The use of *use to* to signal present rather than past habit (e.g. *My mother, she use to go to market daily*);
9. The treatment of mass nouns (in British English) as countable and therefore pluralisable (e.g. *informations*, *luggages*, etc.);
10. The use of *would* in situations where British English would prefer *will* in referring to future situations (e.g. *We sincerely hope this would meet your requirements*).

Many of the same features recur in informal Indian English such as the use of invariant question tags and the treatment of mass nouns as countable (*luggages*, etc.). Other significant grammatical differences observed include:

1. Tense and aspect:
   The more frequent use of the progressive than in British or American English, and its use with stative verbs. (e.g. *She is having many saris*);
   The use of *will* with future reference in temporal and conditional subordinate clauses (e.g. *When you will reach Mumbai, please give me a call*).
2. Question formation:
   The absence of subject-auxiliary inversion in wh-questions; contrasting – rather curiously – with its quite frequent presence in indirect questions (e.g. *What this is made from?*; and *I asked her where does she work*).
3. Verb complementation:
   Rather different complementation patterns from those in British or American English (e.g. *She was prevented to go*).

4. Modal verbs:
   Use of the modal *could* where British English might prefer *be able to* (e.g. *He could do well in his exams because he studied hard*).

5. Miscellaneous:
   For example, use of the locative adverbial *there* where British English speakers would prefer an existential construction (e.g. *What do you want to drink? Coffee is there, tea is there, beer is there*).

6.2.1.3 Lexis

The lexicon is where acculturation, indigenisation and innovation have produced the most obvious differences from British or American English, and where the distinctiveness of Asian and African New Englishes is most abundantly signalled. The linguistic processes involved are borrowing, hybridisation and semantic extension or restriction.

In the case of borrowing, we are talking primarily of single lexical items borrowed from Malay, Chinese, Hindi or any one of a large number of Indian languages to refer to local cultural artefacts or concepts. While some have been assimilated into British and American English, appearing in authoritative dictionaries such as the OED (e.g. *cheroot, pariah, pukka*), the majority have not and thus, though widely used in India or Singapore, would be unfamiliar to British and American speakers: for example, *jaga, padang, makan, kampong* from Singapore English; and *bindi, chota, lathi, swadeshi* from Indian English.[3]

A second category of innovative lexis consists of hybridised items formed by the combination of two or more elements from distinct languages. Examples from Indian English would include *lathi charge* (baton charge) or *bindi mark* (mark on forehead) as well as hybrid collocations such as *satyagraha movement* (insistence on truth movement).

Finally, there are those English lexical items that have undergone semantic extension or restriction. For example, in Singapore English one finds *deep* used in an extended sense to mean 'educated' or 'formal' as in *my father speak the deep Hokkien*; and *last time* used with the meaning of 'previously', as in *last time they had a lot of monkeys in the Botanic gardens*. And in Indian English one encounters such innovative usages as *eating-leaves*, referring to the banana leaves on which food may be served.

Also worthy of notice under the heading of lexis are novel collocations, for instance *yellow journalist*, attested in Indian English; innovative idioms (e.g. *to be on tarmac* from East African English, meaning currently unemployed but looking for a job (Jenkins 2003: 27)); and the use, especially in Indian English, of formal, even archaic, vocabulary where British or American users might prefer more informal, colloquial items.

Beyond the level of the sentence, meanwhile, there are distinctive discoursal phenomena. These include: the different lexico-grammatical realisations of particular speech acts (e.g. offering thanks), differences in genre structure and content (e.g. letters of application), and the use – particularly by creative writers (e.g. Raja Rao, Wole Soyinka, Chinua Achebe) – of rhetorical strategies different from those found in metropolitan varieties, involving, for example, metaphors translated from local languages, local interactional devices in written dialogue and novel collocations (see Kachru 1995).

6.3 THE GENESIS OF NEW ENGLISHES

Moving on from this brief overview of features, we need to consider briefly the developmental, psycholinguistic and socio-cultural processes that have contributed to the emergence of New Englishes, not just because these are interesting in themselves but because they have a bearing on one's stance towards the features mentioned above: are they acceptable deviations from British English or just errors, the product of imperfect learning?

> The main issue that arises is the need to decide when an observed feature of language use is indeed an innovation and when it is simply an error. An innovation is seen as an acceptable variant, while an error is simply a mistake or uneducated usage. (Bamgbose 1998: 2)

Surprisingly perhaps, given the starkness of this contrast between innovation and error, there is a fair measure of agreement regarding the fundamental sources or causes of divergence from metropolitan varieties. Thus, recognising that New Englishes are usually acquired as second languages in complex multilingual environments, both sides in the debate acknowledge the role of transfer from natively spoken local languages (the substrate as it is sometimes called), of universal learning strategies of simplification and complexification and of the superstrate (the variety of English to which acquirers are exposed),[4] even while disagreeing on the relative weight of the contribution of these influences. They tend to agree, moreover, that differences in lexis are substantially attributable to the transplantation of English to new cultural surroundings, where speakers have found it necessary to elaborate vocabulary to refer to the artefacts, situations and institutions of the new setting.

Substrate influence, one might add, is particularly evident in pronunciation, where sounds and stress patterns of the first language tend to be transferred to English, though it also shows up in the grammatical and morphological features of the local English. Singapore Colloquial English (SCE), for example, shows definite substrate influence from Malay and Chinese (e.g. in article usage).

Evidence, meanwhile, for the influence of universal learning processes (e.g. simplification and regularisation) derives from the similarities observed between New Englishes in different parts of the world (e.g. Nigeria, India, Singapore) with respect to deviations from British English. The tendency of these to cluster in morpho-syntactic areas known to be problematic to second language acquirers – preposition use, mass/count nouns, word order in interrogatives, elements of verb morphology – is an indication, some commentators argue, that they may be the consequence of incomplete learning, which generates features that become stabilised in the new speech community.

If there is, as we have suggested, some measure of agreement on the ontogenesis of New Englishes, there is far less on the status of the variation that has arisen as a result, with differing interpretations stemming from the quite different theoretical perspectives through which commentators view such variation. For convenience, the two most important of these can be labelled the SLA/interlanguage paradigm and the macroacquisition/language change paradigm.

6.3.1 New Englishes and SLA: interrogating a paradigm

In the SLA paradigm, successful acquisition is viewed as successive approximation to a target language norm, usually assumed to be a native-like language competence. As individual learners strive to approximate this norm, they pass through a range of interim, intermediate stages – coherent in their own terms but unstable and deviant from target norms. Such stages, or more precisely the individual transitional linguistic systems in operation, are commonly referred to as the learner's inter-language. It is possible, however, and in fact typical, for the learner's interlanguage to stabilise at a point short of the target norm, in which case it is said to have *fossilised*. This, some argue, is precisely the process by which many of the distinctive features of New Englishes arise: learners fall short of the target norm, their interlanguage fossilises and the resultant forms disseminate and are institutionalised within the community. And, of course, from such perspective there is logic to regarding these features not as deviations but as errors.

The logic may be mistaken, however, for – as various commentators (e.g. Kachru 1992b, Sridhar and Sridhar 1992, Stroud 2002, Brutt-Griffler 2002) have pointed out – there are sound reasons for questioning the applicability of an SLA conceptual framework to New Englishes, the fundamental consideration being that in its typical focus on the individual learner, whose target is a standard variety spoken by native speakers, the standard SLA approach discounts external social factors – including, crucially, the complex multilingual environment in which New Englishes are acquired. Below we comment further on this complex context of acquisition, summarising some of the key criticisms made of the SLA/ interlanguage approach.

One cluster of arguments disputes both the feasibility and appropriacy of taking the endpoint of acquisition to be a standard metropolitan variety spoken by native speakers (e.g. standard British English). The relevant points here are as follows:

1. In the contexts where New Englishes are acquired there is very little, or no, input available from metropolitan native speakers. Learning is therefore very largely modelled on the production of variably proficient second language speakers whose speech will be liberally laced with localised features, even while they sometimes believe that it instantiates a standard British English model. In such circumstances, it is unclear whether the variety normally assumed to be the target in standard SLA theory (an idealised native speaker standard) is in fact attainable.

2. Even if attainable, it is questionable whether such a target is appropriate, or in fact the goal of learners. In outer circle countries localised features, divergent from British or American English, very often index a distinctive identity valued by members of the local speech community, and by those acquiring the language primarily for communication with other users of the localised variety. It cannot be taken for granted, therefore, that these learners are actually aiming at mastery of a British or American model. Indeed, too close an emulation of such a model, whether in pronunciation or grammar, may provoke ridicule for its pretentiousness, or else be taken as evidence of the speaker's desire to disassociate from the identity and norms of the local community.

3. Also addressing the appropriacy of an idealised native speaker target is Sridhar and Sridhar's (1992) argument that in the outer circle English is used alongside other languages in speakers' repertoires and for a lesser range of functions than would the case for a monolingual native speaker. It would be wrong, therefore, to expect their competence in English to be a mirror image of that of a monolingual native speaker. Moreover, the transfer features found in some varieties of English spoken by users with a similar bilingual repertoire serve, as suggested previously, as 'effective simplification strategies, modes of acculturation ... and as markers of membership in the community of speakers of a given indigenised variety' (Sridhar and Sridhar 1992: 101).

While these arguments challenge the conventional SLA view of what constitutes the endpoint of successful second language acquisition, and hence the received notion of 'target language', a second cluster, also critical of the SLA/interlanguage approach, brings into focus the distinction between the individual and the social. The key point here is that concepts such as error or fossilisation are appropriate when applied to individuals acquiring a second language whose speech is punctuated by individual idiosyncrasies of grammar, phonology or lexis, marking the individual out as distinct from the group, but are much less appropriate, and problematic, when applied to features that are wildly distributed and accepted in the local community.

6.3.1.1 'Macroacquisition'

This takes us directly to Brutt-Griffler's (2002: 135–6) point, persuasively argued, that the New Englishes are more appropriately conceived as the products not of individual SLA but of social SLA in specific socio-historical circumstances; what she refers to as 'macroacquisition'. Thus, whereas individual SLA gives rise to interlanguages, macroacquisition, the acquisition of the same second language by a whole community of users, gives rise to a new variety that does not antedate but is forged in the process of macroacquisition itself:

Taking second language acquisition as a social process requires conceptual changes in the relation of language and learner. SLA becomes a dynamic process, in which the language no longer appears as a static category, a fixed target, but alters as a result of its acquisition by the learning population. The speech community not only acquires the language but makes the language its own. (Brutt Griffler 2002: 137)

Together, these various arguments are persuasive and suggest that it would be more appropriate to locate features of New Englishes in a conceptual framework of variation and change rather than in one of error, fossilisation and acquisitional deficiency.[5]

6.3.1.2 Discriminating errors and innovations

To do so, however, does not resolve all difficulties. First of all, there remains the delicate matter – highly relevant to teachers and testers (see Davies et al. 2003) – of discriminating forms that are acceptable and widely distributed within a local variety of English from those that are individually idiosyncratic and hence erroneous. The boundaries between the two, between what is and what is not a New Englishes feature, might conventionally be established by codification (see Chapter 2), but, as Bamgbose (1998) observes, there is a continuing dearth of codification of local norms.

It is true, of course, that there is a substantial and growing body of descriptive work on New Englishes, including that based on the International Corpus of English (the ICE corpus), which does offer some guidance, but, as Mesthrie (2003: 451) observes, not all this work conforms to the canons of formal sociolinguistic work. It is not enough, he implies, to document the occurrence of some localised feature. If we wish to separate out errors from features forming part of a legitimate, autonomous variety, we need additional data that only a more formal sociolinguistic investigation can provide: information, for example, on how frequent a feature is, on which 'subgroups use it', on how it is regarded within the local community and on what relationships it contracts with both more standard and more colloquial equivalent constructions (Mesthrie 2003: 451).

A second issue is that accepting New Englishes as legitimate varieties, and viewing diversification as an indicator of vitality rather than decay, does not necessarily commit one to a recommendation that teachers in Singapore, India or elsewhere in the outer circle should teach to a local model of English any more than accepting Tyneside English as a systematic, non-degenerate variety necessarily commits one to explicitly teaching this variety in school. This is because one of the traditional roles of the school has been to teach a prestigious standard written variety of language, a variety that widens opportunities and that permits the individual to transcend the confines of the local. The choice of a model for purposes of education, therefore, involves additional considerations beyond tolerance of diversity and the internal systematicity of particular varieties, and it is to these that we now turn.

6.4 NEW ENGLISHES AND MODELS FOR TEACHING

Our discussion is divided into two main parts: one where we outline the terms of the debate, placing it in historical perspective, and a second where we assess the key arguments. We move first to the historical perspective.

6.4.1 Models for teaching English: the debate in historical perspective

The debate over the models of English that should be employed in teaching the language around the world is a long-standing one, surfacing first in Halliday, MacIntosh and Strevens's (1964: 293) interrogation of the continued dominance of British or American models in a post-colonial era, and in Prator's (1968) riposte titled 'The British Heresy in TESL'. Referring to the views of the former as a 'pernicious heresy', Prator argues that it would be most unwise to recognise second language varieties as teaching models: it is doubtful, he says (1968: 464), whether they really exist 'as coherent, homogenous linguistic systems', and even if they do, they are qualitatively different from, and inherently less stable than, 'mother-tongue types of English'.

Prator's central concern, however, is for intelligibility. English has value for learners because it is an international language, but it can only remain so if mutual intelligibility between different groups of users is maintained. Because second language varieties are less stable than 'mother tongue' varieties, and because change at one linguistic level (e.g. phonology) is not self-contained but impacts on other levels (e.g. syntax/morphology), concessions to what he refers to as 'non-native' models are likely in the long run to encourage the drifting apart of the different varieties of English. The scenario of Latin and its break-up into mutually un-intelligible languages beckons. Prator's (1968: 469) conclusion is that it is prudent to recognise only a native British or American standard English as a model:

> if teachers in many parts of the world aim at the same stable well-documented model, the general effect of their instruction will be convergent … if many diverse models are chosen … the overall effect is bound to be divergent. Widespread intercomprehensibility will be lost with no guaranteed corresponding gain in local intelligibility.

We return to an assessment of these arguments shortly, but staying for the moment with out historical perspective we may note that Prator's 1968 paper foreshadows, almost uncannily, the debate joined nearly twenty years later by Quirk and Kachru on the occasion of the British Council's fiftieth anniversary (1984), and pursued subsequently in the pages of the journal *English Today*, and elsewhere (Quirk 1985, 1988, 1990a; Kachru 1985, 1988, 1991, 1992a).

Disturbed by what he considered to be the diminished respect for the importance of Standard English and by the excessive fascination with varieties, Quirk – like Prator before him – adopts a conservative position, maintaining that 'a single monochrome standard form', exemplified in the production of the BBC World

Service, All India Radio, the *Straits Times* and the *Japan Times* of Tokyo, is the most appropriate model (Quirk 1985: 6). Supporting this position, he argues first that 'non-native' varieties are uncodified and non-institutionalised, and second that there is in any case an important qualitative difference between 'non-native' and 'native' varieties. Here, Quirk adduces psycholinguistic evidence, derived from Coppieters (1987), that natives have 'radically different internalisations' from non-natives', the implication being that 'non-native teachers need to be in constant touch with the native language' (Quirk 1990a: as reprinted in Seidlhofer 2003: 13–14).

Taking a directly opposed outlook and rejecting what he regards as Quirk's deficit view of the New Englishes, Kachru (1985, 1988, 1991, 1992b) argues for a greater degree of sociolinguistic realism, one that would acknowledge that spread inevitably entails some divergence from British or American norms as the language ceases to be the exponent of any one culture, and that would recognise that if English is to be an international language, then the native speakers need to accept that they 'have lost the exclusive prerogative to control its standardisation' (Kachru 1985: 30; see also Widdowson 1994).

He also calls for greater educational realism, making the practical point that it is often simply not possible for teachers in the outer circle to remain in constant touch with the native language as modelled by native speakers. As for the radically different internalisations of native speakers, Kachru (1991) invites us to consider just what these internalisations are internalisations of: native speakers certainly have internalised representations of their native language (their L1), but users of English in the outer circle, some of whom are in fact native speakers of localised varieties, may also have internalisations 'linked to their own multilinguistic, sociolinguistic and sociocultural contexts' (Kachru 1991: as reprinted in Seidlhofer 2003: 21).

Kachru goes on to argue that Quirk's position rests on a set of false assumptions, specifically:

1. That in the outer and expanding circles, English is mainly learnt to interact with native speakers. In fact, Kachru suggests, its main use is in communication with other L2 users, intranationally or internationally;
2. That English is learnt to understand British or American culture. In fact, in the outer circle, it imparts and expresses local cultural values and identities;
3. That 'non-native' varieties are interlanguages, when, in fact, they are 'varieties in their own right rather than stages on the way to a more native-like English';
4. That native speakers – as teachers, administrators and materials developers – are heavily involved in the global teaching of English, when, in fact, most of the teaching of English worldwide lies in the hands of L2 users (Kachru 1991: as reprinted in Seidlhofer 2003: 28).

Kachru's position, then, is that the New Englishes are stable varieties indexing local identities and capable of imparting local cultural values, and that they should therefore have greater recognition in the teaching of English in outer circle contexts.

Surveying recent literature (for example, articles in *English Today* and book-length publications, such as McKay 2002), one senses that in the applied linguistics community, if not among teachers and students at large, the Kachruvian perspective is in the ascendant over that of Quirk. Certainly, this is Seidlhofer and Jenkins's (2003: 142) confidently asserted belief:

> In most outer circle contexts, of course, the long and vigorous struggle for the acknowledgement of their very own sociopolitical identities has been largely successful ... The naive notion of a monolithic, uniform, unadaptable linguistic medium owned by its original speakers and forever linked to their rule(s) has been recognised as simply contrary to the facts, and has therefore given way to the realization that indigenised varieties of English are legitimate Englishes in their own right, accordingly emancipating themselves vis-à-vis British and American Standard English ... Outer circle linguistic independence has, on the whole, been given the linguistic seal of approval.

The same authors go on to make the case for extending the legitimacy already accorded to outer circle Englishes to the expanding circle, to emergent features of English as a Lingua Franca (ELF). We will consider the merits of this case later, but first we turn from an exposition of the history of the debate to an assessment of the central arguments.

6.4.2 Models for teaching English: assessing the arguments

Central to the debate on whether New Englishes should be adopted as teaching models are the recurring issues of intelligibility, identity, practicality, acceptability and standardisation. Interwoven though these are, it may helpful to individuate them, if only for convenience of discussion. Accordingly, we start with intelligibility.

6.4.2.1 The issue of intelligibility

Fears that English may dissolve into mutually unintelligible varieties have featured prominently in the arguments of those opposed to the recognition of second language varieties as teaching models (see above). In one respect, the concern is well-founded: English is only useful as an international language so long as mutual intelligibility between speakers from different world regions can be maintained. On the other hand, the conceptualisation of intelligibility proffered by Prator is not altogether satisfactory.

The initial points one might make are empirical. Nearly forty years on from the publication of Prator's (1968) paper, there are few firm indications that the 'English language complex' (McArthur 1998: xv) is fracturing, as prognosticated, into mutually unintelligible varieties. One reason for this is that, while there are undoubtedly centrifugal tendencies in play, there are also, as various scholars (e.g. Quirk 1985, Crystal 1997, McArthur 1998) have pointed out, countervailing centripetal forces at work – telecommunications, international media, travel and increased individual mobility, for example.

Relevant here also, and important in fact for the entire debate on norms, is the observation made forcefully by Pullum (2002) in his plenary address at the 2002 AILA conference, and reiterated by various other scholars (e.g. Gupta 2001: 370; Crystal 1999: 16), that standard written print English, the English found in the *Straits Times* or the *Japan Times*, is remarkably uniform around the world. True, there are some grammatical differences between different standard and standardising varieties of English, but these are, as Huddleston and Pullum (2002: 5) put it, 'small indeed relative to the full range of syntactic constructions and morphological word forms'. Variability, then, is principally found in speech rather than print, being most marked in pronunciation and vocabulary; not forgetting, of course, the grammatical variation most evident in the non-standard, basilectal or colloquial subvarieties of the New Englishes (e.g. Singlish). The key point here, however, is that against all this variability one needs to set the stabilising, anchoring presence of a relatively uniform standard print English.

Turning now to the conceptual aspect of intelligibility, we also find that it is a more complex concept than Prator seems to suppose, for it may be broken down, as Smith and Nelson (1985: 334) suggest, into a three-level complex, consisting of (1) *intelligibility* (reserved for word/utterance recognition), (2) *comprehensibility* (referring to a grasp of literal propositional content-word/utterance meaning) and (3) *interpretability* (the apprehension of illocutionary force, the speaker's intention).

Jenkins (2000: 78) gives emphasis to intelligibility in the first sense above, pointing out that, due to the relative lack of shared background knowledge, second language users/learners tend to be more reliant on the acoustic signal than fluent (native) users, and that in her experience phonological problems are a more regular cause of misunderstandings for the former category of users than are 'higher level' difficulties of pragmatic interpretation. And this leads her (see below) to give particular attention to pronunciation as one of the graver potential impediments to clear communication. A further point is that intelligibility is as much, or more, a property of the interaction between the speaker and the listener than one inherent in the linguistic forms deployed by the interlocutors. As Jenkins (2000: 79) puts it:

> intelligibility is dynamically negotiable between speaker and listener, rather than statically inherent in a speaker's linguistic forms, even though participants [i.e. second language learners] find the process of negotiation more problematic than do fluent speakers.

An implication may be that in determining what contributes to intelligibility we need to consider, among other things, the attitudes interlocutors bring to the interaction and the effort they are prepared to invest in recovering meaning. And, more pertinently still, who the interlocutors are, and whether intelligibility should continue to be defined solely in terms of intelligibility for the native speaker, as Prator (1968) implies, or more inclusively to encompass mutual intelligibility between users of English as an international lingua franca who happen to have different non-English first languages (L1s).

Jenkins (2000), along with others, adopts the second of these positions, arguing – persuasively – that, given the current demographics and sociolinguistics of English use worldwide, it is no longer appropriate in every circumstance to seek 'to instil (British) L1 pronunciation norms into learners who are rarely likely to communicate with a L1 (especially a RP) speaker of English' (Jenkins 2000: 11). Instead, teachers of English as an international language should take mutual intelligibility between speakers of different L1s as their goal, a stance that implies the adoption of pronunciation norms distinct from those of RP-accented British English, which is in any case, Jenkins (2000: 15) argues – concurring with Smith and Rafiqzad (1979) – by no means the most intelligible accent internationally, or even perhaps in Britain itself.

6.4.2.2 Lingua franca phonological core

Unlike some commentators who might urge the case for a change in pedagogical models and thereafter depart the scene, Jenkins takes matters a stage further, identifying a core of phonological features which are essential for international intelligibility but which are not necessarily identical with any one L1 or L2 variety of English. Excluded, therefore, from the core because they are non-essential for international intelligibility between L2 users, are the following features of British RP-accented English:

1. The consonant sounds /θ/ and /ð/ and the allophone dark 'l';
2. Weak forms (i.e. 'the use of schwa instead of full vowel sounds in, say, 'to', 'from', 'was');
3. Other features of connected speech such as assimilation;
4. Pitch direction, signalling attitude or grammatical meaning;
5. Word stress placement;
5. Stress-timed rhythm.

(Jenkins 2002; 2003: 127)

Included, on the other hand, because they are essential for international intelligibility and constitute therefore the central elements of a new pronunciation syllabus for learners of English as an international language, are the following features of what Jenkins (2000: 124) calls the 'Lingua Franca Core' (LFC):

1. The consonant inventory (except for the dental fricatives /θ/ and /ð/, and allophonic variation within phonemes that does not overlap onto other phonemes);
2. Additional phonetic requirements: aspiration following word-initial voiceless stops /p/, /t/ and /k/; shortening of vowel sounds before fortis consonants and maintenance of length before lenis consonants;
3. Consonant clusters (i.e. no omission of sounds in word-initial clusters (e.g. 'strap'), and omission of sounds in word-final clusters only according to L1 rules of English syllable structure;
4. Vowel sounds: maintenance of the contrast between long and short vowels (e.g. the vowels in words like 'live' and 'leave');

5. Production and placement of nuclear (tonic) stress, especially when used contrastively.

(Jenkins 2000: 159; 2003: 126–7)

These proposals bring to mind previous efforts to define a core English: Ogden's (1930) *Basic English* and Quirk's (1981) *Nuclear English*, for example. Jenkins (2000: 131) points out, however, that her identification of a phonological core differs from earlier constructions in that it is based on empirical research into intelligibility between interlocutors with different L1s and is rooted in actual speech behaviour.

Our own view is that Jenkins's work has substantial merits, not only making a persuasive case for discontinuing universal adherence to L1 British or American pronunciation norms but also bringing forward detailed proposals for an alternative LFC model, and thereby taking pedagogic innovation in pronunciation teaching beyond mere aspiration into the realm of the feasible. A further advantage is that, unlike many innovations, it actually reduces the pedagogic load by removing from the syllabus items that are 'either unteachable or irrelevant' (Jenkins 2000: 160). Whether or not this alternative model passes the final test of acceptability is another matter, however, and one which we will consider shortly. First, however, we turn to the question of identity.

6.4.2.3 Identity and the New Englishes

Language is, of course, not only an instrument of communication but an important means by which speakers and hearers construct, or fashion, particular identities – be these personal, ethnic, social or national (see Joseph 2004). And because this is so, and because many users of the New Englishes wish to project a distinctive identity in, and through, their local variety, it follows, so some argue, that that to deny recognition to local varieties of English is to withhold acceptance of the identities that those varieties express. To appropriate English is to develop a sense of ownership, to claim the language as one's own, but this is not possible if features widespread and stable in the local educated variety continue to be regarded as 'errors' rather than, as Joseph [2004: 161] puts it, 'points at which a distinct ... identity is expressed [or may come to be expressed] in the language'.[6]

Calling for attention here, however, are two main points. The first is that this argument from identity is particularly potent as regards accent and vocabulary, for it is these rather than the morpho-syntax of the acrolectal variety that mark a speaker as, say, distinctively Singaporean. It is true, of course, that the basilect – *Singlish* in this particular instance – also indexes a distinctive Singaporean identity through grammatical features that diverge quite noticeably from standard British English, but this variety is in no sense a candidate for employment as a teaching model. It is a non-standard, uncodified contact variety, which, as Gupta (2001: 378) points out, is functionally constrained:

the leaky diglossia of Singapore English has always leaked in one direction – that H encroaches on the domains of the L – Standard is usable almost everywhere in

Singapore but SCE isn't. If the L variety, SCE (aka Singlish) dies, it may be that it was simply a stage Singapore was going through.[7]

What we are left with, then, is mainly pronunciation and lexis, by no means trivial areas, of course. A pedagogical implication, reinforcing the arguments of Jenkins (2000) above, is that it would be unwise to insist on teaching to British or American pronunciation norms, and not just because to do so would be to infringe against the sensitivities of identity, but because the British RP model is inappropriate on other independent grounds: its prestige is waning, it is the accent of only a minority of Britons and many of its features are either unteachable or difficult for learners to approximate (Jenkins 2000). As regards lexis, there is also, given the rapidity of lexical change within British or American English, a good case for accepting the lexical, and collocational, innovations of the New Englishes, or at least not proscribing them in educational contexts.

The second point has to do with recognition, and different levels of recognition. The fact that particular linguistic features of the New Englishes – grammatical, phonological, lexical, discoursal – index valued identities certainly provides grounds for recognition if one means by recognition an acceptance that these forms, and the varieties of which they are part, are legitimate and should not be stigmatised as in any way sub-standard or 'bad English'. It does not, however, provide sufficient grounds for adopting these varieties as teaching models any more than accepting or recognising Tyneside English, say, as an important constituent of a Geordie[8] identity necessarily commits one to teach that variety in school.

The reason for this is that it has long been regarded (see, for example the Kingman Report 1989) as part of the business of education to impart knowledge of, and skill in using, a standard variety – a variety, that is, that is common and uniform, and has wide currency beyond the local or regional. The standard variety also tends to have the greatest social prestige; not just because the most socially prestigious dialect gets chosen as the standard but because, once selected, it accrues to itself further layers of prestige. And so it becomes that variety, associated with education, that employers and other social agencies expect the educated person to control. It is therefore – and this is a crucial reason for teaching the standard – a variety that confers socio-economic mobility on those with competence in it.

There are, however, different standard and standardising Englishes – British, American, Australian, Indian, Nigerian and so on – to choose between, and this is a complicating factor. But, at least, it is clear that whichever model of English is adopted for teaching, it will, for the reasons mentioned above, very likely be a standard variety. As Davies (1999c: 176) puts it:

Which model is, of course, a matter for those responsible for the examination, normally those with decision-making powers at national level. The choice may be British English, American English, Singapore English, Zimbabwe English: but a standard English it most certainly will be.

6.4.2.4 The nature of the standard

So far, so clear. But there is another complicating factor – the marked uncertainty, even with British Standard English let alone the New Englishes, as to how the standard can be defined. And it is this, the nature of the standard rather than the proposition that the standard should be taught in school that tends to be the locus of the greatest controversy (see Crowley 2003: 254–7, who takes the authors of the Kingman (1989) and Cox Reports (1991) to task for their confused use of the term 'standard').

Although this is not the place for an extended discussion of the standard there is space for a few points, the first being that the standard is, as explained in Chapter 1, more 'an abstract idealisation than empirically verifiable reality' (see Milroy, J. 1999). It is not altogether surprising, therefore, that there should be dispute over the boundaries of the standard. The second is that while the notion of a written standard English is widely accepted, there is, Crowley (2003) remarks, far less consensus regarding the existence of a spoken standard English:

> When the leading experts in the field are consulted, however, the result is striking: there is a lot of confusion, little consensus and a good deal of scepticism towards the idea of 'spoken standard English'. (Crowley 2003: 259)

In the ranks of the sceptical experts, one finds Carter (1999: 165), who – on the basis of extensive study of constructions most typical of spontaneous speech – concludes that it is worrying that the National Curriculum of England and Wales should give so much attention to spoken standard English 'when so little appears to be known about what exactly it is and when it is defined only as "not speaking non-standard English"'; and Cheshire (1999: 129), who points out at the opening of her discussion that 'not only is the concept of spoken standard English problematic in itself, but the grammatical structure of spoken English is far from being well-understood'. There are others, however, equally expert (e.g. Quirk 1990b), who are prepared to concede what is widely taken for granted in political discourse, the existence, namely, of such a thing as spoken standard English, or at least, as Davies (1999c: 177) puts it, that 'the spoken language is not immune from standardisation processes'.

In this zone of uncertainty there are, however, areas of relative consensus. It is widely accepted, for instance, that there is no standard pronunciation, only more or less prestigious accents, and that the concept of the standard has greatest clarity when applied to the written language, and specifically to print English. Few, too, would disagree with Gupta (2001: 320) when she argues that the concept of standardness is relatively weak in phonology and lexis. Indeed Trudgill (1999: 17), in his protests at the common confounding of formal or technical vocabulary with Standard English, goes so far as to assert that 'there is no such thing as Standard English vocabulary'.

One implication of all this is that when we say the model of English adopted for teaching in the outer circle is likely to be a standard variety, we refer primarily to the grammar (the morpho-syntax) of a written print variety, a variety that happens to vary little across regions of the world, and not to lexis or phonology. Clearly, there are other pedagogic implications, but we shall return to these once we have discussed two further important factors: practicality and acceptability.

6.4.2.5 Practicality

Turning first to practicality, we find two considerations recurring with noticeable frequency, though they point in opposing directions: towards the educational recognition of local varieties of English in one case and away from this in the other.

The first has to do with the teaching cadre in outer circle countries such as Nigeria, India, Singapore or Zambia, where the teaching of English has long been in the hands of local teachers who themselves speak an educated indigenised variety of English. It is rather awkward, therefore, even paradoxical, Bamgbose (1992) observes, to insist on forms of speech in class that the teacher herself does not model when speaking out of the classroom:

> One noticeable effect of the refusal to accept the existence of a Nigerian English is the perpetuation of the myth that the English taught in Nigeria is the same as, say, British English ... In our teaching and examinations we concentrate on drilling out of existence forms of speech that even the teachers will use freely when they do not have the textbooks open before them. (Bamgbose 1992: 149)

The point is well made, but there is an opposing consideration to which the same writer draws attention: the relative dearth of codification of indigenised varieties of English, which is important not just because codification is essential to standardisation (see Chapter 1) but because in its absence teachers will be unclear as to what is correct and what not, what is to be discouraged and what tolerated; an uncertainty likely to be aggravated by the complexity of the sociolinguistic environment of English teaching in the outer circle, where local educated varieties coexist with basilectal varieties, mixed varieties and metropolitan standard Englishes.

> Crucial to the entrenchment of innovations and non-native norms is codification. Without it users will continue to be uncertain about what is and what is not correct and, by default, such doubts are bound to be resolved on the basis of existing codified norms, which are derived from an exonormative standard. (Bamgbose 1998: 12)

A similar point is made by Quirk (1988), writing some ten years earlier but from a quite different perspective. For Bamgbose the lack of codification is an obstacle to be overcome by radical reform; for Quirk it functions as a conservative argument for adhering to well-established British or American Standard English models:

> although Kachru has been publishing on Indian English for twenty-five years ... prolifically, eloquently, elegantly ... there is still no grammar, dictionary, or phonological description for any of these non-native norms that is, or could hope

to become, recognised as authoritative in India, a description to which teacher and learner in India could turn for normative guidance and from which pedagogical materials could be derived. (Quirk 1988: 235)

Since Quirk penned these words, significant progress has been made towards developing authoritative descriptions of the New Englishes, not least through the establishment of an International Corpus of English (ICE). Nevertheless, as Bamgbose (1998: 12) says, there is work yet to be done, and codification therefore remains for him 'the priority of the moment'. It needs, moreover, to encompass the implementation of various educational changes: the reform of textbooks, for example, so that they cease to stigmatise localised features as errors, reform in examinations and perhaps most important of all change in teacher education so that all teachers are sensitised to the difference between divergence and error.

6.4.2.6 Acceptability

This leads us to a final factor of equal importance to codification – acceptability, which is, in turn, linked to attitudes and status. It is important because recognition of a new language, or a new standardising variety, depends, it is widely agreed (see Joseph 2004: 139), on both formal linguistic difference and acceptance of that difference as valid, as having status. Bamgbose (1998: 4) acknowledges as much when he remarks with respect to the New Englishes that 'the acceptability factor is the ultimate test of admission of an innovation'.

On the sociolinguistic plane, then, the existence of a New English is at least as much a matter of attitudes, belief and confidence as of linguistic difference. So, if a community of speakers chooses – for reasons of identity or whatever – to describe themselves as speakers, say, of Singapore English, and if they have the confidence to accept their way of using English as an appropriate model for themselves (see Davies 1999c), then these are good grounds for conceding the sociolinguistic reality of the indigenised variety.

Whether the requisite level of acceptance and confidence is actually present in outer circle societies remains unclear, however. Certainly, many ELT teachers and applied linguists no longer regard every deviation from British or American norms as an error: they have moved on conceptually. But it is uncertain to what extent this is true of educated users outside the academic community. Are they prepared to describe themselves as speakers of a standardising Singapore, Indian or Nigerian English, or do native norms still retain, as Bamgbose (1998: 5) implies, a degree of attractiveness as benchmarks of what is taken to be competence in English?

The evidence here is slender, of course, but what little there is does suggest a stubborn residual preference for British or American Standard English norms. Timmis (2002: 248), for example, on the basis of an attitude questionnaire drawing four hundred student responses from fourteen different countries, concludes that 'there is still some desire among students to conform to native speaker norms, and this desire is not necessarily restricted to those students who use or anticipate using English primarily with native speakers', admitting, though, that many of these respondents may not be sensitised to the sociolinguistic issues involved in the debate over the appropriacy of British or American norms. Wright (2004: 176) reports, meanwhile, that European teacher participants at the 2002 Paris TESOL conference displayed a strong attachment to the British Standard English model.

If public attitudes are difficult to determine, there is less uncertainty regarding the stance at the highest levels of government, this tending toward the negative. In Singapore, for instance, the former prime minister Lee Kuan Yew has expressed concern at the popularisation of Singlish in television sitcoms, arguing that prolonged exposure to this colloquial variety might adversely affect school pupils' acquisition of standard English. In the extract below from a speech reported in the (Singapore) *Sunday Herald* he spells out the disadvantages of Singlish and the advantages of what he refers to as 'Standard English'. The context makes clear that in referring to Standard English he has an exonormative rather than endonormative standard in mind.

> We are learning English so that we can understand the world and the world can understand us. It is therefore important to speak and write Standard English. The more the media makes Singlish socially acceptable by popularising it in TV shows, the more we make people believe that they can get by with Singlish. This will be a disadvantage to the less educated half of the population. (Source: *Sunday Herald* 30 January 2000)

In India, too, similar sentiments have been expressed. Quirk (1988: 236), for example, reports a conversation with Indira Gandhi, the late Indian prime minister, in which she expressed horror 'at the idea of India establishing its own standard'.

There is little current evidence,[9] then, of any great enthusiasm in leading political circles for the establishment of an endonormative Standard Indian or Standard Singapore English. And this has significant pedagogical import, for while the conservative views expressed may be sociolinguistically naïve, high-level political endorsement is surely necessary if a local variety, however sociolinguistically valid, is to find adoption as a teaching model.

But even if a standard Indian English, say, were to be codified and authoritatively disseminated as a pedagogical model, it is not inevitable that it would everywhere supplant a British English model. Prestige based on social factors is stubborn and recalcitrant to top-down planning, and so it is not impossible that some Indians at least might seek out institutions advertising themselves as adhering to British standard English and as teaching to British pronunciation norms. And, in these circumstances, it is not impossible to imagine a new hierarchy emerging, related perhaps to class, where British English was taught in private schools and Indian English in state schools (see Sypher 2000).

6.4.3 Teaching models and the New Englishes: some pedagogic conclusions

The remarks above may appear to suggest that it would be easier for the time being to stick with a British or American standard English model. This would not, one suspects, be entirely displeasing to many ELT teachers worldwide, who tend (see Timmis 2002) to be rather conservative in matters of norms for reasons that are not too difficult to understand. First, they have to face the daily practical realities of using textbooks and tests that more often than not remain based on standard British or American English. Second, they are duty-bound to equip students with the skills and knowledge needed to prosper in the world beyond the school, and this constrains them to teach a language variety that is accepted and prestigious in society at large. Third, and perhaps most fundamentally, they – and many others besides – remain wedded to the notion that native-like competence is the ultimate benchmark of learning achievement (Timmis 2002: 243).

However, to argue for a blanket acceptance of British or American norms would be unjustifiable and unsustainable. As we have seen – reviewing Kachru (1992a), Jenkins (2000) and others – shifts in the demographics and sociolinguistics of English use worldwide render anachronistic any continued insistence on the idealised native speaker as the ultimate source of authoritative norms. The fact is New Englishes have emerged that are systematic in their own right, and they are institutionalised in communities that have reshaped the language as they have taken ownership of it, incorporating English-using into their identities. What is needed, then, is a more nuanced position, one that attempts to reconcile, if this is possible, the complex sociolinguistic realities of variation and change with the need for pedagogical clarity, and the demands of international intelligibility with the pull of local identities.

6.4.3.1 Writing and speaking compared

A starting point might be to recognise that the substantial differences between writing and speaking call for different models depending on whether the teaching focus is on speech or writing. We have already argued that the standard is most clearly realised in the grammar of the written language and that, while there are different versions of the standard, there is in fact little variation between these relative to the full range of grammatical constructions in the language (Huddleston and Pullum 2002: 5). Indeed, Crystal (1999: 16) claims there is already an embryonic de facto World Standard Print English (WSPE), a variety that admits only minor regional differences. It may be sensible, therefore, in the case of writing to teach to the model of written grammar codified and available in, say, the Huddleston and Pullum (2002) grammar, especially as this is the literate, written variety that gives access to higher education, international business and science.

Qualifications and caveats are necessary, however, first of all concerning the divergent grammatical features of colloquial subvarieties of the New Englishes – the levelling of the mass/count distinction, innovation in preposition usage and variant verb complementation, for example – all of which could profitably be reconceptualised not as errors but as non-standard dialectal features, and on a par therefore with Tyneside English, say, compared to standard British English. Pedagogically, this would imply a more generous treatment of such features, a policy not of error eradication but of repertoire expansion.

A second qualification concerns lexis, which – as we have seen – is less strongly standardised than grammar, if at all (Trudgill 1999: 17), and more open than other areas to innovations introduced by speakers grappling with new communicative demands. There is also obvious variation between standard varieties, between British and American English for example, and if this is so, and if we allow innovation in native speaker lexis, then we cannot but concede the same licence to creativity to users of English in the outer circle. Pedagogically, this implies accepting novel collocations, semantic extensions and restrictions and coinage of new words for what they are – the inevitable consequence of the transplantation of English to new communicative settings and its appropriation by new users.

That said, the lexical objectives of teaching will need – as ever – to be tailored to the specific needs of the learners. Those wishing to use English as an international lingua franca in science, academia or business will need reminding that not all the items they use will have an international currency. But the same is true, of course, of British native speakers, whose 'unilateral idiomaticity' (Seidlhofer 2002a: 211), the use that is of idioms and metaphors specific to Britain or other inner circle countries, is one of the more regular causes of misunderstandings in lingua franca communication.

The third and final qualification is that the written standard itself is not immune to change. It is possible, for instance, though perhaps unlikely, that a colloquial subvariety of Indian, Singaporean or Nigerian English, once codified, might garner sufficient political support and general acceptance to be introduced as a pedagogical model, and if this were to happen, it would, as Widdowson (2003: 43) puts it, be 'no business … of native speakers in England, the United States, or anywhere else'.

Turning now to speaking, we find a very different situation compared with writing, the most obvious differences being that that there is no standard pronunciation of English and a good deal of regional phonological variation even among those claiming to speak a metropolitan version of standard English. Accent, too, along with vocabulary is one of the more distinctive markers of local, regional or national identities, to the extent that a markedly British or American accent issuing from an outer circle speaker will typically be regarded as signifying affectation rather than high proficiency.

All this, in combination with the tendency to more frequent use of the language with fellow members of the speech community than with inner circle native speakers, suggests that it is no longer appropriate to seek to 'instil L1 pronunciation norms into learners who are rarely likely to communicate with an L1 (especially a RP) speaker of English' (Jenkins 2000: 11). The preferable course may be either to teach to norms that provide for international intelligibility (e.g. Jenkins's 'Lingua Franca Core') or to accept the local educated variety, the acrolect, as a suitable pronunciation model. The latter is in fact more likely because, as Gupta (1999: 70) observes, the accent learners will actually acquire, through a process of 'catching' rather than learning, is the one they are most exposed to.

For aspects of speaking other than pronunciation – lexicogrammar for instance –

the choice of model is complicated by the fact that, unlike writing, there is no international spoken standard English, nor even a definite consensus regarding the boundaries of a putative British spoken Standard English. Some writers (e.g. Crystal 1999: 16) believe that in time a World Standard Spoken English (WSSE) may emerge to stabilise global diversification in the spoken language, but there is no sign of this yet, and no consensus either as to the form it will take, Bamgbose (1998: 12) suggesting that it may be a composite not identical with any national variety and Crystal (1999: 16) that it may be closer in form to American English.

Complicating the picture also is that we now know, thanks to the work of Biber et al. (1999), Carter and McCarthy (1995), Leech (2000) and others, that the lexicogrammar of spontaneous speech is somewhat different from that depicted in grammars based on the written language. The sentence, for instance, is hardly applicable as a unit of analysis, and normal spontaneous speech is characterised by 'normal disfluencies', frequent stand-alone clauses and phrases – many verbless – and constructions specific to speech (e.g. 'heads' and 'tails') that barely qualify as grammatical by the standards of grammars oriented to the written language.

Faced with this complexity, the most realistic course of action once again may be to accept the local acrolect, not the more colloquial basilect, as the most appropriate model for the teaching of the spoken language. This, after all, will be closest in form to the speech of local teachers. At the same time, however, consideration will need to be given to the circumstances and specific purposes of different learners: for many the acrolect will be appropriate and acceptable, but some may wish to be taught what is taken to be British spoken standard English. As ever, acceptability is a significant constraint on pedagogic innovation.

As for the receptive skills, finally, it is highly likely that over their lifetime students will encounter English spoken in a variety of forms and accents, and it will be useful therefore, in teaching listening, to expose students to the diversity of accents and grammatical features found in spoken English worldwide, in the inner as well as the outer and expanding circles.

6.4.3.2 Teacher education

None of these tentative prescriptions could be implemented, however, without some reform of language teacher education. Most useful, specifically, would be a curricular component aimed at raising awareness of features of the New Englishes and alerting teachers to the sociolinguistic complexities of English use worldwide. Such a programme would, one hopes, replace absolutist conceptions of what is proper and correct in language with greater flexibility and principled pragmatism regarding norms and models, yielding more sensitive pedagogic responses to the diversity within English in a world where, as envisaged by Crystal (1999: 16), educated individuals may in future need a multidialectal capacity to switch, as appropriate, between three spoken dialects: a local colloquial variety functioning as a marker of local identity (e.g. Singlish), a (future) standard national variety (e.g. educated Singapore English), and a (future) international standard spoken English (WSSE).

Whether or not these aspirations are actually attainable is, of course, another matter and remains in doubt. Much depends on the priorities of educational authorities, on public attitudes, political will and the resources available. What we can be more confident of is that the struggle to reconcile diversity with international intelligibility will continue to provoke debate over the models that are most appropriate in teaching English around the world.

6.5 A LINGUA FRANCA CODA

So far in this chapter the focus has been on the claims for educational recognition of the New Englishes of outer circle societies.[10] But there is another context of English use to consider, to which recent literature (Jenkins 2000, 2004; Seidlhofer 2001, 2002a, 2002b, 2004) has called attention: the use of English as an international lingua franca, which cuts across outer and expanding circle speakers, and is, Jenkins claims 2000: 195), the most frequent use of spoken English around the world.

Just as increased tolerance has been extended to the New Englishes of the outer circle, so – argue Seidlhofer and Jenkins (2003: 142) – should a greater degree of independence from native speaker norms be accorded to users of English as a lingua franca (ELF), many of whom, as residents of the expanding circle,[11] will hitherto have been taught with almost exclusive reference to a British or American standard English mode. The argument in essence, then, is for a new normative model – a lingua franca (ELF) model – and the reasons are not very dissimilar to those advanced in support of the New Englishes: as an international language English can no longer be the exclusive property of its native speakers; many learn English not to interact with native speakers but with other lingua franca users, and the importance of English in their lives is such that it constitutes an element in their personal identity; and these bilingual users deserve to be identified not as deficient speakers of a British or American native-speaker English but as competent, authoritative users of their own self-sufficient variety.

The trouble is, however, that there is at present no authoritative description of English as a lingua franca (ELF) available that would allow the promulgation of an alternative teaching model, never mind the redesign of curricula, and it is for this reason, to fill what she calls a 'conceptual gap', that Seidlhofer (2001: 146) has initiated the compilation of an ELF corpus (the Vienna-Oxford ELF corpus). Complementing previous research by Jenkins (2000) on the phonology of English as an international language (see above), and work on the pragmatics of ELF by House (1999) and others, this is intended, among other things, to extend knowledge of the lexico-grammatical aspects of ELF spoken interaction between what Seidlhofer (2001: 146) refers to, rather imprecisely, as 'fairly fluent users'. The immediate research objective (Seidlhofer 2001: 147; 2004: 219) is to identify 'salient, common features of ELF use', features that are 'unproblematic in ELF communication' even while ungrammatical in standard L1 English. The long-term goal, though, is the codification of an alternative ELF norm.

Turning now to a brief evaluation of the cogency of these proposals, we can immediately concede that on the socio-political plane they have much to commend them. By repositioning ELF users as competent speakers of their own variety, they would, for instance, contribute to a goal identified as desirable at the end of the last chapter: the democratisation of English. And an ELF norm, if implemented, might hasten the 'de-anglicisation' of English, a process Ammon (2001: 114) believes is necessary if non-native academics/scientists are to have the right to their own 'linguistic peculiarities'.

Neither can there be any objection to the ELF descriptive enterprise. It would clearly be most useful to have more elaborate, empirical descriptions of how English is used as a lingua franca, of what causes misunderstanding and what is redundant to effective communication, since this would, among other things, inform the reassessment of pedagogic priorities and allow more realistic objectives to be set.

Difficulties arise, however, when a move is made from description to prescription, to the proposal that a set of ELF norms be codified and promulgated as a new teaching model. One of these is that English used as a lingua franca is by its very nature likely to be variable between users with different first languages and users of differing levels of proficiency, and it may be more difficult, therefore, than with the closed system of phonology to settle on a common, stable set of features capable of constituting a prescriptive ELF model. Seidlhofer's (2004: 219) ELF corpus, for instance, draws on data from 'fairly fluent' speakers, but it is not clear what level of proficiency this description designates, nor is it obvious against which benchmark it can be assessed. Presumably, some qualifying level of proficiency or fluency is desired, as otherwise an ELF norm might be derived from data supplied by speakers of an indeterminate level of proficiency.

A wider implication here is that in identifying 'salient, common features' of ELF use it may be useful to supplement corpus data with sociolinguistic fieldwork, the reason being that while corpora are certainly useful in determining, for example, the frequency of particular constructions over a wide range of texts, they tend to be less informative about the contextual conditions under which a particular feature was produced. And this surely is relevant, for if we are interested in asserting the linguistic identity of a lingua franca variety of English and establishing a new codified norm, we will need to determine what stability there is in the use of particular forms under what conditions, these being questions that are more satisfactorily resolved when we have fuller information about the speakers involved in particular communicative events and the circumstances as well as variability of their linguistic production.

Also needing clarification is whether any eventual codification of an ELF variety will extend beyond the spoken language to the written. As presently constituted, the Vienna-Oxford corpus, like Mauranen's (2003) corpus of academic lingua franca English, is restricted to spoken data because this, in Seidlhofer's (2001: 146) words, is 'at one remove from the stabilising and standardising influence of writing', and because spoken interaction, being reciprocal, affords greater scope for investigating what is or is not mutually intelligible. Implicit here, perhaps, is a recognition that an ELF model may be more credibly applied to speaking than writing, for, widely accepted around the world there already exists, as previously observed, a fairly uniform standard written print variety, the supplementation of which by some alternative written lingua franca norm would be of questionable utility.

The greatest obstacle, however, to the promulgation of an ELF teaching model, exceeding by far the difficulties just mentioned, is acceptability.[12] As Timmis's (2002: 244) data reveals, and as is corroborated by Wright's (2004: 176) observations, there is still a considerable degree of attachment to standardised native speaker norms, the principal reason being the persistence of the traditional notion that native-speaker-like competence is the ultimate benchmark of learning achievement. Even Seidlhofer (2004: 244) herself, in her opposition to the hegemony of native speaker norms, does not entirely evade what she refers to as a 'conceptual straightjacket', for in outlining 'unproblematic' ELF features posing no obstacle to successful communication she employs negatively loaded vocabulary: for example, '*confusing* the relative pronouns who and which' or '*failing* to use correct forms in tag questions' (our italics); an oversight remedied by Jenkins (2004: 64) in a subsequent article where these terms are enclosed in inverted commas.

Given the deep-rooted nature of these attitudes there is a risk, then, that an ELF model constructed on the lines indicated above will come, like other 'reduced' models before, to be perceived – however unjustifiably – as a second-rate English. It seems unlikely either that European or East Asian students will easily be persuaded that an ELF model is the most suitable one for them on the grounds that they will predominantly, or only, use English as an international lingua franca with other non-natives. They may reason, on the contrary, that their future communication needs are unpredictable, and that, given the still impressive demographics and economic power of native-speaking communities, there is in fact some prospect of encountering native speakers at some future time, in which case a prestige variety of English of wide currency, internationally as well as in the inner circle, will be the best, most flexible bet for them.

The conclusion we are driven to, then, is not that the pursuit of an ELF model is valueless or pointless. Far from it, despite the methodological and conceptual difficulties involved. But rather that gaining acceptance is a formidable obstacle that can probably only be overcome by convincing teachers, students and the wider public not just that English is sociolinguistically in a different position from all other languages, which is obvious, but that this sociolinguistic uniqueness justifies the abandonment of a popular assumption that by and large holds sway for most languages; the assumption, namely, that native-speaker-like proficiency, and conformity to native speaker norms, is the truest measure of achievement in second language learning.

NOTES

1. The distinction between stress-timed and syllable-timed languages is an idealisation; many languages fall on a continuum between these two extremes. Stress-timing refers to a tendency by which stressed syllables occur at regular intervals of time, a characteristic known as 'isochronism'. Syllable-timing refers to the tendency for all syllables in an utterance to receive equal prominence, a characteristic known as 'isosyllablism'.

2. The term 'substrate' is drawn from creole studies, and broadly refers to the input or influence of native L1 languages in the formation of a creole.

3. These Singapore English words are, in fact, borrowings from Malay and refer respectively to a guard, a playing field, food and village. The Indian English words denote a circular red mark placed on the forehead, small or junior, a stick or baton, native or home-grown, respectively.

4. Like 'substrate', the term 'superstrate' derives from creole studies and refers to the dominant language on which the creole is based and from which it usually derives much of its lexis. Mesthrie (2003) argues that the superstrate influence in the formation of New Englishes is both more complex and more substantial than sometimes thought.

5. Lexical innovation, one might add, largely reflects the transplantation of English to a new cultural milieu. It would be curious not to accept the resulting innovations as legitimate at a time when, in the wake of cultural and technological change, British English is itself adding to its lexical stock.

6. Words in square brackets are the author's, not Joseph's.

7. Relevant here is the Singapore government's initiation in 1998 of a campaign to eradicate Singlish from public domains, promoting in its place what they referred to as 'Good English' (see Gupta 2001: 378).

8. A Geordie is a native of the north-east of England, of Newcastle and the surrounding area.

9. Political attitudes are fluid, however, and might well change over time, becoming more favourable to endormative standards.

10. For a certain, still small, sector of the population of outer circle societies, New Englishes are, in fact, acquired as a first, native language.

11. There are, of course, many users of English as an international lingua franca (ELF) resident in the outer circle, which is why ELF cuts across Kachru's three circles of use.

12. Sceptics question the practicality as well as the political and sociolinguistic feasibility of an ELF norm. Görlach (1999: 16), for example, writes as follows:

> For a Euro-English to develop it would need to have prescriptive school norms discarded and to have a billion-fold increase of international communicative events conducted in English. However, it is not a realistic proposition to assume that the French will start talking to each other in English, nor even that they will use English with Germans in unimaginable numbers of speech acts necessary to justify the assumption that a common Continental norm different from BrE is (ever) to develop.

Language education policy and the medium of instruction issue in post-colonial Africa

In this chapter we return to an issue first discussed in relation to minority language speakers in the United States: the medium of instruction, and specifically the role of pupils' home languages in the educational process. On this occasion, however, the focus is on the very different context of the multilingual post-colonial states of Africa, where the choice of instructional medium is the key issue in language planning in education. It is also a highly controversial one, with many academic commentators (e.g. Barrett 1994, Phillipson 1992, Rubagumya 1990, Trappes-Lomax 1990, Williams and Cooke 2002, Stroud 2003, Alidou 2004, Mazrui 2004) calling for the use of English and other former colonial languages to be restricted in favour of a greater role for African languages. This is seen as necessary for (1) promoting the development of indigenous languages, (2) improving the educational performance of pupils, particularly the less able and (3) mitigating the inequalities which are aggravated by the use of official languages of foreign origin over which large sectors of the population have little or no control.

This chapter reviews some of these arguments, but our focus will not so much be on the educational merits of the use of home languages (i.e. local indigenous languages), extensively discussed in Chapter 3, as on the socio-political constraints shaping language education policy. The justification for this selectivity is that advocacy of educationally justifiable policy reforms is more likely in the end to be persuasive if it is borne in mind that policies on instruction media are as much politically as educationally motivated. Indeed, as Tollefson and Tsui (2004b: 2) remark in the introduction to their volume, it is common for the educational case for reform to be trumped by political, social or economic agendas.

Consideration of these agendas in the course of the chapter, and of accompanying socio-political and practical constraints, leads us to the view that there are, in fact, formidable impediments to radical reform, at least in the immediate future. This does not mean, we argue, that applied linguists seeking to influence policy should desist from advocacy of a greater role for indigenous languages, but that they would be well advised to investigate simultaneously how current educational practices might be improved and how the educational disadvantages associated with foreign language media might be mitigated.

We turn first, however, to an overview of current policies on media of instruction in sub-Saharan Africa, and to the problems attached to them.

7.1 CURRENT POLICIES ON MEDIA OF INSTRUCTION: ARTICULATING THE PROBLEM

The tendency in much of anglophone Africa, with a few interesting exceptions,[1] is for education to be conducted through an indigenous language medium[2] for the first three or four years of primary education, with a switch taking place thereafter to exclusively English medium instruction. In Lusophone and Francophone Africa, by contrast, Portuguese and French respectively tend to be the official languages of instruction from the start, though in certain countries (e.g. Mozambique: see Benson 2000) this policy is under review following relatively successful experimentation with bilingual media inclusive of local languages.[3] Table 7.1 summarises the situation in a limited but not unrepresentative range of mainly anglophone countries.

This, of course, is only a portrait of official policies. The actual situation on the ground is a good deal more complicated in that it is very common for teaching in the local language, or some combination of the local indigenous language and the exoglossic official language medium, to continue for some years after the official switch of medium, producing a de facto bilingual medium. One of the principal reasons for this classroom code-switching is simply that teachers find it necessary to make themselves understood by pupils who have only limited proficiency in the official language medium.

7.1.1 Media of education in lower primary school

There is widespread academic agreement that the mother tongue or a local language well known in the community is, in principle, the most suitable medium for education in the initial years of education. Put briefly, the educational argument is that cognitive development and subject learning is best fostered through teaching in a language the child knows well. Instruction in a language familiar to pupils improves immeasurably the quality of interaction between teacher and pupil. It also narrows the psychological gulf between home and school, integrates the school better into the local community and gives recognition to the language and culture the child brings to school with positive effects on the self-esteem of individuals and local communities (see Benson 2002). The work of Cummins (1979, 1984) and others suggests, moreover, that consolidation of the child's L1 facilitates subsequent acquisition of a second language (see Chapter 3).

In spite of equivocal early research findings (e.g. Engle 1975), these arguments are increasingly bolstered by empirical evidence. For example, in a recent study Williams (1996) shows that fifth-year primary pupils in Malawi, where the medium until grade 4 is Chichewa, have no worse reading abilities in English than primary five pupils in Zambia, where the official medium is English from grade 1. Moreover, the

Table 7.1 The medium of education at lower primary level in selected African countries

Years	1	2	3	4	5	6	7	8	9	10	11	12	*Local language medium*
Malawi	▓	▓	▓	▓									Chichewa
Tanzania	▓	▓	▓	▓	▓	▓	▓						Kiswahili
Botswana	▓	▓	▓	▓									Setswana
Burundi	▓	▓	▓	▓									Kirundi
Ghana	▓	▓	▓										various languages
Nigeria	▓	▓	▓										various languages

Key:

▓	Local or indigenous language medium
	Metropolitan language medium

Malawian pupils show far greater reading ability in their local language, Chichewa, than the Zambian pupils do in their local language, Nyanja.[4]

Given, then, that there is that there is little dispute in academic, if not in policy-making circles, that an indigenous, local language, related to the mother tongue, is the most effective medium of early education, the rest of this paper focuses on the more contentious choice of media at the upper primary and secondary levels of education.

7.1.2 Media of instruction at upper primary and secondary levels of education

In many African countries, where English is the medium in the upper primary and secondary education cycles, there is little exposure to English outside class, especially in rural areas, and this coupled with poor teaching of the language in primary school often means that pupils arriving at secondary school have insufficient proficiency to learn subject matter presented in English. The most striking and extreme illustration of this derives from Tanzania where Criper and Dodd's 1984 study found that:

> Most pupils leave primary school unable to speak or understand simple English. A selected few enter secondary school but they are so weak in English that they are unable to understand lessons or read textbooks in English. (Criper and Dodd 1984)

Certainly, Tanzania, for country-specific reasons, is an extreme case, but there are indications that similar problems exist in a number of other African countries. Williams and Cooke (2002: 307), for example, report adverse findings on the situation in upper primary schools in Zambia, Zimbabwe, Zanzibar, Mauritius and Namibia:

> Studies of individuals African countries likewise present a gloomy picture. In Zambia ample evidence shows that the vast majority of primary school pupils cannot read adequately in English, the sole official language of instruction (Nkamba and Kanyika 1998; Williams 1996), and Machingaidze et al. (1998) conclude that in Zimbabwe between 60% and 66% of pupils at grade 6 do not reach 'the desirable levels' … of reading in English. Similar findings for Zanzibar (Nassor and Mohammed 1998), Mauritius (Kulpoo 1998), and Namibia (Voigts 1998) are reported on the basis of large-scale research (carried on behalf of UNESCO by the Southern Africa Consortium for Monitoring Educational Quality).

And in Francophone Africa there are few indications that the situation is significantly better, with Alidou (2003: 108), for example, reporting a 25 per cent drop-out rate between grades 4 and 5 in the primary schools of Burkino Faso, Mali and Niger, and continuing underperformance, relative to international levels, of African students on tests administered in French or English.[5]

There is a body of evidence, then, to indicate that in many African countries education is ineffectively delivered, a situation clearly wasteful of financial and human resources. And, while the causes of this underperformance are multiple and various, relatively successful experimentation with bilingual media incorporating local languages (see Benson 2000, 2002; Fafunwa et al. 1989) provide a reasonably plausible basis for believing that the use of foreign language media, unfamiliar to many pupils, is at least one contributory factor. Certainly, this is a guiding assumption of the many applied linguistics academics (e.g. Rubagumya 1990, Trappes-Lomax 1990, Arthur 1994, Williams 1996, Mazrui 2004, etc.) who have argued that English (or French for that matter) should be replaced by an indigenous language medium, which, because it is better understood by pupils, will produce a better quality of classroom interaction and promote higher levels of scholastic attainment.

This proposal is, as we have seen, theoretically and empirically defensible, and is supported, moreover, by some quasi-experimental evidence. For example, Prophet and Dow (1994) in a Botswana study taught a set of science concepts to an experimental group in Setswana and to a control group in English. They then tested understanding of these concepts and found that form one secondary school students taught in Setswana had developed a significantly better understanding of the concepts than those taught in English. In addition, the latter group experienced some difficulty in expressing their ideas in English. At the form three level, however, they found that 'the language of instruction had no real impact on their under-standing of the science concepts covered in the lesson' (Prophet and Dow 1994: 214). The Setswana and English groups performed equally well.

Given this kind of evidence, the plausibility of the theoretical arguments, and the weight of academic opinion in favour of reform, it may be wondered why English has not long since been replaced by indigenous languages as the medium of instruction. The answer is that choice of medium is not just an educational matter but also a profoundly political one, and that in Africa the tendency, as mentioned earlier, has been for educational considerations to be subordinated to socio-political ones. We now turn to consider these.

7.2 CHANGING THE MEDIA OF INSTRUCTION: CONSTRAINTS ON POLICY

The impediments to policy change on the media of instruction are various: some socio-political, some economic, some practical. We turn first to a consideration of the socio-political constraints.

7.2.1 Socio-political constraints

Historically, one of the more frequent justifications, or explanations, for the retention of former colonial languages as official languages and as media of education is that they are ethnically neutral, and therefore advance rather than retard the cause of nation-building and national unity (see Chapter 1). By contrast, so the argument goes, choosing any one (or more) languages(s) from a range of competing indigenous languages as media of education at upper primary/secondary level would advantage one ethnic group over another and in this way risk political discord or worse.

In some quarters, these arguments are dismissed either as mere self-serving rhetoric, masking the interests of neo-colonialists or those anxious to maintain their privileged position, or as signifying an uncritical attachment to an outmoded European one-nation one-language nationalist ideology. It would be unwise, however, in discussion of a continent troubled, like parts of Europe, by ethnically based conflicts (e.g. in Congo DRC, Ivory Coast, Sudan, Somalia, Uganda), to dismiss them entirely, despite the germs of truth the criticisms contain. (Outside Africa, after all, for instance in Sri Lanka, there are historical grounds for believing that decisions on media of instruction have played a part in the exacerbation of ethnic tensions.)

A brief example from Zambia may help illustrate the point. Van Binsbergen (1994: 144–5) describes in detail the situation in the western province of Zambia, where in colonial and pre-colonial days the Nkoya, a minority ethnolinguistic group, were subjugated and incorporated into a larger Lozi state. Nkoya resentment at Lozi domination persisted into the post-colonial period and they interpreted the lack of official recognition of their language as Lozi oppression.[6] With this history, it is not difficult to imagine the tensions that would arise from the imposition of Silozi as a regional medium of learning, or for that matter the potential for conflict on a national scale occasioned by, say, the imposition of a Silozi medium of instruction on the Bemba. The wider point here is that closer study of the history of the internal politics of regions or subregions, not only in Zambia but elsewhere in Africa, highlights the tensions that could be exacerbated by elevating one indigenous language over another in the educational field.

That said, there are two major considerations to mention, which significantly attenuate the force of the argument from national unity. The first is that while colonial language media may be ethnically neutral, they are far from neutral socio-economically in that they substantially advantage the wealthier, urban class, whose children have easier access to books, satellite television and private English classes over the disempowered rural poor, who have access to none of these things. In this sense, the former colonial language, while ethnically neutral, is socially divisive (see Chapter 5). Paradoxically, however, it is this very propensity to divide socially and to advantage a small but powerful urban social elite that furnishes a motive for the retention of English medium education, as we shall see.

The second point is that in a minority of African states (e.g. Tanzania, Swaziland, Burundi, Botswana), by reason either of extreme multilingual diversity (Tanzania) or relative linguistic homogeneity (Swaziland), there already exists a widely accepted indigenous national language (e.g. Kiswahili in Tanzania), whose selection as an educational medium of secondary education could in no manner be realistically represented as a potential threat to national unity. Yet even here, in the most socio-linguistically propitious circumstances for reform, English remains the medium of secondary education. There must, therefore, be some alternative socio-political or economic explanation for the retention of English.

7.2.1.1 The attractiveness of English

The most important of these, exceeding the national unity factor in explanatory power by far, is the economic power and attractiveness of English. It is a language that is perceived to be, and manifestly functions as, a gatekeeper to educational and employment opportunities, to social advancement. No wonder then that competence in English and English medium education is highly valued by parents, students and the wider public, all of whom see it as a form of 'linguistic capital'.

From a range of countries comes ample evidence of the strong demand for English. In Mozambique, for example, urban employees are willing to spend considerable portions of their small salaries to fund attendance at private English classes, and in many parts of Africa, such as Tanzania, private English-medium schools, principally for children of the political and business elites, are booming (Vavrus 2002: 37; Mafu 2003: 276; see Chapter 5 also). Wright (2004: 81), citing a study by Mafu (2001), notes a strong middle-class antipathy in Tanzania to further Swahilisation of education, this corroborating Criper and Dodd (1984: 22), who – years earlier – had found that proposals to remove English from the curriculum or restrict its teaching were 'universally rejected by all Tanzanians we spoke to, both professionals and others, because it would appear to downgrade education at the primary level'. From South Africa, meanwhile, Broom (2004: 523) reports not just strong parental demand for English but sustained pressure for schools to effect a transition to English medium as early as possible. Where schools do not comply, parents are quite ready to transfer their children to schools where English has been adopted as the medium of instruction.

The attractiveness of English is also partly fuelled by the corresponding un-attractiveness –for parents – of education in indigenous language media. In South Africa, these bear historical connotations of oppression and disempowerment, but there is also a feeling, harboured by many parents here and elsewhere in Africa, that education through indigenous languages is dead-end education, there being relatively little reading material in these languages beyond school books and few well-paid employment opportunities accessed by knowledge of them.

Changing such attitudes is clearly an important matter, but also a large-scale language planning undertaking, involving no less than a complete rehabilitation of the status of African languages. This, in turn, would require changes in the economic status of these languages – to incentivise their study; their use in prestigious public domains – to increase their prestige; and an increase in the variety of reading, educational and entertainment material available in the language(s) to enhance their attractiveness, not to mention, as Broom (2004: 524) suggests, 'the development of a culture of literacy and reading in these languages'. It would seem on the face of it, then, that there is no immediate prospect of rapid attitudinal change

Meanwhile, many of those looking to English to deliver socio-economic advancement will end up disappointed. Many will fail in English, and in countries where only 10 to 20 per cent of children continue to secondary school, many will be excluded from participation in public life and from the modern sector labour market by lack of proficiency in English.

But this does not mean that demand for English is irrational at the individual level (see Chapter 5), even though these preferences in aggregate help maintain a system of education disadvantageous for most, the reason being that, while there is no guarantee of individual mobility with English, without it there is the virtual certainty of exclusion from higher education, salaried positions in the modernised sector of the economy, travel abroad and so on. And it is for these reasons, in King's words (1986: 452), that 'parents and pupils prefer to fail in English rather than be denied it altogether'. The same factors also explain the general reluctance of politicians to embark on a course of action that would restrict access to English or displace it as a secondary school medium, for to do so would be to court considerable public displeasure, or worse.

The wider point here is the familiar one that school reflects society and has limited power of itself to change it. An analogous point was made by Foster (1965) in his seminal study that produced the phrase 'the vocational school fallacy'. In his critique of vocational training as a means of enhancing the relevance of schooling in Ghana, Foster pointed out that unless conditions in the wider labour market changed, an academic curriculum was in fact perceived as vocational because it led to the more desirable modern sector jobs. Vocationally oriented curricula, on the other hand, were regarded as inferior because, no matter how worthy in principle, in practice they led to second-best jobs.

In a similar way, given the present economic order, English in Africa still leads to the more attractive, better paying modern sector jobs, and as long as this situation persists, which is probable given globalisation and the weakness of many African economies, politicians are unlikely to swim against the tide of public opinion by switching the medium away from English.

7.2.1.2 Vested interests

We come finally to another factor sometimes adduced as a reason for the retention of English medium education: the vested interests of ruling elites (see Myers-Scotton 1990). English, it is argued, helps elites maintain their privileged position by excluding the mass of the population, who have less easy access to the language and to the resources needed to develop a high level of proficiency. It is a mechanism, in short, by which elites are able to reproduce their privilege in the succeeding generation, and one, therefore, they are unlikely to dismantle voluntarily.

The argument has some plausibility, in some countries more than others, but it would probably be a mistake to give it too much prominence, for there are other constraints, in all likelihood more powerful, that are also responsible for the ongoing policy inertia. We turn now to a brief consideration of the more salient of these.

7.2.2 Economic and practical constraints

Not to be forgotten in any discussion of medium of instruction policies in Africa is the presence of constraining external forces, the nature of whose operation is perhaps most clearly visible in Tanzania, a country where, as noted above, there are relatively few sociolinguistic impediments to an indigenous national language medium. In 1982 there were, in fact, well-founded expectations that the country would shortly move to Kiswahili medium in secondary education, but not long after, in 1984, these hopes were dashed with an official announcement that English would after all be retained.

Relevant to understanding this apparent policy 'u-turn' are two key factors. First, by the early 1980s Tanzania had entered a period of prolonged economic crisis, increasing the country's dependency on external support and undermining, simultaneously, confidence that the country could successfully implement such a far-reaching reform at a time of financial stringency. Second, the then president, Julius Nyerere, mindful perhaps of this economic weakness, was in favour of maintaining English medium instruction to 'guard against parochialism' and to protect the country's international links within and beyond the African continent. He was fearful too, according to Russell (1990: 370), that 'the use of English might die out altogether if it were taught only as a subject'.

Illustrated here is the not unfounded anxiety, felt by governments in other parts of Africa and indeed elsewhere (e.g. Malaysia: see Gill 2004: 144), that a shift away from English medium at secondary level would isolate the country from the international community, limit inward investment from the richer countries of the North and above all, obstruct access to science and technology – thus diminishing economic competitiveness.[7] These fears, one might add, become especially acute where the country in question (e.g. Tanzania) is economically weak and dependent on external donor support.

Nor can one ignore the influence of globalisation. The autonomy of African states as policy-making units is, in common with nation states elsewhere, increasingly constrained by global economic and political forces. Increasing numbers of African academics, writers, politicians, business executives, financiers, civil servants and university students inhabit a 'globalised landscape' (Fardon and Furniss 1994: 16). Electronic forms of communication (email and the Internet) and improved transport increase the permeability of national boundaries to the flow of information and people. The net effect is greater interdependence, which, in turn, strengthens the need and demand for proficiency in international lingua francas, especially English.

Set alongside these external macro forces are impediments of a more practical nature that can conveniently be grouped into three rough categories: (1) linguistic resources, (2) books and learning materials and (3) financial resources and educational infrastructure.

7.2.2.1 Linguistic resources

One of the more commonly cited, and even more frequently exaggerated, obstacles to the use of African languages as media of instruction is that they lack the requisite level of linguistic resources for performing this function: graphisation, standardisation, codification, scientific and technical terminology and an extensive elaborated vocabulary. Certainly, it is true that many indigenous languages remain understandardised, lacking the developed orthographies and vocabulary that would facilitate their introduction as educational media. It is also true that developing and 'intellectualising' (Liddicoat and Bryant 2002: 10) many languages simultaneously would be a costly undertaking.

That said, considerable progress has been made, especially with regard to national languages. Kiswahili, for example, already possesses the necessary attributes of standardisation, codification and a sufficiently elaborated vocabulary for use as a secondary level medium of instruction, a monolingual dictionary of Kiswahili having been published in 1981 followed in 1990 by a dictionary of scientific terms (Roy-Campbell 2003: 89). In Zimbabwe, likewise, a monolingual Shona dictionary (*Duramazwi RechiShona*) appeared in 1996, with work underway on a similar Ndebele monolingual dictionary as well as glossaries of scientific and technical terms (Roy-Campbell 2003: 92). In South Africa, meanwhile, PanSALB, the main South African language planning agency, has been mandated to elaborate terminology for the nine historically disadvantaged official languages (e.g. Tshivenda, Xitsonga, etc.), which, though partially developed in possessing 'written forms, literary work, dictionaries and terminology lists' (Finlayson and Madiba 2002: 40), require further development in the area of modern terminology.

These instances, and successful corpus planning activity elsewhere on behalf of languages such as Malay[8] – which is now a medium in tertiary education – show that the cultivation/intellectualisation of indigenous African languages is perfectly feasible technically. The greater obstacle, then, is not so much the technical operations of elaboration or standardisation, administratively and logistically complex though these may be (Finlayson and Madiba 2002: 48), as the availability of resources and the political willingness to commit them, which, in turn, hinges on attitudes to these languages.

This leads us to a further point of some importance, which is that it is by no means obvious that corpus planning should always and necessarily precede the implementation of a given language as a medium of instruction. Form tends to follow function, and, as Nadkarni (1984: 154) suggests, if a language is not first put to use in a given function, it is hardly likely to develop the relevant linguistic resources.

> It is not so much the ready availability of scientific and technical terminology in a language that is crucial … as the actual use of the language to 'do' science and to 'do' technology … what comes first, is scientific discourse … It is the quality and quantity of scientific and technical discourse and not the creation of terminology that is the crucial factor in the modernisation of languages. (Nadkarni 1984: 154)

It may be, then, that linguistic development and enhanced prestige is a consequent of, rather than a necessary condition for, the adoption of a language as a medium of education.

7.2.2.2 Books and learning materials

Another much cited practical obstacle to adopting indigenous language media is the relative dearth of textbook and learning materials in these languages, the only solution for which would be the large-scale production, or translation, of books across a range of curricular subjects, a matter not just of finding suitably qualified authors or translators but also the necessary paper, publishers and distributors. Not impossible, of course, but clearly a costly and time-consuming business. Boyle (1995: 294), for example, points out how the 1984 Hong Kong Educational Commission, which recommended the publication of textbooks in both Chinese and English, seriously underestimated the 'enormity' of the task. And anyone with experience of donor-supported textbook production projects involving, for example, the supply of a single English language textbook to schools throughout a developing country, can testify to the considerable effort and administration required.

Again, this is not to say the provision of textbooks in a new language medium is an insuperable obstacle. Recent developments in desktop publishing technology may help, though, as far as we aware, there is – as yet – no conclusive demonstration of this. It is to say, rather, that implementation of a change of this magnitude, which would additionally involve accustoming teachers to teaching subjects in a language they had not themselves been taught in, would require confidence, commitment and, above all, money – a crucial factor to which we now turn.

7.2.2.3 Financial resources and educational infrastructure

Central, and critical, in discussions of media of instruction in the context of the resource-weakened education systems found in parts of Africa is the question of financial resources, to which we have already alluded in previous discussion. Here it is useful at the outset to recall the very adverse conditions in which schooling often takes place.

In Malawian and Zambian primary schools, for instance, Williams (1996) depicts the following kind of conditions: large classes of fifty or more pupils and a shortage of desks for pupils to sit at, paralleling a shortage of classrooms with some classes held in the open air as a result. In Ghanaian primary schools, Al-Hassan (personal communication) testifies to not dissimilar conditions: the rationing of teachers' supplies of chalk and the marked shortage of textbooks. In many countries it is not that unusual for the teacher to hold the only copy of a key textbook. From Mozambique, Benson (2002: 307; 2004: 266) also reports adverse conditions: chronic illness among pupils, and frequent school closures due to strikes or teacher absence. Across a swathe of countries teachers are poorly paid and frequently poorly trained, if at all (see Cleghorn and Rollnick 2002: 350 on Kenya), and it is unsurprising, therefore, that the methods employed to teach the second/foreign language often leave much to be desired. Finally, many primary school systems are characterised by high drop-out rates and less than universal enrolment, particularly among girls. Secondary schools, meanwhile, tend to cater to a small, relatively select sector of the age-population.

This somewhat depressing catalogue of problems has not been assembled for its own sake, however, but to make three main points. The first is that ministries of education in sub-Saharan Africa have many problems to cope with and many competing spending priorities. Given the conditions outlined above, and their fundamental task of delivering basic education to the population, it would be unsurprising, even justifiable, if they elected to commit their available financial resources to the improvement of the basic educational infrastructure – books, desks, teacher-training – rather than to a change of instructional medium, necessary though that might also be.

Second, given the scale of spending required to ameliorate school conditions, and given the fact that in many countries as much as 90 per cent of the primary education budget is allocated to recurrent expenditure on teachers' salaries – leaving little over for books, equipment or maintenance, it is likely that a policy directed at changing the medium of instruction, whether at primary or secondary level, would require substantial multilateral or bilateral external donor support. Whether such support will be forthcoming, however, is an uncertain and controversial matter. Mazrui (2004: 45) for example, alleges that the World Bank speaks with a forked tongue on this matter, espousing – on the one hand – a rhetoric supportive of the use of the mother tongue in early primary education but refraining, on the other, from committing resources to the 'linguistic Africanisation of all primary education' because it has, Mazrui (2004: 49) claims, a vested interest in the maintenance of European languages of instruction.

Comparatively little empirical evidence is advanced, however, to support the stronger of these claims. Certainly, there are good grounds for believing that past structural adjustment policies[9] of the IMF-World Bank were not helpful to educational development, and that the World Bank has taken little interest in pushing forward an agenda of 'linguistic Africanisation' beyond the initial stages of primary school. But there are indications that it is prepared to fund experimental programmes using local languages as media in early primary education, the primary bilingual education project in Mozambique (1993–97) being a case in point (Benson 2000: 50).

The third and perhaps most important point is that, given the circumstances described above, we need to question the proposition that a change to an indigenous language medium at upper primary or secondary level would of itself resolve the problems of educational underachievement, whose causes are, in fact, more plausibly conceived of as multiple, including: imperfect understanding of the language in which instruction is delivered, a lack of books and learning materials, the ineffective teaching of English as a subject, inappropriate syllabuses and teaching methodologies and the variable quality of teachers. In view of this complex causality, it seems likely that much-needed improvements in educational quality require not just changes in policy but simultaneous micro-level change in educational practices, in resource provision and the implementation of policy, the two being interdependent. As Cummins (1998) has pointed out (see Chapter 3), use of the home language is no educational panacea; bilingual education can be effectively as well as poorly delivered. Thus, while the use of a familiar indigenous language medium may well, the evidence suggests,[10] make a substantial contribution to improved educational performance, this contribution is most likely to be realised if it is accompanied by other necessary changes. Too great a burden of expectation placed on policy reform, or, indeed, change in any one single factor, is likely, experience suggests, to lead only to disappointment.

7.2.2.4 The influence of higher education

Talk here of educational infrastructure leads us to a final factor constraining changes in instructional media at secondary level, the influence, namely, of higher education. The reason this is significant is that the different levels of the education system interlock, the output of one level generally constituting the input of another, with lower levels often seen as preparatory in some measure for the level immediately above. The effect is that higher levels of education tend to exert considerable, often undue, influence on curricular provision at the level below. Thus, where English (or some other former colonial language) is the medium at university, as it so often is in post-colonial Africa[11] – especially in science and social science subjects – pressure develops for that language to be employed also as a medium at secondary school. The pressure comes largely from parents and pupils, who harbour aspirations, no matter how unrealistic in practice, of progressing to university; and is evident not just in Africa but beyond. In Hong Kong, for instance, this is one of the factors, along with the economic, that explains parental demand for English medium secondary education, even where many, perhaps most, understand the educational benefits of the mother tongue medium (Tsui 2004: 100).

One could argue, of course, that effective teaching of English as a secondary school subject could, and should, equip students with the requisite proficiency to study through English at university. Experience suggests, however, that this is unduly optimistic, as is illustrated by the Malaysian case. Here, the 1993 reintroduction of English medium for science, technical and medical courses at public universities[12] placed the Malay medium secondary sector under increased pressure to deliver students with sufficient proficiency to cope with university level study in English. For a time, EAP (English for Academic Purposes) courses were entrusted with remedying the shortfalls in the proficiency of students entering university, but in 2002, realising that that this was insufficient in an era of higher education expansion, the government took the decision to extend English medium to science and mathematics at secondary school (Gill 2004: 150).

In Africa, meanwhile, concern that students graduating from nominally English medium secondary schools possess insufficient proficiency to cope with university study in English has prompted the establishment of communication skills units in many universities (e.g. in Kenya), catering mainly to the needs of first year students. It is not unreasonable to suppose, therefore, that abandoning English medium at secondary level would only exacerbate these difficulties. One obvious solution, of course, would be to adopt an indigenous national language medium at university level, but such a course of action would run up against many of the constraints we have already outlined, and more besides.

7.3 THE MEDIUM OF INSTRUCTION ISSUE AND THE ROLE OF THE APPLIED LINGUIST

This is a suitable juncture at which to take stock of the preceding arguments and examine the implications for applied linguistic interventions at the level of both policy and pedagogy. The first point to emphasise is that we have not been arguing for the retention of English medium at secondary or any other level. On the contrary, there is ample evidence, theoretical and empirical, of the educational benefits instruction in a familiar indigenous language can deliver, some of which we have drawn attention to. Laudable, too, and amply justified on other grounds – the reduction of social inequalities, for example – is the rehabilitation of the status of African languages, to which their use as educational media can make a significant contribution.

There are, however, as we have argued, significant obstacles of a political, practical and economic kind to the realisation of these goals, and if advocacy of change is to carry conviction beyond the academic world it is necessary not just that the supporting arguments are grounded in educational theory but that they show awareness of the political and, above all, economic realities that constrain action. Previous discussion also suggests that the rehabilitation of African languages cannot be brought about by language planning interventions alone (see Chapter 1), for it is bound up with and dependent on long-term economic developments, which may, if favourable, restore their economic attractiveness and prestige, relative to the former colonial languages, and generate the funds necessary for their promotion and development.

The unavoidable conclusion, then, is that radical change in policies on media of instruction beyond early primary schooling is unlikely in the near future. English medium is strongly entrenched, particularly at secondary level, for reasons that have little to do with any educational rationale or merit. The principal implication is that applied linguists might be well advised to complement continued advocacy of policy reform with investigation of measures that might – in the meantime – mitigate some of the adverse effects of the use of foreign language media. Taking this as a cue, we outline very briefly some of the ameliorative measures that might be considered, at the level of both policy and pedagogy. The tentative and programmatic nature of what follows indicates the scope of the research that still needs to be undertaken.

7.3.1 Ameliorating a difficult situation

7.3.1.1 Bilingual education

The medium of instruction issue in sub-Saharan Africa is sometimes presented, in political circles at least, as if it were a matter of a binary choice between either English/French/Portuguese or some indigenous language. But, of course, as previously discussed, this is not the case at all. Bilingual education, the use of two languages as media of instruction – whether for different subjects or at different times of day (see Jacobsen and Faltis 1990 for a full range of language alternation possibilities) – is an obvious alternative option with merits applied linguists could usefully draw to the attention of policy-makers. Aside from the educational ones, already discussed in Chapter 3, it may allow the popular demand for English to be reconciled with the continued development of pupils' skills in a language more closely related to their home language, skills that will positively impact on the acquisition of English as a second language. It is a strategy that makes sense, too, in a sociolinguistic environment where speakers are already accustomed to using different languages for different purposes. And it accords well with Laitin's (1992) useful 3 ± 1 language 'rationalisation' formula for language-in-education planning, which proposes that – for optimal functioning in a multilingual African society – an individual's language repertoire should include between two and four languages: four if they are members of a linguistic minority and two if their mother tongue happens to be also the national language. The three base languages in the formula are (1) a former colonial language as language of wider communication (LWC), (2) an indigenous national language and (3) a local or regional official language.

This is not to deny that the implementation of a bilingual education strategy will be formidably difficult, or feasible on any other than a gradual, piecemeal basis (see Benson 2002: 313). But at least experimental bilingual programmes (in Mozambique, for example) show that it can – even if imperfectly executed – deliver educational benefits, which may be why the Mozambique government is considering extending the experimental scheme to further primary schools on a voluntary basis (Benson 2004: 307). Their very existence suggests, meanwhile, that official discourses in which indigenous languages were viewed as inevitably and necessarily in opposition to former colonial languages may be giving way to greater policy flexibility.

Nor is to deny that bilingual education already has an unofficial existence, taking the form of widespread classroom code-switching (CS) by teachers who feel instinctively that it is necessary for pupils to learn through an imperfectly understood foreign language. And, significantly, the evidence suggests (Ferguson, 2003, Martin-Jones 1995) that they are right, that CS is a useful resource for mitigating the difficulties of learning through a foreign language. There is a good case, then, for moderating official hostility to CS, for acknowledging its prevalence and, indeed, for incorporating awareness of CS as a resource into teacher education curricula.[13]

7.3.1.2 Transitioning between media

Remaining at the level of policy, another matter calls out for closer attention: the transition from one language medium to another, a switch that in Africa usually takes place at the end, or in the middle years, of primary education, and one that is typically not as well managed as it might be. Reform efforts here could potentially focus on (1) the timing of the switch, (2) the phasing of the switch or (3) preparation for the switch.

As regards timing, there is a good educational case for delaying the switch to a foreign language medium for one or two years so that in Botswana, for example, English medium would be officially introduced in grade 5 or 6, not 4, and in Tanzania in, say, year 3 of secondary school rather than year 1. The advantages of such delay have already been made clear: it allows more time for the consolidation of vital L1 literacy skills, facilitates subject content learning in the middle years of primary school and enhances the status of indigenous languages. A further benefit is that it may allow more efficient use to be made of the limited numbers of primary school teachers with sufficient English language proficiency to teach effectively through the language, a common problem being (and not just in Africa) that there are too few such individuals to cover many primary grades (see Davies 1999a: 70).

Standing in the way of such a reform, however, looms the familiar obstacle of public and political reluctance to embrace any circumscription of the educational role of English. In which case greater weight may need to fall not on timing but on the preparation for, and phasing of, the switch to English medium. Phasing refers to the gradual implementation of the switch of medium over a number of years subject by subject, starting first, as Clegg (1995: 16) suggests, with contextually supportive subjects. The rationale, of course, is that this alleviates some of the stress many pupils suffer when the switch is made more abruptly. Helpful here would be the devolution of some decision-making powers to school level so that headteachers and their staff can decide – in the light of locally available teaching resources – which subjects should make the switch first.

As regards preparation, meanwhile, a variety of potentially helpful measures come to mind. One is the reintroduction of the intensive crash courses of L2 instruction that once immediately preceded the switch of medium – for example in the Tanzania of the late 1960s and early 1970s, where there used to operate a six-week intensive course based around Isaac's textbook *Learning Through Language*. Of note, too, though not necessarily feasible in the African context, is the former practice in Malaysia of the so-called one year 'remove', whereby pupils moving from Tamil or Chinese medium primary schools to a Bahasa Malaysia medium secondary school would undergo a one-year period of intensive language preparation in a 'remove' class.

7.3.1.3 Curriculum innovation

Another potentially helpful measure might be the introduction, or reintroduction rather, from upper primary school onwards of the programmes of extensive reading that were a prominent feature of secondary school syllabuses in East Africa in the 1960s and Malaysia in the 1970s, and which have since been successfully implemented in English medium Hong Kong secondary schools (Hill 1992: 2). Properly implemented (Hill 1992), these can significantly increase exposure to the target language with beneficial effects, the evidence suggests (Day and Bamford 1998; Hill 1992; Krashen 1993), on reading fluency, vocabulary learning and overall proficiency in the second language. Thus far, unfortunately, there appears to be few widely accessible accounts, or evaluations, of such schemes in African education systems, an exception being Cunningham (1990), who reports on the problems and successes of an extensive reading programme in Zanzibar.

Attention, too, could usefully be given to redesigning the English language subject curriculum in such a way as to systematically prepare pupils for the forthcoming switch to English medium. Desiderata here would include (1) an increased emphasis on reading and listening skill development prior to the switch; (2) the use of instruction material with content reflecting the future necessity of study reading in such subjects as geography, science and mathematics; and (3) a vocabulary development component aimed at equipping pupils with the type and size of vocabulary necessary for studying through an L2 medium (see Clegg 1995: 16), a further justification, incidentally, for an extensive reading programme.

7.3.1.4 Learning materials: quantity and readability

Moving on now to issues of materials, classroom pedagogy and teacher education, we turn first to the crucial matter of L2 learning materials, starting with the simple question of quantity and availability. One of the more robust findings of studies conducted by the World Bank and other agencies (e.g. Fuller 1987, Fuller and Heyneman 1989, Heyneman et al. 1983) into factors associated with school quality is that in situations where there is a shortage of textbooks, as is the case in many African schools, an increase in their quantity, improving the ratio of pupils per textbook, is one of the most effective single inputs towards raising levels of pupil achievement. No medium can be effective without textbooks, and it is plainly important, then, that the basic resources are made available.

Quantity, however, will not suffice if the textbooks are not used properly and if they are not readable. The latter point is a particular matter of concern in view of accumulating evidence (see e.g. Chimombo 1989) that many of the books currently in use are linguistically unsuitable because they take little account of the fact that readers are learning through an L2 medium. Peacock (1995: 394), for example, refers to research from a range of countries showing that 'the demands of science texts are often above the level and capacities of the primary school children they are intended for'. He also cites MacDonald's (1990) South African study, which exposed a substantial gap between the language used in science texts and that taught in the English language syllabus up to that same stage both in terms of vocabulary ('from 38 per cent to 55 per cent of the vocabulary used was not taught in the (English) schemes') and previously untaught logical connectives (Peacock 1995: 393).

Clearly, then, there is ample scope for research into the readability of the textbooks used across the curriculum in L2 medium situations, the aim of which would be to generate guidelines for textbook authors and publishers. Such research would need to take account not just of vocabulary and syntax, the usual inputs to traditional readability formulas, but also other factors impinging on comprehensibility: discourse, lay-out, visual support, use of metaphor and analogy, and rate of information unloading, not forgetting important non-textual factors that play a role, specifically the manner in which teachers mediate L2 medium texts (see Martin 1999).

7.3.1.5 Classroom pedagogy and teacher education

This last point leads us directly to the crucial area of effective pedagogy in a second language, which, in turn, connects with questions of teacher education. As regards pedagogy, Clegg (1995: 17) urges teachers to carry out routine analyses of the linguistic demands of the material they are about to teach so that they consider ways of modifying their input communicatively to maximise comprehensibility and devise appropriate presentation strategies. These are sensible suggestions, clearly, but of doubtful feasibility in situations where teachers are poorly paid and sometimes poorly motivated, where they lack confidence in their English proficiency and where pedagogical training for the particular demands of L2 medium instruction may be rudimentary.

One of the more reliable routes to improved classroom pedagogy, then, may lie in revised and improved teacher education, and it is here that the ideas just mentioned may best find expression, for they draw attention to the fact that in an L2 medium system all teachers, whatever their subject, are condemned to be language teachers with a responsibility to attend to their own as well as pupils' use of the various languages in their repertoires. The implication is clear: components on bilingual education, second language learning theory, L2 language improvement and language awareness could profitably feature on the training curriculum of teachers of, say, biology or geography as well as on that of language arts teachers, particularly at secondary level (see Benson 2004: 215 for further suggestions on teacher training in developing countries). The latter, meanwhile, could benefit from curricular components imparting knowledge of principles of bilingual education and modelling second language teaching methods, with both supplemented by study visits to effective schools.

7.3.2 Concluding remarks

Many of the measures proposed above are not new, and many may well turn out not to be feasible. But this is testimony in itself to the need for further research and experimentation, and at least the preceding discussion may contribute to the elaboration of a fresh research agenda focusing on practice as well as policy. Such an agenda is needed, for much current education is inefficient, wasteful and inimical to development, and, while changes in the medium of instruction policy may resolve some of these problems, there is, as argued earlier, little immediate prospect of radical policy change. Also, while there is a large literature on policy, empirical studies of the processes of L2 medium instruction in Africa, and of how those processes might be made more efficient, are rather less abundant. There still remains, then, much work for applied linguists to do.

NOTES

1. One exception is Zambia, where English functions as the official medium from grade 1 of primary school.

2. Terms used in this chapter to refer to various different types of language or language variety (e.g. 'mother tongue' or 'indigenous language') are problematic. 'Mother tongue', for example, is unsatisfactory because in Africa many children grow up with bilingualism as their 'mother tongue'. And 'mother tongue education' may be a misnomer because, while the language used at home and in early primary education may bear the same name, they may in fact be quite different varieties. 'Indigenous language', too, is problematic when used to contrast with 'former colonial language', for many Africans do, in fact, speak English, or to an even greater extent Portuguese (see Vilela 2002: 308), as their native, first language, albeit in an Africanised form. That said, as a matter of convenience we shall persist with these terms because they are widely used and seem unlikely in the present context, given this caveat, to provoke serious misunderstanding.

3. There is a long tradition of experimentation with bilingual primary schooling, incorporating local languages as media of instruction, in Francophone countries such as Burkino Faso, Mali and Niger. But even after twenty years of experimentation there have been no moves to extend the use of bilingual media to all mainstream primary schools in the state sector (Alidou 2003: 110).

4. Chichewa and Nyanja are in fact very closely related languages.

5. Alidou (2003: 106–8) draws on UNESCO research data (UNESCO 2000 *Status and Trends 2000: Assessing Learning Achievement*. Paris: UNESCO).

6. Having lived in Kaoma (formerly Mankoya), the centre of the Nkoya heartland, from 1977 to 1982, the author can confirm the reality of such tensions.

7. These very factors feature prominently in the explanation given by the then Malaysian prime minister, Dr Mahathir Mohamed, of the government's 1993 decision to reinstate English as medium of higher education in science, engineering and medical courses after many years of Bahasa Malaysia medium (see Gill 2004: 144).

8. The Malaysian corpus planning agency, *Dewan Bahasa dan Pustaka*, has played a leading role in elaborating a corpus of scientific and technical terms in Malay (see Chapter 2), greatly facilitating the completion in 1983 of a switch from English to Malay medium instruction in all subjects in public university education (Gill 2004: 142).

9. The heyday of 'structural adjustment' policies was the 1980s and early 1990s. Imposed by the IMF-World Bank (in part as a remedy for the heavy burden of external debt servicing), they prescribed, among other things, privatisation of state enterprises, liberalisation of capital controls and the reduction of public expenditure, including expenditure on education.

10. One source of evidence is the success of experimental programmes using local languages as media of instruction (e.g. in Mozambique). Yet even here, caution in interpretation is necessary, for it is notoriously difficult to replicate the success of an experimental program across the whole of an education system, the reason being that experimental programs tend to be so nurtured with attention and resources that they are, in Crossley's (1984: 84) words, 'doomed to success'.

11. The overwhelming dominance of English in published academic writing and the problems of elaborating indigenous national languages have tended to render efforts to dislodge the former colonial language from its role at this level very difficult. In the great majority of African post-colonial states, therefore, the former colonial language remains the medium of education at university.

12. Most private universities already operated through English medium.

13. Regrettably, space constraints disallow any more detailed consideration of this important phenomenon. For a review of official attitudes to classroom CS, and of its merits as a pedagogical resource, see Ferguson (2003). For an overview of research on classroom CS, see Martin-Jones (1995).

Discussion questions, exercises and further reading

CHAPTERS 1 AND 2: OVERVIEWS OF LANGUAGE PLANNING

1. Consider the language situation in your own country, or one with which you are familiar. Which languages and language varieties are spoken/used, in which domains and for which functions? Is there a designated official and national language? Which languages are used as media of instruction in the education system? Prepare a short description.

   Can you describe any recent language planning activity undertaken by the government or other official agencies. What was the purpose of this activity, and to what extent has it been successful?

2. Spolsky (2004: 17) writes as follows:

   > Looking at the policy of established nations, one commonly finds major disparities between the language policy laid down in the constitution and the actual practices in the society.

   Is this true of your own country, or a country with which you are familiar? If so, what is the nature of the disparity between policy and practice?

3. Ó'Riagáin, P. (1997) is one of several commentators who are sceptical about the power of language policy / language planning to effect intended outcomes. He writes (1997: 170–1) as follows, with Ireland particularly in mind:

   > The power of state policies to produce intended outcomes is severely constrained by a variety of social, political and economic structures which sociolinguists have typically not addressed, even though their consequences are profound and of far more importance than language policies themselves.

   Do you agree with Ó'Riagáin? If so, can you think of specific instances/examples that would support his argument?

Suggestions for further reading

Still well worth reading are the 'classic' volumes on language planning, for example: Rubin and Jernudd (ed.) 1971; Fishman, Ferguson and Das Gupta (ed.) 1968; Fishman (ed.) 1974; not forgetting the seminal books and papers by Haugen 1966a, 1966b, 1966c. Moving forward in time, Cooper 1989 and Kaplan and Baldauf 1997 are also very useful sources.

The most recent general books on language policy and language planning are Spolsky 2004 and Wright 2004, both of which are stimulating and illuminating. On the theme of nationalism and language, I have found Barbour and Carmichael (eds) 2000 a very helpful collection, with individual papers focusing on different regions of Europe. Not to be overlooked, finally, are the two relatively new journals in the field, *Language Policy* and *Current Issues in Language Planning*.

CHAPTER 3: EDUCATIONAL AND POLITICAL DIMENSIONS OF BILINGUAL EDUCATION: THE CASE OF THE UNITED STATES

1. Assess the relative merits and disadvantages of the maintenance and the transitional models of bilingual education as applied to the education of immigrant linguistic minority pupils.

2. Do you agree with the following remarks of former US president Ronald Reagan in 1981 on bilingual education in the United States. Why or why not?

   It is absolutely wrong … to have a bilingual program that is now openly, admittedly dedicated to preserving their [the immigrants'] language and never getting them adequate in English so they can go out into the job market and participate.

3. On page 201 is an extract from a *New York Times* editorial of September 1995.

   • To what extent, if at all, do you agree with the sentiments expressed in the *New York Times* editorial?

   • Were you so minded, how would you respond the points made in the editorial? What points would you make in support of bilingual education?

4. How do language education policies for immigrant linguistic minorities in the United States (e.g. California) compare with those for similar minorities in Western Europe (e.g. the Netherlands, the UK)?

   (The volumes by Extra and Gorter 2001 and Extra and Yağmur 2004 are a useful starting-point for a study of the situation of immigrant language minorities in Europe.)

New York's Bilingual 'Prison'

Instruction in English alone may not be the perfect method of helping immigrant students into the mainstream. But neither is a system that dragoons children into bilingual programs that reinforce the students' dependency on their native language and then makes escape impossible.

The Board of Education made this point last year in a scalding report on bilingual education in New York. Its broad conclusion was that new immigrants instructed in English alone performed better than students in bilingual education programs, where comparatively little English is spoken. In a lawsuit based mainly on the board's report, a Brooklyn parents group charged this week that tens of thousands of immigrant children were being warehoused in bilingual classes well beyond the three years specified in state law, and taught neither English nor anything else very well.

… Moreover, once enrolled in a bilingual program, the student is soon trapped in what lawyers for the Brunswick Parents Organization call a 'prison'. The students speak so little English each day that they learn the language too slowly to test out of the program within the mandated three years.

… The Bushwick parents also complain that children are often kept in bilingual classes despite protest from parents, who want their children mainstreamed. They also fault the State Department of Education for routinely issuing waivers that permit children to remain in the classes beyond the three year limit. The department claims that the waiver process is in keeping with the law and that the suit 'has no merit'.

That is too glib an answer for a program that according to the Board of Education's own evaluation is failing. Whatever the merits of bilingual education, the present approach may be harming more students than it helps.

(Source: *New York Times* 21 September 1995.)

Suggestions for further reading

Recommended are the following: Baker 2001, an excellent, wide-ranging introductory textbook on bilingual education and bilingualism, and Cummins 2000. Baker and Hornberger 2001 is a very useful collection of some of Cummins's more influential papers.

August and Hakuta 1997, Arias and Casanova 1993 and Crawford 1997 are all worth reading on the educational aspects of bilingual education (BE) in the United States, alongside Schmidt 2000 and Schmid 2001 on the political/identity dimension. Crawford 1999, meanwhile, is a readable account of the recent history and politics of bilingual education. Finally, there are a large number of websites on bilingual education in the United States, one of the more useful being that run by Crawford at http://ourworld.compuserve.com/homepages/jwcrawford .

CHAPTER 4: MINORITY LANGUAGES AND LANGUAGE REVITALISATION

1. What arguments are commonly advanced for protecting endangered languages? Are some more convincing than others? Which ones?

Are there circumstances where you think intervention to defend endangered languages is more, or less, justified? Which? Consider particular examples of endangered languages from a region with which you are familiar.

2. Consider your own ethnic group membership. What are the most important elements that define group membership: language, religion, descent myths, something else? How do they rank in importance relative to each other?

3. Consider situations where language teaching has been a significant element in language revitalisation efforts (e.g. the cases of Irish, Basque, Maori, Scots Gaelic, Hebrew, etc.). Compare these with the cases of Welsh and Breton discussed in this chapter. Has teaching played a more significant role in some cases more than others? And has revitalisation made greater progress in some case more than others? Why? What factors explain different levels of success or failure?

Suggestions for further reading

Dorian 1989, Crystal 2000 and Nettle and Romaine 2000 are useful starting points for those interested in language endangerment, and Fishman's 1991 and 2001a volumes are essential reading on the topic of language revitalisation. Likely to be of interest for the topic of minority language rights are May 2001 and Kymlicka and Patten 2003.

As regards Welsh and Breton, I have found Jones, M. 1998a, Aitchison, J. and Carter, H. 2000, Jenkins, G. and Williams, A. (eds) 2000, and Williams, C. 2000b particularly useful resources, the last mentioned covering revitalisation in Wales and elsewhere. The papers by Jones, M. 1998b, Humphreys 1993, Kuter 1989, Moal 2000 and Texier and O'Neill 2000 are helpful on the Breton situation.

CHAPTER 5: THE GLOBAL SPREAD OF ENGLISH: CAUSE, AGENCY, EFFECTS AND POLICY RESPONSES

1. Identify a country with which you are particularly familiar and consider the role of English within that country, reflecting on the following points:

   • The place of English in the education system (at what stage is English introduced into the school curriculum? Is it a medium of instruction at any level? What percentage of the school population study English?).

   • The place of English in public institutions (e.g. in administration, the press and media) and business.

   • Public attitudes toward English, and discourses about English (e.g. in news-papers, magazines and the broadcast media).

   In the light of your reflections, can you comment on:

   • The effect of English on other languages in the society. Is English a threat to other languages? Does English diminish the vitality of other languages by, for example, occupying prestigious functions that might be discharged by some other language?

- The effect of English on inequalities in society. Do you believe that English contributes to, or exacerbates, social inequalities in the country? If so, how?
- The effect of English on the cultural life of the society. Does English contribute to the undermining of local cultures and customs? Is it, in your opinion, a vector of Americanisation?

2. 'English as a global language is now a factor that needs to be taken into account in its language policy by any nation state' (Spolsky 2004: 91).

    To what extent, if at all, can language planning / language policy at the nation state level control, or counter, the spread of English? Do you think it would be politically feasible in a democratic state to curtail English language teaching in state-funded schools?

3. Are there any circumstances in which it would be appropriate for British or American government agencies, or non-governmental agencies (NGOs), to give aid in support of English language teaching in a developing country? If you feel that such circumstances do exist, what are they? And what criteria, if any, should govern the provision of such assistance?

Suggestions for further reading

Those wishing to pursue the topics discussed in this chapter further should sample critical work on the global spread of English (e.g. Phillipson 1992, 2000a, Phillipson and Skuttnab-Kangas 1996, Pennycook 1994, 2001 (chapter 3)) as well as that which is critical of the critical approach (e.g. Davies 1996, Bisong 1995 and Ridge 2000). Worth reading also are Brutt-Griffler 2002 on the spread of English and its implications, and De Swaan 2001a, who discusses the place of English within the dynamics of the global language system.

CHAPTER 6: NEW ENGLISHES AND TEACHING MODELS: THE CONTINUING DEBATE

1. Variation in preposition usage and the treatment of mass nouns as countable are among the most commonly noticed features of the New Englishes. Below are a few attested examples:

    a) When the police arrived, a small crowd was discussing about the robbery.
    b) He isn't coping up with the amount of work he has to do.
    c) The same names keep cropping in when they discuss about bad behaviour.
    d) He was congratulated for his success in the exam.
    e) Thank you for looking after all the equipments at the farm.
    f) I lost a lot of furnitures in the robbery.
    g) Can you provide us with some advices about the exam?

As a teacher, how would you respond to the above forms? Would your response vary with the context in which they occurred? If so, how?

Do you think the forms above should be treated as correct if they occurred in the context of an international test of English such as TOEIC or TOEFL? Why or why not?

2. The text below is from the *Deccan Herald*. Are there any features – grammatical, lexical, stylistic, discoursal – that might identify the text as Indian English as opposed to, say, British English? If so, are these mainly a matter of grammar or lexis, or something else? Are any parts of the text difficult to understand?

Blame public for decline in snakes

It is ironical that the snakes which are held in high esteem when it comes to prayer, are being hacked, apparently for fear, whenever they make a surprise appearance in residential areas.

However, snakes have a role to play in the food chain. Their staple diet, rodents, cause much loss to farmers as they gulp down more than 15 per cent of agricultural produce in an year.

But snakes are facing a major threat, particularly in rural areas, as the people are devoid of information on the necessity of snakes in the food chain.

The number of poisonous snakes are just a handful, but the residents have been ruthless in eliminating their nemesis for fear.

In urban areas, however, people are becoming quite aware about the necessity to protect snakes.

Even if a snake makes an appearance in a residential locality, people capture the reptile and release it into the forest.

According to the Wildlife Conservation Act, killing snakes is banned, but it is yet to be fully implemented. However, snake lovers hope that people will take the initiative in protecting a species which may soon become endangered.

(Source: *Deccan Herald* 13 May 2005.)

---

3. Do you agree with Seidlhofer and Jenkins (2003:142) that a greater degree of independence from native speaker norms should now also be accorded to users of English as a lingua franca in the Expanding Circle (i.e. in countries like Italy, Japan, China, Greece, etc.), where English has traditionally been taught with almost exclusive reference to British or American Standard English? Are there obstacles to so doing?

Suggestions for further reading

Kachru's 1992a edited volume *The Other Tongue*, and the papers by Quirk 1988, 1990a, Kachru 1988 and 1991 and Bamgbose 1998 are recommended reading for those interested in following the debate over models for teaching English around the world. Meanwhile, Jenkins 2000, Gnutzmann 1999 and Seidlhofer 2001, 2004 all have interesting and illuminating things to say about the emergence of English as a lingua franca (ELF) and the implications for pedagogy. Jenkins 2003, finally, is a good textbook on the general topic of World Englishes.

CHAPTER 7: LANGUAGE EDUCATION POLICY AND THE MEDIUM OF INSTRUCTION ISSUE IN POST-COLONIAL AFRICA

1. 'Equality of educational opportunity has two complementary parts to it. The first is the right, **wherever feasible**, to be educated in the variety of language one learned at home, or at a basic minimum when this is not feasible, to be educated in a school that shows full respect for that variety and its strengths and potentials … The second is the right to learn in the best way feasible the standard or official language or languages of wider communication selected for the society as a whole.' (Spolsky 1986: 189)

   Note the phrase 'wherever feasible' in this quotation from Spolsky. With particular reference to the African context, are there any factors that might render education through the home language not feasible? What measures might enhance the feasibility of education in the home language?

2. Over twenty years ago Bahasa Malaysia (Malay) was implemented as the medium of instruction of secondary education in Malaysia, replacing English. In Tanzania English, not Kiswahili, remains the medium of secondary education. What factors (economic, political, social, educational, etc.) could explain this contrast?

3. Consider the role of private education (i.e. non state-funded education) in any multilingual post-colonial society you are familiar with (e.g. Kenya, Tanzania, India, Nigeria, Malaysia, etc.). What is the size of the private school sector? Which kind of people attend private schools? Do private schools predominately operate in English medium or not? If English medium instruction were discontinued in state-funded schools, what would be the consequences for the private school sector?

4. In this chapter a number of measures were proposed to mitigate the educational difficulties of studying through a foreign language medium. Do you think these measures would actually assist? Why or why not? Can you suggest any other measures not already mentioned?

Suggestions for further reading

Although Africa is somewhat underrepresented (relative to post-colonial Asia), Tollefson and Tsui 2004a would be a very useful starting point for further study. Williams 1996 and Williams and Cooke 2002 are also stimulating reads on the themes of development, educational efficiency, and media of instruction. Benson's

2002 article makes an effective case for bilingual education in developing countries, and Alidou and Roy-Campbell's 2003 papers in the volume edited by Makoni et al. 2003 present interesting critical analyses of the social consequences of retaining ex-colonial languages as media of instruction.

References

Achebe, C. (1976), *Morning Yet On Creation Day*, New York: Anchor.

Achebe, C. (1987), *No Longer At Ease*, London: Heinemann.

Aitchison, J. and H. Carter (2000), *Language, Economy and Society: The Changing Fortunes of the Welsh Language in the Twentieth Century*, Cardiff: University of Wales Press.

Alexander, N. (2000), 'Why the Nguni and Sotho languages in South Africa should be harmonised', in Deprez, K. and T. Du Plessis (eds), *Multilingualism and Government*, Pretoria: Van Schaik, pp. 171–5.

Alidou, H. (2003), 'Language policies and language education in Francophone Africa: a critique and a call to action', in Makoni, S., G. Smitherman, A. Ball, A. Spears (eds), *Black Linguistics: Language, Society, and Politics in Africa and the Americas*, London: Routledge, pp. 103–16.

Alidou, H. (2004), 'Medium of instruction in post-colonial Africa', in Tollefson, J. and A. Tsui (eds), *Medium of Instruction Policies: Which Agenda, Whose Agenda?*, Mahwah, NJ: Lawrence Erlbaum, pp. 195–214.

Alishjahbana, S. (1974), 'Language policy, language engineering and literacy in Indonesia and Malaysia', in Fishman, J. (ed.), *Advances in Language Planning*, The Hague: Mouton, pp. 391–416.

Alishjahbana, S. (1976), *Language Planning for Modernization: The Case of Indonesia and Malaysia*, The Hague: Mouton.

Alishjahbana, S. (1984), 'The concept of language standardisation and its application to the Indonesian language', in Coulmas, F. (ed.), *Linguistic Minorities and Literacy: Language Policy Issues in Developing Countries*, Berlin: Mouton de Gruyter, pp. 47–55.

Ammon, U. (1990), 'German or English? The problems of choice experienced by German-speaking scientists', in Nelde, P. (ed.), *Language Conflict and Minorities*, Bonn: Dümmler, pp. 33–51.

Ammon, U. (2000), 'Towards more fairness in international English: linguistic rights of non-native speakers?', in Phillipson, R. (ed.), *Rights to Language, Equity and Power in Education*, Mahwah, NJ: Lawrence Erlbaum, pp. 111–16.

Ammon, U. (2001b), 'English as a future language of science at German universities? A question of difficult consequences, posed by the decline of German as a language of science', in Ammon, U. (2001a) (ed.), *The Dominance of English as a Language of Science*, Berlin: Mouton de Gruyter, pp. 343–61.

Ammon, U. (2003), 'The international standing of the German language', in Maurais, J. and M. Morris (eds), *Languages in a Globalising World*, Cambridge: Cambridge University Press, pp. 231–49.

Anderson, B. (1991), *Imagined Communities: Reflections on the Origin and Spread of Nationalism* (2nd edition), London and New York: Verso.

Annamalai, E. (2004), 'Medium of power: the question of English in education in India', in

Tollefson, J. and A. Tsui (eds), *Medium of Instruction Policies: Which Agenda? Whose Agenda?*, Mahwah, NJ: Lawrence Erlbaum, pp. 177–94.

Arias, M. and U. Casanova (eds) (1993), *Bilingual Education: Politics, Practice and Research*, Chicago: National Society for the Study of Education/University of Chicago Press .

Arthur, J. (1994), 'English in Botswana primary classrooms: functions and constraints', in Rubagumya, C. (ed.), *Teaching and Researching Language in African Classrooms*, Clevedon: Multilingual Matters, pp. 63–78.

August, D. and K. Hakuta (1997), *Improving Schooling for Language-Minority Children*, Washington, DC: National Academy Press.

Baker, C. (1993), 'Bilingual education in Wales', in Beardsmore, B. (ed.), *European Models of Bilingual Education*, Clevedon: Multilingual Matters, pp. 7–29.

Baker, C. (1997), 'Bilingual education in Ireland, Scotland and Wales', in Cummins, J. and D. Corson (eds), *Encyclopedia of Language and Education, Volume 5: Bilingual Education*, Amsterdam: Kluwer Publishers, pp. 127–42.

Baker, C. (2001), *Foundations of Bilingual Education and Bilingualism* (3rd edition), Clevedon: Multilingual Matters.

Baker, C. (2002), 'Bilingual education', in Kaplan, R. (ed.), (2002), *Oxford Handbook of Applied Linguistics*, Oxford: Oxford University Press, pp. 229–42.

Baker, C. (2003a), 'Education as a site of language contact', *Annual Review of Applied Linguistics* 23, 95–112.

Baker, C. (2003b), 'Language planning: a grounded approach', in Dewaele, J.-M., A. Housen and Li Wei (eds), *Bilingualism: Beyond Basic Principles*, Clevedon: Multilingual Matters, pp. 88–111.

Baker, K. and A. de Kanter (1981), *Effectiveness of Bilingual Education: A Review of Literature*, Washington, DC: Office of Planning, Budget, and Evaluation, US Department of Education.

Baldauf, R. Jnr (1994), '"Unplanned" language policy and planning', in Grabe, W. (ed.), 'Language Policy and Planning', *Annual Review of Applied Linguistics* 14, 82–9.

Baldauf, R., R. Kaplan and R. Baldauf Jnr (eds) (2000), *Language Planning in Nepal, Taiwan and Sweden*, Clevedon: Multilingual Matters.

Baldauf, R. and R. Kaplan (eds) (2004), *Language Planning and Policy in Africa, Vol. 1: Botswana, Malawi, Mozambique and South Africa*, Clevedon: Multilingual Matters.

Bamgbose, A. (1992), 'Standard Nigerian English: issues of identification', in Kachru, B. (ed.), *The Other Tongue: English Across Cultures* (2nd edition), Urbana and Chicago: University of Illinois Press, pp. 125–47.

Bamgbose, A. (1994), 'Pride and prejudice in multilingualism', in Fardon, R. and G. Furniss (eds), *African Languages, Development and the State*, London: Routledge, pp. 33–43.

Bamgbose, A. (1998), 'Torn between the norms: innovations in World Englishes', *World Englishes* 17, 1, 1–14.

Bamgbose, A. (2000), 'Language planning in West Africa', *International Journal of the Sociology of Language* 141, 101–17.

Barber, B. (1995), *Jihad Versus McWorld*, New York: Random House.

Barbour, S. (2000a), 'Nationalism, language, Europe', in Barbour, S. and C. Carmichael (eds), *Language and Nationalism in Europe*, Oxford: Oxford University Press, pp. 1–17.

Barbour, S. (2000b), 'Germany, Austria, Switzerland, Luxembourg: the total coincidence of nations and speech communities?', in Barbour, S. and C. Carmichael (eds), *Language and Nationalism in Europe*, Oxford: Oxford University Press, pp. 151–67.

Barbour, S. (2000c), 'Britain and Ireland: the varying significance of language for nationalism', in Barbour, S. and C. Carmichael (eds), *Language and Nationalism in Europe*, Oxford: Oxford University Press, pp. 18–43.

Barrett, J. (1994), 'Why is English still the medium of education in Tanzanian secondary schools?', *Language, Culture and Curriculum* 7, 1, 3–28.

Bennicini, F. and W. Strang (1995), *An Analysis of Language Minority and Limited English Proficient Students from NELS:88*, Arlington, VA: Development Associates.

Benson, C. (2000), 'The primary bilingual education experiment in Mozambique, 1993–1997', *International Journal of Bilingual Education and Bilingualism* 3, 3, 149–66.

Benson, C. (2002), 'Real and potential benefits of bilingual programmes in developing countries', *International Journal of Bilingual Education and Bilingualism* 5, 6, 303–17.

Benson, C. (2004), 'Do we expect too much of bilingual teachers? Bilingual teaching in developing countries', *International Journal of Bilingual Education and Bilingualism* 7, 2 and 3, 204–21.

Biber, D., S. Johansson, G. Leech, S. Conrad and E. Finegan (eds) (1999), *Longman Grammar of Spoken and Written English*, London: Longman.

Billig, M. (1995), *Banal Nationalism*, London: Sage.

Bisong, J. (1995), 'Language choice and cultural imperialism: a Nigerian perspective', *ELT Journal* 49, 2, 122–32.

Block, D. and D. Cameron (eds) (2002), *Globalization and Language Teaching*, London: Routledge.

Blommaert, J. (1996), 'Language planning as a discourse on language and society: the linguistic ideology of a scholarly tradition', *Language Problems and Language Planning* 20, 3, 199–222.

Blommaert, J. (2001), 'The Asmara Declaration as a sociolinguistic problem: reflections on scholarship and linguistic rights', *Journal of Sociolinguistics* 5, 1, 131–55.

Bokhorst-Heng, W. (1999), 'Singapore's Speak Mandarin Campaign: language ideological debates in the imagining of the nation', in Blommaert, J. (ed.), *Language Ideological Debates*, Berlin: Mouton de Gruyter, pp. 235–65.

Boran, I. (2003), 'Global linguistic diversity, public goods and the principle of fairness', in Kymlicka, W. and A. Patten (eds), *Language Rights and Political Theory*, Oxford: Oxford University Press, pp. 189–209.

Bourdieu, P. (1991), *Language and Symbolic Power*, Cambridge: Polity Press.

Bourhis, R. (2001), 'Reversing language shift in Quebec', in Fishman, J. (ed.) (2001a), *Can Threatened Languages be Saved?*, Clevedon: Multilingual Matters, pp. 101–41.

Boyle, J. (1995), 'Hong Kong's educational system: English or Chinese', *Language, Culture and Curriculum* 8, 3, 291–304.

Braine, G. (ed.) (1999), *Non-Native Educators in English Language Teaching*, Mahwah, NJ: Lawrence Erlbaum.

Broom, Y. (2004), 'Reading English in multilingual South African primary schools', *International Journal of Bilingual Education and Bilingualism* 7, 6, 506–28.

Bruthiaux, P. (2002), 'Hold your courses: language education, language choice, and economic development', *TESOL Quarterly* 36, 3, 275–96.

Bruthiaux, P. (2003), 'Squaring the circles: issues in modelling English worldwide', *International Journal of Applied Linguistics* 13, 2, 159–78.

Brutt-Griffler, J. (2002), *World English: A Study of its Development*, Clevedon: Multilingual Matters.

Burchfield, R. (ed.) (1994), *The Cambridge History of the English Language, Volume 5: English in Britain and Overseas: Origins and Development*, Cambridge: Cambridge University Press.

Campbell, L. and M. Muntzel (1989), 'The structural consequences of language death', in Dorian, N. (ed.), *Investigating Obsolescence: Studies in Language Contraction and Death*, Cambridge: Cambridge University Press, pp. 181–96.

Canagarajah, A. (1996), '"Nondiscursive" requirements in academic publishing, material resources of periphery scholars, and the politics of knowledge production', *Written Communication* 13, 4, 435–72.

Canagarajah, A. (2000), 'Negotiating ideologies through English: strategies from the periphery', in Ricento, T. (ed.), *Ideology, Politics and Language Policies: Focus on English*,

Amsterdam: John Benjamins, pp. 121–32.

Carmichael, C. (2000), 'Conclusions: language and national identity in Europe', in Barbour, S. and C. Carmichael (eds), *Language and Nationalism in Europe*, Oxford: Oxford University Press, pp. 280–89.

Carter, R. (1999), 'Standard grammars, spoken grammars: some educational implications', in Bex, T. and R. Watts (eds), *Standard English: The Widening Debate*, London: Routledge, pp. 149–66.

Carter, R. and M. McCarthy (1995), 'Grammar and the spoken language', *Applied Linguistics* 16, 2, 141–58.

Cheshire, J (ed.), (1991), *English around the World: Sociolinguistic Perspectives*, Cambridge: Cambridge University Press.

Cheshire, J. (1999), 'Spoken standard English', in Bex, T. and R. Watts (eds), *Standard English: The Widening Debate*, London: Routledge, pp. 129–48.

Chimombo, M. (1989), 'Readability of subject texts: implications for ESL teaching in Africa', *English for Specific Purposes* 8, 3, 255–64.

Christian, D. (1989), 'Language planning: the view from linguistics', in Newmeyer, F. (ed.), *Language: the Socio-Cultural Context*, Cambridge: Cambridge University Press, pp. 193–209.

Clegg, J. (1995), 'Education through the medium of a second language: time to get serious about results', in The British Council (1995), *Dunford House Seminar Report*, Manchester: The British Council, pp. 12–19.

Cleghorn, A. and A. Rollnick (2002), 'The role of English in individual and societal development: a view from African classrooms', *TESOL Quarterly* 36, 3, 347–72.

Cook, V. (1999), 'Going beyond the native-speaker in language teaching', *TESOL Quarterly* 33, 2, 185–209.

Cooper, R. (1989), *Language Planning and Social Change*, Cambridge: Cambridge University Press.

Coppieters, R. (1987), 'Competence differences between native and near-native speakers', *Language*, 544–73.

Coulmas, F. (1991), *Language Policy for the European Community: Prospects and Quandaries*, Berlin: Mouton de Gruyter.

Coulmas, F. (1992), *Language and Economy*, Oxford: Blackwell.

Coulmas, F. (2002), 'Language policy in modern Japanese education', in Tollefson, J. (ed.), *Language Policies in Education*, Mahwah, NJ: Lawrence Erlbaum, pp. 203–23.

Cox, C. (1991), *Cox on Cox: an English Curriculum for the 1990s*, London: Hodder and Stoughton.

Crawford, J. (1997), *Best Evidence: Research Foundations of the Bilingual Education Act*, Washington DC: National Clearinghouse for Bilingual Education.

Crawford, J. (1999), *Bilingual Education: History, Politics, Theory and Practice* (4th edition), Los Angeles: Bilingual Educational Services.

Crawford, J. (2000), *At War with Diversity: US Language Policy in an Age of Anxiety*, Clevedon: Multilingual Matters.

Crawford, J. (2002), 'The Bilingual Education Act 1968–2002: an obituary', at http://ourworld.compuserve.com/homepages/jwcrawford/T7obit.htm

Criper, C. and W. Dodd (1984), *Report on the Teaching of the English Language and Its Use as a Medium in Education in Tanzania*, London: ODA/British Council.

Crossley, C. (1984), 'Strategies for curriculum change and the question of international transfer', *Journal of Curriculum Studies* 16, 1, 75–88.

Crowley, T. (2003), *Standard English and the Politics of Language* (2nd edition), Basingstoke: Palgrave Macmillan.

Crystal, D. (1995), *The Cambridge Encyclopedia of the English language*, Cambridge: Cambridge University Press.

Crystal, D. (1997), *English as a Global Language*, Cambridge: Cambridge University Press.

Crystal, D. (1999), 'The future of Englishes', *English Today* 15, 2, 10–20.

Crystal, D. (2000), *Language Death*, Cambridge: Cambridge University Press.

Cummins, J. (1976), 'The influence of bilingualism on cognitive growth: a synthesis of research findings and explanatory hypotheses', in *Working Papers on Bilingualism* 1–43, Toronto: Ontario Institute for Studies in Education. (Reprinted in Baker, C. and N. Hornberger (eds), *An Introductory Reader to the Writings of Jim Cummins*, Clevedon: Multilingual Matters, pp. 26–55.)

Cummins, J. (1979), 'Linguistic interdependence and the educational development of bilingual children', *Review of Educational Research* 49, 222-51. (Reprinted in Baker, C. and N. Hornberger (eds), *An Introductory Reader to the Writings of Jim Cummins*, Clevedon: Multilingual Matters, pp. 63–95.)

Cummins, J. (1980), 'The entry and exit fallacy in bilingual education', *NABE Journal* 4, 25–60. (Reprinted in Baker, C. and N. Hornberger (eds), *An Introductory Reader to the Writings of Jim Cummins*, Clevedon: Multilingual Matters, pp. 110–38.)

Cummins, J. (1981), 'Age on arrival and immigrant second language learning in Canada: a reassessment', *Applied Linguistics* 1, 132–49.

Cummins, J. (1984), *Bilingualism and Special Education: Issues in Assessment and Pedagogy*, Clevedon: Multilingual Matters.

Cummins, J. (1988), 'The role and use of educational theory in formulating language policy', *TESL Canada Journal* 5, 11–19. (Reprinted in Baker, C. and N. Hornberger (eds), *An Introductory Reader to the Writings of Jim Cummins*, Clevedon: Multilingual Matters, pp. 240–7.)

Cummins, J. (1991), 'The politics of paranoia: reflections on the bilingual education debate', in Garcia, O. (ed.), *Bilingual Education: Focusschrift in Honor of Joshua Fishman* (volume 1), Amsterdam: John Benjamins, pp. 183–99.

Cummins, J. (1996), *Negotiating Identities: Education for Empowerment in a Diverse Society*, Los Angeles: California Association for Bilingual Education.

Cummins, J. (1998), *Beyond Adversarial Discourse: Searching for Common Ground in the Education of Bilingual Students*, Presentation to the California State Board of Education, Sacramento, CA, February 1998, at http://ourworld.compuserve.com/homepages/jwcrawford/cummins.htm

Cummins, J. (1999), 'Alternative paradigms in bilingual education research: does theory have a place?' *Educational Researcher* 28, 2, 99–107. (Reprinted in Baker, C. and N. Hornberger (eds), *An Introductory Reader to the Writings of Jim Cummins*, Clevedon: Multilingual Matters, pp. 326–41.)

Cummins, J. (2000), *Language, Power and Pedagogy*, Clevedon: Multilingual Matters.

Cummins, J. (2003), 'Bilingual education: basic principles', in Dewaele, J., A. Housen and Li Wei (eds), *Bilingualism: Beyond Basic Principles*, Clevedon: Multilingual Matters, 56–66.

Cunningham, R. (1991), 'The Zanzibar English Reading Programme', *Reading in a Foreign Language* 8, 1, 663–75.

Dauenhauer, N and R. Dauenhauer (1998), 'Technical, emotional and ideological issues in reversing language shift: examples from South-east Alaska', in Grenoble, L. and L. Whaley (eds), *Endangered Languages*, Cambridge: Cambridge University Press, pp. 57–98.

Davies, A. (1996), 'Ironising the myth of linguicism', *Journal of Multilingual and Multicultural Development* 17, 6, 485–96.

Davies, A. (1999a), *An Introduction to Applied Linguistics*, Edinburgh: Edinburgh University Press.

Davies, A. (1999b), 'Native speaker', in Spolsky, B. (ed.), *Concise Encyclopedia of Educational Linguistics*, Amsterdam: Kluwer, pp. 532–9.

Davies, A. (1999c), 'Standard English: discordant voices', *World Englishes* 18, 2, 171–86.

Davies, A. (2003), *The Native Speaker: Myth and Reality*, Clevedon: Multilingual Matters.

Davies, A., E. Hamp-Lyons and C. Kemp (2003), 'Whose norms? International proficiency tests in English', *World Englishes* 22, 4, 571–84.

Day, R. and J. Bamford (1998), *Extensive Reading in the Second Language Classroom*, Cambridge: Cambridge University Press.

De Klerk, V. (ed.) (1996), *Focus on South Africa: Varieties of English around the World*, Amsterdam: John Benjamins.

Department of Education and Science (1989), *Report of the Committee of Enquiry into the Teaching of English Language*. [The Kingman Report], London: HMSO.

De Swaan, A. (1998), 'A political sociology of the world language system (1): the dynamics of language spread, *Language Problems and Language Planning* 22, 1, 63–75.

De Swaan, A. (2001a), *Words of the World*, London: Polity Press.

De Swaan, A. (2001b), 'English in the social sciences', in Ammon, U. (ed.), *The Dominance of English as a Language of Science*, Berlin: Mouton de Gruyter, pp. 71–83.

Dixon, R. (1997), *The Rise and Fall of Languages*, Cambridge: Cambridge University Press.

Dorian, N. (1981), *Language Death: The Life Cycle of a Scottish Gaelic Dialect*, Philadelphia: University of Pennsylvania Press.

Dorian, N. (ed.) (1989), *Investigating Obsolescence: Studies in Language Contraction and Death*, Cambridge: Cambridge University Press.

Dorian, N. (1998), 'Western language ideologies and small-language prospects', in Grenoble, L. and L. Whaley (eds), *Endangered Languages*, Cambridge: Cambridge University Press, pp. 3–21.

Edwards, J. (1994), *Multilingualism*, London: Routledge.

Edwards, J. (2003), 'Language and the future: choices and constraints', in Tonkin, H. and T. Reagan (eds), *Language in the 21st Century*, Amsterdam: John Benjamins, pp. 35–45.

Engle, P. (1975), 'The use of vernacular languages in education', *Papers in Applied Linguistics: Bilingual Education Series No 3*, Virginia, Center for Applied Linguistics.

Eurydice (2000), *Key Data on Education in Europe 1999–2000*, Luxembourg: Office for Publications of the European Communities (available at http://www.eurydice.org/Search/frameset_en.html).

Eurydice (2002), *Key Data on Education in Europe*, Luxembourg: Office for Publications of the European Communities (available at http://www.eurydice.org/Documents/cc/2002/en/CC2002_EN_home_page.pdf).

Evans, S. (2002), 'Macaulay's Minute revisited: colonial language policy in nineteenth-century India', *Journal of Multilingual and Multicultural Development* 23, 4, 260–81.

Extra, G. and D. Gorter (eds) (2001), *The Other Languages of Europe: Demographic, Sociolinguistic and Educational Perspectives*, Clevedon: Multilingual Matters.

Extra, G. and K. Yağmur (eds) (2004), *Urban Multilingualism in Europe: Immigrant Minority Languages at Home and School*, Clevedon: Multilingual Matters.

Fafunwa, B., J. Iyabode Macauley and J. Sokoya (eds) (1989), *Education in the Mother Tongue: The Primary Education Research Project (1970–78)*, Ibadan, Nigeria: University Press Ltd.

Faltis, C. (1997), 'Bilingual education in the United States', in Cummins, J. and D. Corson (eds), *Encyclopedia of Language and Education, Volume 5: Bilingual Education*, Dordrecht: Kluwer, pp. 189–97.

Fardon, R. and G. Furniss (1994b), 'Introduction: frontiers and boundaries – African languages as political environment', in Fardon, R. and G. Furniss (eds) (1994a), *African Languages, Development and the State*, London: Routledge, pp. 1–29.

Ferguson, C. (1968), 'Language development', in Fishman, J., C. Ferguson and J. Da Gupta (eds), *Language Problems of Developing Nations*, London: John Wiley, pp. 27–35.

Ferguson, G. (2003), 'Classroom code-switching in post-colonial contexts: functions, attitudes and policies', in Makoni, S. and U. Meinhof (eds), *Africa and Applied Linguistics*, *AILA Review* 16, Amsterdam: John Benjamins, pp. 38–51.

Fettes, M. (1997), 'Language planning and education', in Wodak, R. and D. Corson (eds),

Encyclopedia of Language and Education, Volume 1: Language Policy and Political Issues in Education, Amsterdam: Kluwer, pp. 13–22.

Finlayson, R. and M. Madiba (2001), 'The intellectualisation of the indigenous languages of South Africa: challenges and prospects', *Current Issues in Language Planning* 3, 1, 40–61.

Fishman, J. (1968), 'Sociolinguistics and the language problems of developing countries', in Fishman, J., C. Ferguson and J. Das Gupta (eds), *Language Problems of Developing Nations*, London: John Wiley, pp. 3–16.

Fishman, J (ed.) (1974a), *Advances in Language Planning*, The Hague: Mouton.

Fishman, J. (1974b), 'Language modernization and planning in comparison with other types of national modernization and planning', in Fishman, J. (ed.), *Advances in Language Planning*, The Hague: Mouton, pp. 79–102.

Fishman, J. (1991), *Reversing Language Shift*, Clevedon: Multilingual Matters.

Fishman, J. (1996), 'Summary and interpretation: post-imperial English 1940–1990', in Fishman, J., A. Conrad and A. Rubal-Lopez (eds), *Post-Imperial English: Status Change in Former British and American Colonies 1940-1990*, Berlin: Mouton de Gruyter, pp. 623–41.

Fishman, J. (2000), 'The status agenda in corpus planning', in Lambert, R. and E. Shohamy (eds), *Language Politics and Pedagogy: Essays in Honor of Ronald Walton*, Amsterdam: John Benjamins, pp. 43–52.

Fishman, J. (ed.) (2001a), *Can Threatened Languages be Saved?*, Clevedon: Multilingual Matters.

Fishman, J. (2001b), 'From theory to practice (and vice-versa): review, reconsideration and reiteration', in Fishman, J. (ed.) (2001a), *Can Threatened Languages be Saved?*, Clevedon: Multilingual Matters, pp. 451–83.

Fishman, J., A. Conrad and A. Rubal-Lopez (eds) (1996a), *Post-Imperial English: Status Change in Former British and American Colonies 1940–1990*, Berlin: Mouton de Gruyter.

Fishman, J., C. Ferguson and J. Da Gupta (eds) (1968), *Language Problems of Developing Nations*, London: John Wiley.

Foley, W. (1997), *Anthropological Linguistics: An Introduction*, Oxford: Blackwell.

Foster, P. (1965), 'The vocational school fallacy in development planning', in Anderson, A. and M. Bowman (eds), *Education and Economic Development*, Chicago: Aldine Publishing Company, pp. 142–66. (Also reprinted in Karabel, J. and H. Halsey (eds), *Power and Ideology in Education*, Oxford: Oxford University Press, pp. 356–65.)

Fuller, B. (1987), 'What school factors raise achievement in the third world?', *Review of Educational Research* 57, 3, 255–92.

Fuller, B. and S. Heyneman (1989), 'Third world school quality: current collapse, future potential', *Educational Researcher* 18, 2, 12–19.

Gandara, P. (1999), *Review of Research on the Instruction of Limited English Proficient Student: A Report to the California Legislature*, Santa Barbara, CA: University of California, Linguistic Minority Research Institute.

Gandara, P. and R. Rumberger (2003), *The Inequitable Treatment of English Learners in California's Public Schools*, University of California Linguistic Minority Research Institute Working Paper. (Available at http://lmri.ucsb.edu/resdiss/2/pdf_files/gandara_rumberger.pdf)

Gardner, N., M. Serralvo and C. Williams (2000), 'Language revitalization in comparative context: Ireland, the Basque Country and Catalonia', in Williams, C. (ed.), *Language Revitalization: Policy and Planning in Wales*, Cardiff: University of Wales Press, pp. 311–55.

Gellner, E. (1983), *Nations and Nationalism: New Perspectives on the Past*, Oxford: Blackwell.

Giddens, A. (1999), 'Runaway world: how globalization is reshaping our lives', The 1999 BBC Reith lectures, at http://www.lse.ac.uk/Giddens/reith_99 (Also published as *Runaway World*. London: Profile Books.)

Giddens, A. (2004), 'Globalisation – the state of the debate and the challenge for Europe', Lecture at the University of Sheffield 15 June 2004, at http://www.sheffield.ac.uk/

escus/Giddens_transcript.pdf

Giles, H., R. Bourhis and D. Taylor (1977), 'Towards a theory of language in ethnic group relations', in Giles, H. (ed.), *Language, Ethnicity and Intergroup Relations*, London: Academic Press, pp. 307–48.

Gill, S. K. (2004), 'Medium of instruction policy in higher education in Malaysia: nationalism versus internationalization', in Tollefson, J. and A. Tsui (eds), *Medium of Instruction Policies: Which Agenda? Whose Agenda?*, Mahwah, NJ: Lawrence Erlbaum, pp. 135–52.

Gnutzmann, C. (ed.) (1999), *Teaching and Learning English as a Global Language*, Tübingen: Stauffenberg Verlag.

Gonzalez, R. and I. Melis (2000), *Language Ideologies: Critical Perspectives on the Official English Movement, Volume 1: Education and the Social Implications of Official Language*, Mahwah, NJ: Lawrence Erlbaum.

Görlach, M. (1995), *More Englishes: New Studies in Varieties of English 1988–1994*, Amsterdam: John Benjamins.

Görlach, M. (1999), 'Varieties of English and language teaching', in Gnutzmann, C. (ed.), *Teaching and Learning English as a Global Language*, Tübingen: Stauffenberg Verlag, pp. 3–21.

Görlach, M. (2002), *Still More Englishes*, Amsterdam: John Benjamins.

Graddol, D. (1997), *The Future of English?*, London: The British Council.

Graddol, D. (1999), 'The decline of the native speaker', in Graddol, D. and U. Meinhof (eds), *English in a Changing World, AILA Review* 13, Oxford: AILA, 57–68.

Gramley, S and K. Pätzold (1992), *A Survey of Modern English*, London: Routledge.

Gramsci, A. (1971), 'Selections from the prison notebooks', in Hoare, Q and G. Nowell-Smith (eds), *Selections from the Prison Notebooks of Antonio Gramsci*, New York: International Publishers, pp. 77–80, 82–3.

Greene, J. (1997), 'A meta-analysis of the Rossell and Baker review of bilingual education research', *Bilingual Research Journal* 21, 2 and 3, 103–22.

Grillo, R. (1989), *Dominant Languages: Language and Hierarchy in Britain and France*, Cambridge: Cambridge University Press.

Grillo, R. (1998), *Pluralism and the Politics of Difference*, Oxford: Oxford University Press.

Grin, F. (2001), 'English as economic value: facts and fallacies', *World Englishes* 20, 1, 65–78.

Grin, F. (2002), *Using Language Economics and Education Economics in Language Education Policy*, Strasbourg: Language Policy Division, Council of Europe.

Grin, F. (2003a), *Language Policy Evaluation and the European Charter for Regional or Minority Languages*, London: Palgrave Macmillan.

Grin, F. (2003b), 'Language planning and economics', *Current Issues in Language Planning* 4, 1, 1–67.

Guitarte, G. and R. Quintero (1974), 'Linguistic correctness and the role of the academies in Latin America', in Fishman, J. (ed.), *Advances in Language Planning*, The Hague: Mouton, pp. 315–68.

Gunnarsson, B.-L. (2001), 'Swedish, English, French or German – the language situation at Swedish universities', in Ammon, U. (2001a) (ed.), *The Dominance of English as a Language of Science*, Berlin: Mouton de Gruyter, pp. 267–315.

Gupta, A. F. (1999), 'Standard Englishes, contact varieties, and Singapore Englishes', in Gnutzmann, C. (ed.), *Teaching and Learning English as a Global Language*, Tübingen: Stauffenberg Verlag, pp. 59–72.

Gupta, A. F. (2001), 'Realism and imagination in the teaching of English', *World Englishes* 20, 5, 365–81.

Guzman, M. (2002), 'Dual language programs: key features and results', *Directions in Language and Education* 14, 1–16. National Clearinghouse for Bilingual Education.

Haarman, H. and E. Holman (2001), 'The impact of English as a language of science in Finland and its role for the transition to network society', in Ammon, U. (ed.), *The*

Dominance of English as a Language of Science, Berlin: Mouton de Gruyter, pp. 229–60.

Hakuta, K., Y. Butler and D. Witt (2000), *How Long Does It Take English Learners to Attain Proficiency?*, Santa Barbara, CA: University of California Linguistic Minority Research Institute Policy Report. (Available at http://www.stanford.edu/%7Ehakuta/Docs/HowLong.pdf)

Halliday, M., A. MacIntosh and P. Strevens (1964), *The Linguistic Sciences and Language Teaching*, London: Longman.

Haugen, E. (1959), 'Planning for a standard language in Norway', *Anthropological Linguistics* 1, 3, 8–21.

Haugen, E. (1966a), *Language Conflict and Language Planning: The Case of Modern Norwegian*, Cambridge, MA: Harvard University Press.

Haugen, E. (1966b), 'Linguistics and language planning', in Bright, W. (ed.), *Sociolinguistics: Proceedings of the UCLA Sociolinguistics Conference, 1964*, The Hague: Mouton, pp. 50–71.

Haugen, E. (1966c), 'Dialect, language and nation', *American Anthropologist* 68, 4, 41–61. (Reprinted in Pride, J. and J. Holmes (eds), *Sociolinguistics*, Harmondsworth: Penguin, 97–111.)

Haugen, E. (1983), 'The implementation of corpus planning: theory and practice', in Cobarrubias, J. and J. Fishman (eds), *Progress in Language Planning: International Perspectives*, Berlin: Mouton, pp. 269–89.

Heyneman, S., D. Jamison and X. Montenegro (1983), 'Textbooks in the Philippines: evaluation of the pedagogical impact of a nationwide investment', *Educational Evaluation and Policy Analysis* 6, 139–50.

Hill, D. (1992), *The EPER Guide to Organising Programmes of Extensive Reading*, Edinburgh: Institute for Applied Language Studies, University of Edinburgh.

Hinton, L. and K. Hale (eds) (2001), *The Green Book of Language Revitalization in Practice*, San Diego: Academic Press.

Hobsbawm, E. (1983), 'Introduction: inventing traditions', in Hobsbawm, E. and T. Ranger (eds), *The Invention of Tradition*, Cambridge: Cambridge University Press, pp. 13–14.

Holborow, M. (1999), *The Politics of English*, Newbury: Sage.

Hornberger, N. and K. King (2001), 'Reversing Quechua language shift in South America', in Fishman, J. (ed.), *Can Threatened Languages Be Saved?*, Clevedon: Multilingual Matters, pp. 166–94.

House, J. (1999), 'Misunderstanding in intercultural communication: interactions in English as a lingua franca and the myth of mutual intelligibility', in Gnutzmann, C. (ed.), *Teaching and Learning English as a Global Language*, Tübingen: Stauffenberg Verlag, pp. 73–89.

Howell, R. (2000), 'The Low Countries: a study in contrasting nationalisms', in Barbour, S. and C. Carmichael (eds), *Language and Nationalism in Europe*, Oxford: Oxford University Press, pp. 130–50.

Huddleston, R. and G. Pullum (2002), *The Cambridge Grammar of the English Language*, Cambridge: Cambridge University Press.

Humphreys, L. (1991), 'The geolinguistics of Breton', in Williams, C. H. (ed.), *Linguistic Minorities, Society and Territory*, Clevedon: Multilingual Matters, pp. 96–120.

Humphreys, L. (1993), 'The Breton Language: its present position and historical background', in Ball, M. (ed.), *The Celtic Languages*, London: Routledge, pp. 606–43.

Hutchinson, J. and A. Smith (eds) (1994), *Nationalism*, Oxford: Oxford University Press.

Jacobson, R. and C. Faltis (eds) (1990), *Language Distribution Issues in Bilingual Schooling*, Clevedon: Multilingual Matters.

Jenkins, G. and A. Williams (eds) (2000), *Let's Do Our Best for the Ancient Tongue: The Welsh Language in the Twentieth Century*, Cardiff: University of Wales Press.

Jenkins, J. (1998), 'Which pronunciation norms and models for English as an international language?', *ELT Journal* 52, 2, 119–26.

Jenkins, J. 2000, *The Phonology of English as an International Language*, Oxford: Oxford

University Press.

Jenkins, J. (2002), 'A sociolinguistically based, empirically researched pronunciation syllabus for English as an international language', *Applied Linguistics* 23, 1, 83–103.

Jenkins, J. (2003), *World Englishes*, London: Routledge.

Jenkins, J. (2004), 'ELF at the gate: the position of English as lingua franca', *The European English Messenger* 13, 2, 63–9.

Jenkins, J., M. Modiano and B. Seidlhofer (2003), 'Euro-English', *English Today* 17, 4, 13–19.

Johnstone, R. (2002), 'Addressing the age factor: some implications for language policy', in *Guide for the Development of Language Education Policies in Europe: From Linguistic Diversity to Plurilingual Education*, Strasbourg: Language Policy Division, Directorate of School, Out-of-School and Higher Education, Council of Europe.

Jones, Mari (1994), 'A tale of two dialects: standardization in modern spoken Welsh', in Parry, M., W. Davies and R. Temple (eds), *The Changing Voices of Europe: Social and Political Changes and their Linguistic Repercussions, Past, Present and Future: Papers in Honour of Glanville Price*, Cardiff: University of Wales Press, pp. 243–64.

Jones, Mari (1998a), *Language Obsolescence and Revitalization*, Oxford: Clarendon Press.

Jones, Mari (1998b), 'Death of a language, birth of an identity: Brittany and the Bretons', *Language Problems and Language Planning* 22, 2, 129–42.

Jones, Robert (1993), 'The sociolinguistics of Welsh', in Ball, M. (ed.), *The Celtic Languages*, London: Routledge, pp. 536–605.

Joseph, J. (2004), *Language and Identity*, Basingstoke: Palgrave Macmillan.

Judge, A. (2000), 'France: 'one state, one nation, one language'', in Barbour, S. and C. Carmichael (eds), *Language and Nationalism in Europe*, Oxford: Oxford University Press, pp. 44–82.

Kachru, B. (1985), 'Standards, codification and sociolinguistic realism: the English language in the outer circle', in Quirk, R. and H. Widdowson (eds), *English in the World: Teaching and Learning the Language and the Literatures*, Cambridge: Cambridge University Press in association with The British Council, pp. 11–30.

Kachru, B. (1988), 'The spread of English and sacred linguistic cows', in Lowenberg, P. (ed.), *Language Spread and Language Policy: Issues, Implications, and Case Studies: Georgetown University Round Table on Languages and Linguistics 1987*, Washington, DC: Georgetown University Press, pp. 207–28.

Kachru, B. (1991), 'Liberation linguistics and the Quirk concern', *English Today* 25, 3–13. (Reprinted in Seidlhofer, B. (ed.), *Controversies in Applied Linguistics*, Oxford: Oxford University Press, pp. 19–32.)

Kachru, B. (ed.) (1992a), *The Other Tongue: English across Cultures* (2nd edition), Urbana and Chicago: University of Illinois Press.

Kachru, B. (1992b), 'Models for non-native Englishes', in Kachru, B. (ed.), *The Other Tongue; English across Cultures* (2nd edition), Urbana and Chicago: University of Illinois Press, pp. 48–74.

Kachru, B. (1994), 'English in South Asia', in Burchfield, R. (ed.), *The Cambridge History of the English Language, Volume 5: English in Britain and Overseas: Origins and Development*, Cambridge: Cambridge University Press, pp. 497–552.

Kachru, B. (1995), 'Transcultural creativity in world Englishes and literary canons', in Cook, G. and B. Seidlhofer (eds), *Principle and Practice in Applied Linguistics: Studies in Honour of H. G. Widdowson*, Oxford: Oxford University Press, pp. 271–87.

Kaiser, S. (2003), 'Language and script in Japan and other East Asian countries: between insularity and technology', in Maurais, J. and M. Morris (eds), *Languages in a Globalising World*, Cambridge: Cambridge University Press, pp. 188–202.

Kamwangamalu, N. (2003), 'When 2 + 9 = 1: English and the politics of language planning in a multilingual South Africa', in Mair, C. (ed.), *The Politics of English as a World Language*, ASNEL papers 7, Amsterdam: Rodopi, pp. 235–46.

Kaplan, R. and R. Baldauf Jnr (1997), *Language Planning: From Practice to Theory*, Clevedon: Multilingual Matters.

Kaplan, R. and R. Baldauf (eds) (1999), *Language Planning in Malawi, Mozambique and the Philippines*, Clevedon: Multilingual Matters.

Kaplan, R. and R. Baldauf (eds) (2003), *Language and Language-in-Education Planning in the Pacific Basin*, Dordrecht: Kluwer Academic Publishers.

Karam, F. (1974), 'Toward a definition of language planning', in Fishman, J. (ed.), *Advances in Language Planning*, The Hague: Mouton, pp. 103–24.

Kedourie, E. (1960), *Nationalism*, London: Hutchinson.

Kennedy, C. (ed.) (1984), *Language Planning and Language Education*, London: Allen and Unwin.

Kindler, A. (2002), *Survey of the States' Limited English Proficient Students and Available Educational Programs and Services, 2000–2001 Summary Report*, Washington, DC: National Clearinghouse for English Language Acquisition and Language Educational Programs.

King, K. (1986), 'Conclusion', in Davies, A. (ed.), *Language in Education in Africa*, Seminar Proceedings 26, Edinburgh: Centre of African Studies, University of Edinburgh.

Kloss, H. (1967), '*Abstand* and *Ausbau* languages', *Anthropological Linguistics* 9, 90–101.

Kloss, H. (1969), *Research Possibilities on Group Bilingualism*, Quebec: International Center for Research on Bilingualism.

Kloss, H. (1977), *The American Bilingual Tradition*, Rowley, MA: Newbury House.

Knapp, K. (2002), 'The fading out of the non-native speaker', in Knapp, K and C. Meierkord (eds), *Lingua Franca Communication*, Frankfurt: Peter Lang, pp. 217–44.

Krashen S. (1993), *The Power of Reading*, Eaglewood Colorado: Libraries Unlimited.

Krashen, S. (2001), 'Bilingual education: arguments for and (bogus) arguments against', in Alatis, J. and T. Ai-Hui (eds), *Language in Our Time: Georgetown University Round Table on Language and Linguistics 1999*, Washington, DC: Georgetown University Press.

Krauss, M. (1992), 'The world's languages in crisis', *Language* 68, 4–10.

Kuter, L. (1989), 'Breton vs French: language and the opposition of political, economic, social and cultural values', in Dorian, N. (ed.), *Investigating Obsolescence: Studies in Language Contraction and Death*, Cambridge: Cambridge University Press, pp. 75–89.

Kymlicka, W. (1995), *Multicultural Citizenship: A Liberal Theory of Minority Rights*, Oxford: Clarendon Press.

Laitin, D. (1992), *Language Repertoire and State Construction in Africa*, Cambridge: Cambridge University Press.

Lambert, R. (1999), 'A scaffolding for language policy', *International Journal of the Sociology of Language* 137, 3–25.

Lambert, W. (1975), 'Culture and language as factors in learning and education', in Wolfgang, A. (ed.), *Education of Immigrant Students*, Toronto: Ontario Institute for Studies in Education.

Leech, G. (2000), 'Grammars of spoken English: new outcomes of corpus-oriented research', *Language Learning* 50, 4, 675–724.

Lewis, G. (1992), *Just a Diplomat* (translation of Kuneralp, Z. (1981), *Sadece Diplomat*), Istanbul: Isis Press.

Lewis, G. (1999), *The Turkish Language Reform: A Catastrophic Success*, Oxford: Oxford University Press.

Liddicoat, A. and P. Bryant (2002), 'Intellectualisation: a current issue in language planning', *Current Issues in Language Planning* 3, 1, 1–4.

Lieberson, S. (1982), 'Forces affecting language spread: some basic propositions', in Cooper, R. (ed.), *Language Spread: Studies in Diffusion and Social Change*, Bloomington, IN: Indiana University Press, pp. 37–62.

Lindholm, K. (1997), 'Two-way bilingual education programs in the United States', in

Cummins, J. and D. Corson (eds), *Encylopedia of Language and Education, Volume 5: Bilingual Education*, Dordrecht: Kluwer, pp. 271–80.

Lindholm-Leary, K. (2001), *Dual Language Education*, Clevedon: Multilingual Matters.

Linn, A. (1997), *Constructing the Grammars of a Language: Ivar Aasen and Nineteenth-Century Norwegian Linguistics*, Münster: Nodus Publikationen.

Linn, A. (2004), *Johan Storm*, Oxford: Blackwell.

Lo Bianco, J. and M. Rhydwen (2001), 'Is the extinction of Australia's indigenous languages inevitable?', in Fishman, J. (ed.), *Can Threatened Languages Be Saved?*, Clevedon: Multilingual Matters, pp. 391–422.

Lucas, T. and A. Katz (1994), 'Reframing the debate: the roles of native languages in English-only programs for language minority students', *TESOL Quarterly* 28, 3 537–61.

Luke, A., A. McHoul and J. Mey (1990), 'On the limits of language planning: class, state and power', in Baldauf, R. and A. Luke (eds), *Language Planning and Education in Australasia and the South Pacific*, Clevedon: Multilingual Matters, pp. 25–4.

Lyons, J. (1995), 'The past and future directions of federal bilingual policy', reprinted in Garcia, O. and C. Baker (eds), *Policy and Practice in Bilingual Education*, Clevedon: Multilingual Matters, pp. 1–14.

Macdonald, C. (1990), *School-Based Learning Experiences: A Final Report of the Threshold Project*, Pretoria: Human Sciences Research Council.

Machin, D. and T. Van Leeuwen (2003), 'Global schemas and local discourses in *Cosmopolitan*', *Journal of Sociolinguistics* 7, 4, 493–512.

Macias, R. (2000), 'The flowering of America: linguistic diversity in the United States', in McKay, S. and S. Wong (eds), *New Immigrants in the United States*, Cambridge: Cambridge University Press, pp. 11–57.

MacLean, C. (1999), 'Language diffusion policy', in Spolsky, B. (ed.), *Concise Encyclopedia of Educational Linguistics*, Amsterdam: Kluwer, pp. 92–101.

Mafu, S. (2003), 'Postcolonial language planning in Tanzania: what are the difficulties and what is the way out?', in Mair, C. (ed.), *The Politics of English as a World Language*, Amsterdam: Rodopi, pp. 267–78.

Makerere (1961), *Report of the Commonwealth Conference on the Teaching of English as a Second Language*, Entebbe, Uganda: Government Printer.

Makoni, S. and U. Meinhof (2003b), 'Introducing applied linguistics in Africa', in Makoni, S. and U. Meinhof (eds), *Africa and Applied Linguistics. AILA Review* 16, Amsterdam: John Benjamins, pp. 1–12.

Marivate, C. (2000), 'The mission and activities of the Pan South African Language Board', in Deprez, K. and T. du Plessis (eds), *Multilingualism and Government*, Pretoria: Van Schaik, pp. 130–7.

Martin, P. (1999), 'Bilingual unpacking of monolingual texts in two primary classrooms in Brunei Darussalam', *Language and Education* 13, 1, 38–58.

Martin-Jones, M. (1995), 'Code-switching in the classroom: two decades of research', in Milroy, L. and P. Muysken (eds), *One Speaker, Two Languages: Cross-Disciplinary Perspectives on Code-Switching*, Cambridge: Cambridge University Press, pp. 90–111.

Mauranen, A. (2003), 'The corpus of English as lingua franca in academic settings', *TESOL Quarterly* 37, 3, 513–27.

May, S. (1999), 'Extending ethnolinguistic democracy in Europe: the case of Wales', in Smith, D. and S. Wright (eds), *Whose Europe? The Turn towards Democracy*, Oxford: Blackwell/ Sociological Review, pp. 142–67.

May, S. (2000), 'Uncommon languages: the challenges and possibilities of minority language rights', *Journal of Multilingual and Multicultural Development* 21, 5, 366–85.

May, S. (2001), *Language and Minority Rights*, Harlow: Longman.

Mazrui, Alamin (2002), 'The English language in African education: dependency and decolonization', in Tollefson, J. (ed.), *Language Policies in Education: Critical Issues,*

Mahwah, NJ: Lawrence Erlbaum, pp. 267–81.

Mazrui, Alamin (2004), *English in Africa after the Cold War*, Clevedon: Multilingual Matters.

Mazrui, Ali and Alamin Mazrui (1998), *The Power of Babel: Language and Governance in the African Experience*, Oxford: James Currey.

McArthur, T. (1998), *The English Languages*, Cambridge: Cambridge University Press.

McChesney, R. (1999), 'The new global media' from *The Nation*, Illinois: Illinois University Press. Reprinted in Held, D. and A. McGrew (eds) (2003), *The Global Transformations Reader* (2nd edition), Oxford: Polity Press, pp.260–68.

McDonald, M. (1989), *We Are Not French: Language, Culture and Identity in Brittany*, London: Routledge.

McKay, S. (2002), *Teaching English as an International Language*, Oxford: Oxford University Press.

McKay, S. (2003), 'Toward an appropriate EIL pedagogy: re-examining common ELT assumptions', *International Journal of Applied Linguistics* 13, 1, 1–22.

McLean, D. and K. McCormick (1996), 'English in South Africa: 1940–1996', in Fishman, J., A. Conrad and A. Rubal-Lopez (eds), *Post-Imperial English: Status Change in Former British and American Colonies 1940–1990*, Berlin: Mouton de Gruyter, pp. 307–37.

McMahon, A. (1994), *Understanding Language Change*, Cambridge: Cambridge University Press.

Mercator-Education (2003), *The Breton Language in Education in France* (2nd edition), Regional Dossier, Leewarden, Netherlands: Mercator–Education. (Available at http://www.mercator-education.org/15/12/03)

Mesthrie, R. (2003), 'The world Englishes paradigm and contact linguistics: refurbishing the foundations', *World Englishes* 22, 4, 449–61.

Milroy, J. (1999), 'The consequences of standardisation in descriptive linguistics', in Bex, T. and R. Watts (eds), *Standard English: The Widening Debate*, London: Routledge, pp. 16–39.

Milroy, L. (1999), 'Standard English and language ideology in Britain and the United States', in Bex, T. and R. Watts (eds), *Standard English: The Widening Debate*, London: Routledge, pp. 173–206.

Milroy, J. and L. Milroy (1998), *Authority in Language: Investigating Language Prescription and Standardisation* (3rd edition), London: Routledge.

Moal, S. (2000), 'Broadcast media in Breton: dawn at last?', *Current Issues in Language and Society* 7, 2, 17–134.

Moss, M. and M. Puma (1995), *Prospects: The Congressionally Mandated Study of Educational Growth and Opportunity: First Year Report on Language Minority and Limited English Proficient Students*, Cambridge, MA: ABT Associates.

Mphahlele, E. (1963), 'Polemics: the dead end of African literature', *Transition* 2, 11, 7–9.

Mufwene, S. (2001), *The Ecology of Language Evolution*, Cambridge: Cambridge University Press.

Mufwene, S. (2002), 'Colonisation, globalisation, and the future of languages in the twenty-first century', *International Journal on Multicultural Societies*, vol. 4, no. 2, http://www.unesco.org/most/vl4n2mufwene.pdf

Mühlhäusler, P. (1996), *Linguistic Ecology: Language Change and Linguistic Imperialism in the Pacific Region*, London: Routledge.

Mühlhäusler, P. (2000), 'Language planning and language ecology', *Current Issues in Language Planning* 1, 306–67.

Murray, H. and S. Dingwall (2001), 'The dominance of English at European universities: Switzerland and Sweden compared', in Ammon, U. (ed.), *The Dominance of English as a Language of Science*, Berlin: Mouton de Gruyter, pp. 85–112.

Myers-Scotton, C. (1990), 'Elite closure as boundary maintenance: the case of Africa', in B. Weinstein (ed.), *Language Policy and Political Development*, Norwood: Ablex, pp. 25–32.

Nadkarni, K. (1984), 'Cultural pluralism as a national resource: strategies for language education', in Kennedy, C. (ed.), *Language Planning and Language Education*, London: Allen and Unwin, pp. 151–9.

National Assembly for Wales (2002), *Our Language, its Future: Policy Review of the Welsh Language*, Cardiff: National Assembly for Wales.

National Assembly for Wales (2003), *Digest of Welsh Statistics 2002*, Cardiff: National Assembly for Wales.

Nettle, D. and S. Romaine (2000), *Vanishing Voices*, Oxford: Oxford University Press.

Ngugi wa Thiong'o (1986), *Decolonising the Mind: The Politics of Language in African Literature*, London: Heinemann.

Nunan, D. (2003), 'The impact of English as a global language on educational policies and practices in the Asia-Pacific region', *TESOL Quarterly* 37, 4, 589–613.

Oakey, R. (2000), 'Lesser-used languages and linguistic minorities in Europe since 1918: an overview', in Jenkins, G. and A. Williams (eds), *Let's Do Our Best for the Ancient Tongue: The Welsh Language in the Twentieth Century*, Cardiff: University of Wales Press, pp. 627–56.

OECD (2003), *OECD in Figures: Statistics on the Member Countries, Volume 2003*, Paris: OECD Publications. (Available at http://www1.oecd.org/publications/e-book/0103061E.PDF)

Ogbu, J. (1978), *Minority Education and Caste*, New York: Academic Press.

Ogbu, J. (1992), 'Understanding cultural diversity and learning', *Educational Researcher* 21, 8, 5–14 and 24.

Ogden, C. (1930), *Basic English*, London: Kegan Paul, Trench and Trubner.

O'Hare, W. (1992), 'America's minorities – the demographics of diversity', *Population Bulletin* 47, 4, 2–47.

Ohly, R. and A. Gibbe (1982), 'Language development: lexical elaboration of Kiswahili to meet educational demands', in Trappes-Lomax, H., R. Besha and Y. Mcha (eds), *Changing Language Media*, Dar-es-Salaam: University of Dar-es Salaam.

Omar Asmah Haji (1992), *The Linguistic Scenery in Malaysia*, Kuala Lumpur: Dewan Bahasa dan Pustaka, Ministry of Education.

Ó'Riagáin, P. (1997), *Language Policy and Social Reproduction: Ireland 1893–1993*, Oxford: Clarendon Press.

Ó'Riagáin, P. (2001), 'Irish language production and reproduction 1981–1996', in Fishman, J. (ed.), *Can Threatened Languages Be Saved?*, Clevedon: Multilingual Matters, pp. 195–214.

Ovando, C. (2003), 'Bilingual education in the United States: historical development and current issues', *Bilingual Research Journal* 27, 1–24.

Pakir, A. (2004), 'Medium of Instruction policy in Singapore', in Tollefson, J. and A. Tsui (eds), *Medium of Instruction Policies*, Mahwah, NJ: Lawrence Erlbaum, pp. 117–33.

Parekh, B. (2000), *Rethinking Multiculturalism: Cultural Diversity and Political Thought*, Basingstoke: Macmillan Press.

Patten, A. (2003), 'What kind of bilingualism?', in Kymlicka, W. and A. Patten (eds), *Language Rights and Political Theory*, Oxford: Oxford University Press, pp. 296–321.

Patten, A. and W. Kymlicka (2003), 'Introduction: language rights and political theory: contexts, issues and approaches', in Kymlicka, W. and A. Patten (eds), *Language Rights and Political Theory*, Oxford: Oxford University Press, pp. 1–51.

Peacock, A. (1995), 'An agenda for research on text material in primary science for second language learners of English in developing countries', *Journal of Multilingual and Multicultural Development* 16, 5, 389–401.

Peal, E. and W. Lambert (1962), 'The relationship of bilingualism to intelligence', *Psychological Monographs* 76, 27, 1–23.

Pennycook, A. (1994), *The Cultural Politics of English as an International Language*, London: Longman.

Pennycook, A. (1995), 'English in the world / The world in English', in Tollefson, J. (ed.), *Power and Inequality in Language Education*, Cambridge: Cambridge University Press, pp. 34–58.

Pennycook, A. (2000), 'English, politics, ideology: from colonial celebration to postcolonial peformativity', in Ricento, T. (ed.), *Ideology, Politics and Language Policies: Focus on English*, Amsterdam: John Benjamins, pp. 107–19.

Pennycook, A. (2001), *Critical Applied Linguistics: A Critical Introduction*, Mahwah, NJ: Lawrence Erlbaum.

Phillipson, R. (1992), *Linguistic Imperialism*, Oxford: Oxford University Press.

Phillipson, R. (1997), 'Realities and myths of linguistic imperialism', *Journal of Multilingual and Multicultural Development* 18, 3, 238–47.

Phillipson, R. (2000a), 'English in the new world order: variations on a theme of linguistic imperialism and 'world' English', in Ricento, T. (ed.), *Ideology, Politics and Language Policies: Focus on English*, Amsterdam: John Benjamins, pp. 87–106.

Phillipson, R. (ed.) (2000b), *Rights to Language, Equity and Power in Education*, Mahwah, NJ: Lawrence Erlbaum.

Phillipson, R. (2001), Global English and local language policies: what Denmark needs', *Language Problems and Language Planning* 25, 1, 1–24.

Phillipson, R. (2003), *English-Only Europe? Challenging Language Policy*, London: Routledge.

Phillipson, R. and T. Skutnabb-Kangas (1995), 'Linguistic rights and wrongs', *Applied Linguistics* 16, 4, 483–504.

Phillipson, R. and T. Skuttnab-Kangas (1996), 'English only worldwide or language ecology?' *TESOL Quarterly* 30, 3, 429–52.

Phillipson, R. and T. Skuttnab-Kangas (1997), 'Linguistic human rights and English in Europe', *World Englishes* 16, 1, 27–43.

Phillipson, R. and T. Skutnabb-Kangas (1999), 'Englishisation: one dimension of globalization', in Graddol, D. and U. Meinhof (eds), *English in a Changing World*, *AILA Review* 13, 19–36.

Platt, J. and H. Weber (1980), *English in Singapore and Malaysia: Status, Features and Functions*, Oxford: Oxford University Press.

Platt, J., H. Weber and M. Ho (1984), *The New Englishes*, London: Routledge.

Porter, R. (1990), *Forked Tongue: The Politics of Bilingual Education*, New York: Basic Books.

Prator, C. (1968), 'The British heresy in TESL', in Fishman, J., C. Ferguson and J. Das Gupta (eds), *Language Problems of Developing Nations*, New York: John Wiley, pp. 459–76.

Press, I. (1994), 'Breton speakers in Brittany, France and Europe: constraints on the search for an identity', in Parry, M., W. Davies and R. Temple (eds), *The Changing Voices of Europe*, Cardiff: University of Wales Press, pp. 213–26.

Price, Glanville (1984), *The Languages of Britain*, London: Arnold.

Price, Glanville (2000), 'The other Celtic languages in the twentieth century', in Jenkins, G. and A. Williams (eds), *Let's Do Our Best for the Ancient Tongue: The Welsh Language in the Twentieth Century*, Cardiff: University of Wales Press, pp. 601–26.

Pride, J. (1986), *New Englishes*, Rowley, MA: Newbury House.

Prophet, R. and J. Dow (1994), 'Mother tongue language and concept development in science: a Botswana case study', *Language, Culture and Curriculum* 7, 3, 205–17.

Quirk, R. (1981), 'Nuclear English', in Smith, L. (ed.), *English for Cross-Cultural Communication*, London: Macmillan, pp. 151–65.

Quirk, R. (1985), 'The English language in a global context', in Quirk, R. and H. Widdowson (eds), *English in the World: Teaching and Learning the Language and the Literatures*, Cambridge: Cambridge University Press in association with The British Council, pp. 1–10.

Quirk, R. (1988), 'The question of standards in the international use of English', in Lowenberg, P. (ed.), *Language Spread and Language Policy: Issues, Implications, and Case Studies, Georgetown University Round Table on Languages and Linguistics 1987*, Washington,

DC: Georgetown University Press, pp. 229–41.

Quirk, R. (1990a), 'Language varieties and standard language', *English Today* 21, 3–10. (Reprinted in Seidlhofer, B. (ed.), *Controversies in Applied Linguistics*, Oxford: Oxford University Press, pp. 9–19.)

Quirk, R. (1990b), 'What is standard English?', in Quirk, R. and G. Stein, *English in Use*, London: Longman, pp. 112–25.

Ramirez, J. (1992), 'Executive summary', *Bilingual Research Journal* 16, 1 and 2, 1–62.

Ramirez, J., S. Yuen and D. Ramey (1991), *Executive Summary: Final Report: Longitudinal Study of Structured English Immersion, Early-Exit and Late-Exit Transitional Bilingual Education Programs for Language-Minority Children* (report submitted to the US Department of Education), San Mateo, CA: Aguirre International.

Raz, J. (1994), *Ethics in the Public Domain: Essays in the Morality of Law and Politics*, Oxford: Clarendon Press.

Ricento, T. (1996), 'Language policy in the United States' in Herriman, M. and B. Burnaby (eds), *Language Policy in English-Dominant Countries: Six Case Studies*, Clevedon: Multilingual Matters, pp. 122–58.

Ricento, T. (1998), 'National language policy in the United States', in Ricento, T. and B. Burnaby (eds), *Language and Politics in the United States and Canada*, Mahwah, NJ: Lawrence Erlbaum, pp. 85–112.

Ricento, T. (ed.) (2000a), *Ideology, Politics and Language Policies: Focus on English*, Amsterdam: John Benjamins.

Ricento, T. (2000b), 'Historical and theoretical perspectives in language policy and planning', in Ricento, T. (ed.) (2000a), *Ideology, Politics and Language Policies: Focus on English*, Amsterdam: John Benjamins, pp. 9–24.

Ridge, S. (2000), 'Mixed motives: ideological elements in the support for English in South Africa', in Ricento, T. (ed.), *Ideology, Politics and Language Policies: Focus on English*, Amsterdam: John Benjamins, pp. 151–72.

Ritzer, G. (1996), *The McDonaldization of Society*, London: Sage.

Romaine, S. (2002), 'The impact of language policy on endangered languages', *International Journal on Multicultural Societies* 4, 2, 1–28.

Rossell, C. and K. Baker (1996), 'The educational effectiveness of bilingual education', *Research in the Teaching of English* 30, 1, 7–74.

Roy-Campbell, Z. (2003), 'Promoting African languages as conveyors of knowledge in educational institutions', in Makoni, S., G. Smitherman, A. Ball and A. Spears (eds), *Black Linguistics: Language, Society, and Politics in Africa and the Americas*, London: Routledge, pp. 83–102.

Rubagumya, C. (ed.) (1990), *Language in Education in Africa: a Tanzanian Perspective*, Clevedon: Multilingual Matters.

Rubin, J. (1971), 'Evaluation and language planning', in Rubin, J. and B. Jernudd (eds), *Can Language Be Planned? Sociolinguistic Theory and Practice for Developing Nations*, Honolulu, East-West Center: Hawaii University Press, pp. 271–52.

Rubin, J. and B. Jernudd (eds) (1971), *Can Language Be Planned? Sociolinguistic Theory and Practice for Developing Nations.* Honolulu, East-West Center: Hawaii University Press.

Ruiz, R. (1984), 'Orientations in language planning', *NABE Journal* 8, 2, 15–34.

Rumberger, R. (2000), *Educational Outcomes and Opportunities for English Language Learners*, University of California Linguistic Minorities Research Institute.

Russell, J. (1990), 'Success as a source of conflict in language planning: the Tanzanian case', *Journal of Multilingual and Multicultural Development* 11, 5, 363–75.

Safran, W. (1999), 'Politics and language in contemporary France: facing supranational and intranational challenges', *International Journal of the Sociology of Language* 137, 39–66.

Schiffman, H. (1996), *Linguistic Culture and Language Policy*, London: Routledge.

Schmid, C. (2001), *The Politics of Language: Conflict, Identity and Cultural Pluralism in*

Comparative Perspective, Oxford: Oxford University Press.

Schmidt, R. (1998), 'The politics of language in Canada and the United States: explaining the differences', in Ricento, T. and B. Burnaby (eds), *Language and Politics in the United States and Canada*, Mahwah, NJ: Erlbaum, pp. 37–70.

Schmidt, R. (2000), *Language Policy and Identity Politics in The United States*, Philadelphia: Temple University Press.

Schmied, J. (1991), *English in Africa: An Introduction*, Harlow: Longman.

Schneider, E. (ed.) (1997), *Englishes Around the World 1: Studies in Honour of Manfred Gorlach*, Amsterdam: John Benjamins.

Scovel, T (2000a), '"The younger, the better" myth and bilingual education', in Gonzalez, R. and I. Melis, *Language Ideologies: Critical Perspectives on the Official English Movement, Volume 1: Education and the Social Implications of Official Language*, Mahwah, NJ: Lawrence Erlbaum, pp. 114–36.

Scovel, T. (2000b), 'A critical review of the critical period research', *Annual Review of Applied Linguistics* 20, 213–23.

Seidlhofer, B. (1999), 'Double standards: teacher education in the expanding circle', *World Englishes* 18, 2, 233–45.

Seidlhofer, B. (2001), 'Closing a conceptual gap: the case for the description of English as a lingua franca', *International Journal of Applied Linguistics* 11, 2, 133–58.

Seidlhofer, B. (2002a), '*Habeas corpus* and *divide et impera*: "global English" and applied linguistics', in Spelman-Miller, K. and P. Thompson (eds), *Unity and Diversity in Language Use*, London: British Association of Applied Linguistics in association with Continuum, pp. 198–217.

Seidlhofer, B. (2002b), 'The shape of things to come? Some basic questions about English as a lingua franca', in Knapp, K. and C. Meierkord (eds), *Lingua Franca Communication*, Frankfurt: Peter Lang, pp. 269–302.

Seidlhofer, B. (2004), 'Research perspectives on teaching English as a lingua franca', *Annual Review of Applied Linguistics* 24, 209–39.

Seidlhofer, B. and J. Jenkins (2003), 'English as a lingua franca and the politics of property', in Mair, C. (ed.), *The Politics of English as a World Language*, ASNEL Papers 7, Amsterdam: Rodopi, pp. 139–54.

Shuibhne, N. (2001), 'The European Union and minority language rights: respect for the cultural and linguistic diversity', *International Journal on Multicultural Societies* 3, 2, 67–83. (Accessible at www.unesco.org/shs/ijms/vol 3)

SIPRI (Stockholm International Peace Research Institute) (2003), 'Armaments, disarmament and international security', in the *SIPRI Yearbook 2003*, Oxford: Oxford University Press. (Data on military expenditure accessed from SIPRI website http://editors.sipri.org/pubs/yb03/ch10.html, 21/01/04)

Skuttnab-Kangas, T. (2000), *Linguistic Genocide in Education or Worldwide Diversity and Human Rights?*, Mahwah, NJ: Lawrence Erlbaum.

Skuttnab-Kangas (2003), 'Linguistic diversity and biodiversity: the threat from killer languages', in Mair, C. (ed.), *The Politics of English as a World Language*, ASNEL papers 7, Amsterdam: Rodopi, pp. 31–52.

Smith, L. and C. Nelson (1985), 'International intelligibility of English: directions and resources', *World Englishes* 4, 3, 333–42.

Smith, L. and K. Rafiqzad (1979), 'English for cross-cultural communication: the question of intelligibility', *TESOL Quarterly* 13, 3, 371–80.

Snow, C., H. Cancino, J. De Temple and S. Schley (1991), 'Giving formal definitions: a linguistic or metalinguistic skill?', in Bialystok, E. (ed.), *Language Processing in Bilingual Children*, Cambridge: Cambridge University Press, pp. 90–112.

Spolsky, B. (1986),, 'Overcoming language barriers to education in a multilingual world', in Spolsky, B (ed.), *Language and Education in Multilingual Settings*, Clevedon: Multilingual

Matters, pp. 182–91.

Spolsky, B. (2003), Preface in Kaplan, R. and R. Baldauf (eds) (2003), *Language and Language-in-Education Planning in the Pacific Basin*, Dordrecht: Kluwer, pp. xi–xii.

Spolsky, B. (2004), *Language Policy*, Cambridge: Cambridge University Press.

Sridhar, K. and S. Sridhar (1992), 'Bridging the paradigm gap: second-language acquisition theory and indigenized varieties of English', in Kachru, B. (ed.), *The Other Tongue: English across Cultures* (2nd edition), Urbana and Chicago: University of Illinois, pp. 91–107.

Stiglitz, J. (2002), *Globalization and its Discontents*, London: Penguin Books.

Stroud, C. (2002), *Toward a Policy for Bilingual Education in Developing Countries*, New Education Division Documents Number 10, Stockholm: Swedish International Development Agency.

Stroud, C. (2003), 'Postmodernist perspectives on local languages: African mother-tongue education in times of globalisation', *International Journal of Bilingual Education and Bilingualism* 6, 1, 17–36.

Sypher, C. (2000), *New Englishes: An investigation into the Debate on New Englishes as Pedagogical Models in TESL*, unpublished M.Sc. Dissertation, University of Edinburgh.

Tardy, C. (2004), 'The role of English in scientific communication: lingua franca or Tyrannosaurus Rex', *Journal of English for Academic Purposes* 3, 3, 247–69.

Tay, M. (1982), 'The uses, users and features of English in Singapore', in Pride, J. (ed.), *New Englishes*, Rowley, MA: Newbury House, pp. 51–70.

Taylor, C. (1994), 'The politics of recognition', in Gutmann, A. (ed.), *Multiculturalism*, Princeton, NJ: Princeton University Press.

Temple, R. (1994), 'Great expectations? Hope and fears about the implications of political developments in western Europe for the future of France's regional languages', in Parry, M., W. Davies and R. Temple (eds), *The changing voices of Europe: Social and Political Changes and their Linguistic Repercussions, Past, Present and Future: Papers in Honour of Glanville Price*, Cardiff: University of Wales Press, pp. 193–207.

Texier, M. and C. O'Neill (2000), 'The Nominoe study of the Breton language compiled from field research', at http://www.breizh.net/icdbl/saozg/nominoe.htm

Thomas, B. (1987), 'A cauldron, a rebirth: population and the Welsh language in the nineteenth century', *Welsh History Review* 13, 418–37.

Thomas, G. (1991), *Linguistic Purism*, London: Longman.

Thomas, W. and V. Collier (1997), *School Effectiveness for Language Minority Students*, Washington, DC: National Clearing house for Bilingual Education.

Thomas, W. and V. Collier (2002), *A National Study of School Effectiveness for Language Minority Students' Long-Term Academic Achievement*, Washington, DC: Center for Research, Diversity and Excellence. (Available at http://www.crede.ucsc.edu/research/llaa/1.1_final.html)

Thomason, S. (2001), *Language Contact: An Introduction*, Edinburgh: Edinburgh University Press.

Thompson, J. (2003), 'The globalization of communication', in Held, D. and A. McGrew (eds), *The Global Transformations Reader* (2nd edition), London: Polity Press, pp. 246–59.

Thorburn, T. (1971), 'Cost-benefit analysis in language planning', in Rubin, J. and B. Jernudd (eds), *Can Language Be Planned? Sociolinguistic Theory and Practice for Developing Nations*, Honolulu, East-West Center: Hawaii University Press, pp. 283–305.

Thorne, D. (1994), '"Tafodieithoedd Datguddiad Duw": the change in the voice of the Welsh Bible', in Parry, M., W. Davies and R. Temple (eds), *The Changing Voices of Europe*, Cardiff: University of Wales Press, pp. 265–79.

Timm, L. (1980), 'Bilingualism, diglossia and language shift in Brittany', *International Journal of the Sociology of Language* 25, 29–41.

Timmis, I. (2002), 'Native speaker norms and international English: a classroom view', *ELT Journal* 56, 3, 240–9.

Tollefson, J. (1991), *Planning Language, Planning Inequality*, London: Longman.

Tollefson, J. (ed.) (2002a), *Language Policies in Education*, Mahwah, NJ: Lawrence Erlbaum.

Tollefson, J. (2002b), 'Limitations of language policy and planning', in Kaplan, R. (ed.), *Oxford Handbook of Applied Linguistics*, Oxford: Oxford University Press, pp. 416–25.

Tollefson, J. and A. Tsui (eds) (2004a), *Medium of Instruction Policies: Which Agenda, Whose Agenda?*, Mahwah, NJ: Lawrence Erlbaum.

Tollefson, J. and A. Tsui (2004b), 'The centrality of medium-of-instruction policy in sociopolitical processes', in Tollefson, J. and A. Tsui (eds), *Medium of Instruction Policies: Which Agenda, Whose Agenda?*, Mahwah, NJ: Lawrence Erlbaum, pp. 1–18.

Tomlinson, J. (1997), 'Cultural globalization and cultural imperialism', in Mohammadi, A. (ed.), *International Communication and Globalization*, London: Sage Publications, pp. 170–90.

Torrance, E., J. Gowan, J. Wu and N. Aliotti (1970), 'Creative functioning of monolingual and bilingual children in Singapore', *Journal of Educational Psychology* 61, 72–5.

Trappes-Lomax, H. (1990), 'Can a foreign language be a national medium?', in Rubagumya, C. (ed.), (1990), *Language in Education in Africa: a Tanzanian Perspective*, Clevedon: Multilingual Matters, pp. 94–104.

Truchot, C. (2001), 'The language of science in France: public debate and language policies', in Ammon, U. (ed.), *The Dominance of English as a Language of Science*, Berlin: Mouton de Gruyter, pp. 319–28.

Trudgill, P. (1999), 'Standard English: what it isn't', in Bex, T. and R. Watts (eds), *Standard English: The Widening Debate*, London: Routledge, pp. 117–28.

Trudgill, P. (2000), 'Greece and European Turkey: from religious to linguistic identity', in Barbour, S. and C. Carmichael (eds), *Language and Nationalism in Europe*, Oxford: Oxford University Press, pp.240–63.

Tsuda, Y. (1994), 'The diffusion of English: its impact on culture and communication', *Keio Communication Review* 16, 49–61.

Tsui, A. (2004), 'Medium of instruction in Hong Kong: one country, two systems, whose language?', in Tollefson, J. and A. Tsui (eds), *Medium of Instruction Policies: Which Agenda, Whose Agenda?*, Mahwah, NJ: Lawrence Erlbaum, pp. 97–116.

US English (2003), US English home page, http://www.us-english.org/inc

Van Binsbergen, W. (1994), 'Minority language, ethnicity and the state in two African situations: the Nkoya of Zambia and the Kalanga of Botswana', in Fardon, R. and G. Furniss (eds), *African Languages, Development and the State*, London: Routledge, pp. 142–88.

Vavrus, F. (2002), 'Postcoloniality and English: exploring language policy and the politics of development in Tanzania', *TESOL Quarterly* 26, 3, 373–97.

Veltman, C. (2000), 'The American linguistic mosaic', in McKay, S. and S. Wong (eds), *New Immigrants in the United States*, Cambridge: Cambridge University Press, pp. 58–93.

Verhoeven, and R. Aarts (1998), 'Attaining functional literacy in the Netherlands', in Verhoeven, L. and A. Durgunoglu (eds), *Literacy Development in a Multilingual Context*, Mahwah, NJ: Lawrence Erlbaum, pp. 111–34.

Vikør, L. (2000), 'Northern Europe: languages as prime markers of ethnic and national identity', in Barbour, S. and C. Carmichel (eds), *Language and Nationalism in Europe*, Oxford: Oxford University Press, pp. 105–29.

Vilela, M. (2002), 'Reflections on language policy in African countries with Portuguese as an official language', *Current Issues in Language Planning* 3, 3, 306–16.

Voluntary Service Overseas (VSO) (2001), *English and Disadvantage: A Study of the Impact of VSO'S ELT Programme in China*, London: Voluntary Service Overseas. (Available at www.vso.org.uk)

Voluntary Service Overseas (VSO) (2002), *English Language Teaching: The Criteria for Supporting ELT as Part of a VSO Country Programme*, London: Voluntary Service Overseas.

(Available at www.vso.org.uk)

Weinstock, D. (2003), 'The antinomy of language policy', in Kymlicka, W. and A Patten (eds), *Language Rights and Political Theory*, Oxford: Oxford University Press, pp. 250–70.

Welsh Language Board (1999), *Continuity in Welsh Language Education*, Cardiff: Welsh Language Board.

Widdowson, H. (1994), 'The ownership of English', *TESOL Quarterly* 28, 2, 377–89.

Widdowson, H. (2001), 'The monolingual teaching and bilingual learning of English', in Cooper, R., E. Shohamy and J. Walters (eds), *New Perspectives and Issues in Educational Language Policy: in Honor of Bernard Dov Spolsky*, Amsterdam: John Benjamins, pp. 7–18.

Widdowson, H. (2003), *Defining Issues in English Language Teaching*, Oxford: Oxford University Press.

Williams, C. H. (ed.) (1991a), *Linguistic Minorities, Society and Territory*, Clevedon: Multilingual Matters.

Williams, C. H. (1991b), 'Conclusion: sound language planning is holistic in nature', in Williams, C. H. (ed.), *Linguistic Minorities, Society and Territory*, Clevedon: Multilingual Matters, pp. 315–22.

Williams, C. H. (1994), *Called Unto Liberty*, Clevedon: Multilingual Matters.

Williams, C. H. (2000a), 'Restoring the language', in Jenkins, G. and A. Williams (eds), *Let's Do Our Best for the Ancient Tongue: The Welsh Language in the Twentieth Century*, Cardiff: University of Wales Press, pp. 657–81.

Williams, C. H. (ed.) (2000b), *Language Revitalization: Policy and Planning in Wales*, Cardiff: University of Wales Press.

Williams, C. H. (2001), 'Welsh in Great Britain', in Extra, G. and D. Gorter (eds), *The Other Languages of Europe*, Clevedon: Multilingual Matters, pp. 59–81.

Williams, E. (1995), *Images of Europe – Television and Lesser-used Languages*, Brussels: European Bureau for Lesser-Used Languages.

Williams, E. (1996), 'Reading in two languages at year five in African primary schools', *Applied Linguistics* 17, 2, 182–209.

Williams, E. and J. Cooke (2002), 'Pathways and labyrinths: language and education in development', *TESOL Quarterly* 36, 3, 297–322.

Williams, Glyn. (1992), *Sociolinguistics: A Sociological Critique*, London: Routledge.

Williams, Glyn and D. Morris (2000), *Language Planning and Language Use*, Cardiff: University of Wales Press.

Willig, A. (1985), 'A meta-analysis of selected studies on the effectiveness of bilingual education', *Review of Educational Research* 55, 3, 269–317.

Willig, A. and J. Ramirez (1993), 'The evaluation of bilingual education', in Arias, M. and U. Casanova (eds), *Bilingual Education: Politics, Practice and Research*, Chicago: National Society for the Study of Education/University of Chicago Press, pp. 65–87.

Wood, A. (2001), 'International scientific English: the language of research scientists', in Flowerdew, J. and M. Peacock (eds), *Research Perspectives on English for Academic Purposes*, Cambridge: Cambridge University Press, pp. 71–83.

Wright, S. (2004), *Language Policy and Language Planning*, Basingstoke: Palgrave Macmillan.

Index